What a Character!

Character Study as a Guide to Literary
Meaning Making in Grades K–8

Nancy L. Roser
University of Texas at Austin
Austin, Texas, USA

Miriam G. Martinez
University of Texas at San Antonio
San Antonio, Texas, USA

Editors

With Junko Yokota
and Sharon O'Neal

INTERNATIONAL
Reading Association
800 BARKSDALE ROAD, PO BOX 8139
NEWARK, DE 19714-8139, USA
www.reading.org

IRA BOARD OF DIRECTORS

MaryEllen Vogt, California State University Long Beach, Long Beach, California, President • Richard Allington, University of Florida, Gainesville, Florida, President-elect • Timothy Shanahan, University of Illinois at Chicago, Chicago, Illinois, Vice President • Cathy Collins Block, Texas Christian University, Fort Worth, Texas • James Flood, San Diego State University, San Diego, California • Victoria J. Risko, Peabody College of Vanderbilt University, Nashville, Tennessee • Charline J. Barnes, Adelphi University, Garden City, New York • Rita M. Bean, University of Pittsburgh, Pittsburgh, Pennsylvania • Carrice L. Cummins, Louisiana Tech University, Ruston, Louisiana • David Hernandez, III, Washington DC Public Schools, Washington, DC • Susan Davis Lenski, Portland State University, Portland, Oregon • Jill Lewis, New Jersey City University, Jersey City, New Jersey • Alan E. Farstrup, Executive Director

The International Reading Association attempts, through its publications, to provide a forum for a wide spectrum of opinions on reading. This policy permits divergent viewpoints without implying the endorsement of the Association.

Director of Publications Dan Mangan
Editorial Director, Books and Special Projects Teresa Curto
Managing Editor, Books Shannon T. Fortner
Acquisitions and Developmental Editor Corinne M. Mooney
Associate Editor Charlene M. Nichols
Production Editor Amy Messick
Assistant Editor Elizabeth C. Hunt
Books and Inventory Assistant Rebecca A. Zell
Permissions Editor Janet S. Parrack
Assistant Permissions Editor Tyanna L. Collins
Production Department Manager Iona Muscella
Supervisor, Electronic Publishing Anette Schütz
Senior Electronic Publishing Specialist R. Lynn Harrison
Electronic Publishing Specialist Lisa M. Kochel
Proofreader Stacey Lynn Sharp
Project Editor Shannon T. Fortner

Cover Design, Linda Steere; Art © Vicki Wehrman/Images.com

Copyright 2005 by the International Reading Association, Inc.

All rights reserved. No part of this publication may be reproduced or transmitted in any form or by any means, electronic or mechanical, including photocopy, or any information storage and retrieval system, without permission from the publisher.

Web addresses in this book were correct as of the publication date but may have become inactive or otherwise modified since that time. If you notice a deactivated or changed Web address, please e-mail books@reading.org with the words "Website Update" in the subject line. In your message, specify the Web link, the book title, and the page number on which the link appears.

Library of Congress Cataloging-in-Publication Data
What a character! : character study as a guide to literary meaning making in grades K-8 / Nancy L. Roser, Miriam G. Martinez, editors.
        p. cm.
  Includes bibliographical references and index.
  ISBN 0-87207-563-X
  1. Characters and characteristics in literature--Study and teaching (Elementary) 2. Creative writing (Elementary education) 3. Children's literature--Study and teaching (Elementary) 4. Children--Books and reading. I. Roser, Nancy. II. Martinez, Miriam G., 1948- III. International Reading Association.
  PN56.4.W43 2005
  372.64'044--dc22
                                                                        2005003018

Contents

Part I
The Importance of Character

Part II
Creating Characters

Part III
Supporting Children's Understanding of Characters

Why Character?

Nancy L. Roser and Miriam G. Martinez

O F ALL THE LITERARY ELEMENTS ABOUT WHICH AN entire book could be spun, why focus on character? The central reason is that it is through characters that readers come to care about and connect with literature; characters entice us to stick around and make literary meaning. It's likely that Harry Potter (Rowling, 1998) has made more students into readers than Hester Prynne (Hawthorne, 1850/1999) has (Toppo, 2004). Characters like Harry (stick-with-me-through-my-travails-and-I'll-give-you-a-wild-ride-with-something-to-think-about-at-the-end characters) convince students of the potential satisfactions of sticking with characters like Hester.

Some authors argue that characters are central to literary texts because they propel the action. Others just as soundly disagree. But *character* as literary element does not have to be the most important component of literature to be deserving of careful inspection. Teachers intuitively know that characters enlist readers, hold their interest, unravel plots—and affect lives. Not too shabby for a list of literary functions.

As characters pull students into and through books, they stretch students' perspectives; they help them live out adventure and drama and conflict at a safe distance. Characters make the roadway seem traversable. They make plot comprehensible (and manageable). Characters lead students to deep, satisfying, and meaningful experiences with literature. In fact, students become more insightful about the human experience through the characters who tussle with critical moral and ethical dilemmas.

What a Character! Character Study as a Guide to Literary Meaning Making in Grades K–8 edited by Nancy L. Roser and Miriam G. Martinez, with Junko Yokota and Sharon O'Neal. Copyright 2005 by the International Reading Association.

Because understanding character is so central to reading literature deeply and well, teachers need to ensure that students learn how to make sense of characters. And understanding characters—from Owen and his blanket (Henkes, 1993) to Cassie Logan (Taylor, 1976) to Elizabeth Bennett (Austen, 1813/2003)—means considering their traits and perspectives, understanding their motivations and goals, exploring their feelings, and probing their relationships. Not all at once of course, and not with a checklist. Rather, teachers must guide students to consider character thoughtfully using tools such as writing, visual representations, and drama.

Asked what a character is, 9-year-old Jose replied, "It's the player." Yes, character is the player revealed by actions, speech, appearance, and the responses and descriptions of others; character is the player for whom the stage is set and the plot derived.

The Origins of This Book

The teachers, researchers, and children's book authors whose work appears in this volume believe that there are pragmatic reasons for bringing character study to center stage in classrooms. Not only can character study motivate readers, it also has the potential to help them become more thoughtful readers of literature. Almost all of us were contributors to a 2002 International Reading Association Annual Convention preconvention institute that focused on character as an important meaning-making element in children's literature. "What a good idea it is to focus on character," we said to each other. "It should be a book," people told us. After all, characterization is a complex construct; there are many facets of character to which good readers attend—character traits, motives, feelings, goals, relationships. Although character is typically addressed in the curriculum, in some instances consideration of character does not extend much beyond identifying main characters. Yet given the potential of character exploration as a pathway to deeper literary understanding, there seemed to be good reason for a book focusing on character.

How to Best Use This Book

This volume is composed of five parts, and each part plays a specific role. Together these five parts help readers grasp "the big picture" of character study—why it is important for students to delve into characterization, how authors craft their characters, how children understand those characters, and how teachers can thoughtfully select books for character study and guide students in their explorations of literary characters.

Part I explores the importance of character as a focus of study. For stories to develop, as Donald Graves points out in chapter 1, characters must *want* something—and want it badly. Without desire, and the character's movement toward satisfying it, there is no action, no plot. In addition, chapter 2 offers current research showing that, as students mature, their understandings keep pace with the increasing complexity of characters in books. Recognition of how students' understanding of character grows and changes puts teachers in a better position to gently propel their students forward in their explorations of characters.

Part II is composed of chapters by children's book authors—some of the best creators of character. Their essays examine character in powerful and original ways. These seven authors share some of the ways in which they infuse their characters with life—by making a character *want* something, by unveiling a character's shifting feelings, and by revealing characters through the smallest of moments, to name a few. Teachers can use these very pathways to help students gain insights into the characters they meet in books.

Part III offers voices from classrooms in which teacher research and practice have generated fresh ways of examining and extending students' understanding of character. Marjorie Hancock suggests ways of stretching students' insights into character through reflective writing, and Lee Galda shows how children make meaning for characters by playing out roles. Susan Keehn and her colleagues share techniques for helping students step into character through Readers Theatre, and Caitlin Dooley and Beth Maloch provide a range of ways to visually represent students' grasp of the dimensions of characters. Karen Smith shows how student literature groups focus on the gaps in a story to start their character discussions.

Part IV takes a close look at some of the best character-rich picturebooks and chapter books for elementary and middle school students, paying close attention to artistry and appeal. Lawrence Sipe and Maria Ghiso examine specific picturebook titles and show how characters are revealed in the details. Junko Yokota and William Teale describe the types of characters that populate books for young readers, providing detailed examples. Janis Harmon and her colleagues present some of the most memorable characters in young adult literature, selected by middle school students. Through discussion of both text and illustrations, as well as the inclusion of students' talk about books, the chapters in this section suggest ways in which teachers can select books for character study and guide students to better understand those characters.

In Part V, Maria Nikolajeva presents scholarly work aimed at developing a theory of character interpretation in children's literature. She provides background that sheds light on the characters in children's literature across time.

A major theme of this collection is that characters (whether fleshed out, flat, dynamic, or static) guide readers through text. This volume is intended to help teachers better understand how authors craft literary characters and how they can select books for character study, guide character study, and observe children's understandings that emerge through character study.

REFERENCE

Toppo, G. (2004, May 24). Contemporary vs. classic: High school reading has changed with the times. *USA Today*, p. D6.

LITERATURE CITED

Austen, J. (2003). *Pride and prejudice.* New York: Penguin. (Original work published 1813)

Hawthorne, N. (1999). *The scarlet letter.* New York: Penguin. (Original work published 1850)

Henkes, K. (1993). *Owen.* New York: Greenwillow.

Rowling, J.K. (1998). *Harry Potter and the sorcerer's stone.* New York: Scholastic.

Taylor, M. (1976). *Roll of thunder, hear my cry.* New York: Penguin.

Contributors

Franny Billingsley
Author
Simon & Schuster
Lake Forest, Illinois, USA

Edward Bloor
Author
Harcourt, Inc.
Winter Garden, Florida, USA

Kate DiCamillo
Writer
Minneapolis, Minnesota, USA

Caitlin McMunn Dooley
Doctoral Student
University of Texas at Austin
Austin, Texas, USA

Lee Galda
Professor of Children's Literature
University of Minnesota
Minneapolis, Minnesota, USA

Maria Paula Ghiso
Doctoral Student
University of Pennsylvania
Philadelphia, Pennsylvania, USA

Donald H. Graves
Professor Emeritus
University of New Hampshire
Jackson, New Hampshire, USA

Nikki Grimes
Author
Curtis Brown, Ltd.
New York, New York, USA

Marjorie R. Hancock
Professor of Language Arts
Kansas State University
Manhattan, Kansas, USA

Janis M. Harmon
Associate Professor of Literacy
    Education
University of Texas at San Antonio
San Antonio, Texas, USA

Kimberly Willis Holt
Writer
Amarillo, Texas, USA

Susan Keehn
Associate Professor of Reading
University of Texas at San Antonio
San Antonio, Texas, USA

Michelle S. Kenney
Reading Teacher
Kirby Middle School
San Antonio, Texas, USA

Beth Maloch
Assistant Professor of Language
    and Literacy Studies
University of Texas at Austin
Austin, Texas, USA

Miriam G. Martinez
Professor of Literacy Education
University of Texas at San Antonio
San Antonio, Texas, USA

Maria Nikolajeva
Professor of Literature
Stockholm University
Stockholm, Sweden

Katherine Paterson
Writer
Barre, Vermont, USA

Nancy L. Roser
Professor of Language and
   Literacy Studies
University of Texas at Austin
Austin, Texas, USA

Lawrence R. Sipe
Associate Professor of Education
University of Pennsylvania
Philadelphia, Pennsylvania, USA

Karen Smith
Associate Professor of Education
Arizona State University
Tempe, Arizona, USA

William H. Teale
Professor of Education
University of Illinois at Chicago
Chicago, Illinois, USA

Deborah Wiles
Writer
Atlanta, Georgia, USA

Terri Willeford
Reading Teacher
Bradley Middle School
San Antonio, Texas, USA

Junko Yokota
Professor of Curriculum
   and Instruction
National-Louis University
Evanston, Illinois, USA

Part I

THE
Importance
OF
Character

1

The Centrality of Character

Donald H. Graves

It is the character, according to Donald Graves, who brings the life into stories—and it is through focus on character that teachers and students give life to classroom discussions. Taking time for character study, says Graves, will reengage all of us in the joyful adventure of reading.

I BEGIN WITH A QUOTE FROM NEIL SIMON FROM an interview in *The Paris Review*: "The key word is *want*. In every comedy, every drama, somebody has to want something and want it bad" (as cited in Lipton, 1992, p. 170).

For the past five years, I have been walking every Wednesday in the town where I live with my friend, Rob, a psychiatrist. We test each other continually with our questions and theories. My friend experiments on me with questions that he often uses with his clients. Here's one that's in the territory of Neil Simon's insight: "What is there that there's not enough of for you, right now, this very minute?"

I think my response was, "There's not enough time."

What a Character! Character Study as a Guide to Literacy Meaning Making in Grades K–8 edited by Nancy L. Roser and Miriam G. Martinez, with Junko Yokota and Sharon O'Neal. Copyright 2005 by the International Reading Association.

"Time for what?" he quickly asked.

Time to love the ones nearest to me. Time to do the things I most enjoy. Reading is one of those things, and I count some of the characters I've met in books as folks I'd like to spend more time with.

In an age when there is such an emphasis on testing and scores in the classroom, taking time for "stepping into character" too often gets short shrift. Instead, innocuous test paragraphs with multiple-choice questions and one right answer rob students of time they might have spent with the richly developed characters of the best children's books.

It takes time to develop *and* respond to characters. Why? Perhaps because mulling over a deserving character often leads to the discovery of a paradox. Characters have wants, which often lead to tough choices. Students find characters mirroring the same tough decisions they have to make. Such questions as "Why do you think she made that particular decision?" and "What do you think he wanted?" are only simple on the surface. They have great peeling potential. As students peel back the wants of a character, the needs and potential of their own lives are revealed to them. If the curriculum bypasses character study, then educators bypass their students, and the full dimension of what it means to be a reader of literature—in its broadest sense—is lost.

But in classrooms where teachers and students take time to read and discuss authentic literature, and to allow characters to take center stage, wonderful things happen. In those classrooms, children both understand and craft increasingly rich characterizations of their own.

Children's understanding of characters in stories appears to parallel, in many ways, the characters they develop in their own fiction writing. In classrooms where students select their own books to read, and where they discuss and write to peers and teachers about these books, I found that understanding of character develops in a predictable order (Graves, 1989):

1. Children concentrate first on "what happens." They mention characters but focus on retelling the story.

2. As children learn to abstract the story, telling the essential plot in a few lines, characters come more to the fore.

3. Children focus on character motives and link the plot to the nature of the characters.

4. Children critique the writer in light of the plausibility of events that come from the nature of the characters in the book.

5. Children discuss the interrelationships of characters in the story.

6. Children discuss characters in one book in relation to other books or in relation to their own personal interests and motives.

These rough sequences are important because they are general guidelines to trace children's development as writers of fiction. By examining children's writing, I have found that their progress can be traced along a pathway as they learn to develop characters (Graves, 1989).

In general, the first characters children create in their writing exist more to serve their plot. Children are rightfully fascinated by plot. They have been immersed in a television world that stresses plot and high action far more than character. On the other hand, there are real consequences to what characters want and do. Therefore, children need to be immersed in literature in order to feel and know what effects humans have on the world around them. Only when children begin to give a character identity— a name, dialogue, description—does plot begin to seem "a consequence of character revelation" (p. 778).

I have completed three drafts of a novel, *The Eye of the Whale*. The book has truly humbled me as no other writing has because I've chosen to reenact the third chapter of Genesis and become God creating people. Mine is the story of a boy, Joshua, who wants to find the story behind a piece of scrimshaw depicting a harpooner trying to dart a sperm whale. His father says, "It takes a lot of courage to look a whale in the eye. And some day this scrimshaw will be yours." But Joshua wants it now, and an argument ensues. The father goes to sea, and the boy ends up with the scrimshaw only because his father goes down at sea with all hands in a hurricane.

The boy is distraught at coming into possession of the scrimshaw, has to move, is furious with his mother and with a grandmother who insists that the cure for grief is work. What does Joshua want? He wants friends, he wants out of a dark, dreary home. He wants his mother. He wants to be away from his grandmother. He is grieving and quite basically, if the truth were known, he'd like to be held. If we ask Joshua what there isn't enough of for him, he might say, "Friends, time with my mother, and time out of this prison." But what he can't quite say is, "I'd like to find my father in the mystery of the scrimshaw." Perhaps the reader can surmise what Joshua really wants before Joshua himself knows.

Perhaps never has understanding of character been so important. I wrote *Bring Life Into Learning* (Graves, 1999) because, as I visited classrooms, there was less and less emphasis on characters in class discussions and much more on plot. Students deserve vivid characters—characters who are funny, flawed, hopeful, and triumphant. We who teach and read to children need to ensure their capacity and opportunities to become lost in books, immersed in the characters who lead them through patterns of living—patterns that are near to them, or wonderfully imagined.

According to author David McCullough, people often ask if he is working on a book. "I say yes," McCullough acknowledged, "because that's what they asked, but in fact they've got the wrong preposition. I'm *in* the book, *in* the subject, *in* the time and the place" (as cited in Gaffney & Howe, 1999, p. 146). It is a question we should ask readers: "Whose skin are you living *in*?"

REFERENCES

Gaffney, E., & Howe, B. (1999, Fall). The art of biography II. *The Paris Review, 152,* 138–160.

Graves, D.H. (1989). Research currents: When students respond to fiction. *Language Arts, 66*(7), 776–783.

Graves, D.H. (1999). *Bring life into learning.* Portsmouth, NH: Heinemann.

Lipton, J. (1992, Winter). Neil Simon: The art of theater X. *The Paris Review, 125,* 167–213.

2

Students' Developing Understanding of Character

Miriam G. Martinez and Nancy L. Roser

In the stories they read, children—even young children—often encounter well-rounded characters who grow and change over the course of a story. Miriam Martinez and Nancy Roser explore children's understanding of character and how that understanding changes as children move from the early elementary grades and into middle school.

O BECOME THOUGHTFUL READERS OF LITERATURE, students must first learn to "step into" and "move through" the world of the story (Langer, 1995). Students are often drawn into and through stories by the characters they find there. Eventually, young readers learn to linger within a story's web and, again, it is often story characters who seem to invite this willingness to pause, consider, and develop insights. That is, characters not only help move readers *into* and *through* text, but affect what those readers *come away with* as well.

Many traditional stories intended for children are notable for their action or plot line rather than rich characterization (see chapter 16, this

What a Character! Character Study as a Guide to Literary Meaning Making in Grades K–8 edited by Nancy L. Roser and Miriam G. Martinez, with Junko Yokota and Sharon O'Neal. Copyright 2005 by the International Reading Association.

volume). Yet, even in some picturebooks, students meet characters with distinctive personalities who may experience an array of emotions and even grow and change—in just 32 pages. As students move into lengthier books, they begin to regularly meet more rounded characters who face complex problems (Nikolajeva, 2002). We believe that understanding characters—their desires, feelings, thoughts, and beliefs—may lie at the very heart of literary meaning making (Emery, 1996). In fact, it is by seeking to understand characters' intentions and conflicts that readers reach for and achieve thematic insights (Golden & Guthrie, 1986). Certainly, there are authors and other authorities who don't subscribe to the centrality of character in strong narratives (e.g., Lukens, 1999). Even so, it is when readers want to understand what motivates characters, and to engage with the moral and ethical dimensions of characters' decisions and actions, that they work for deeper understandings (Martinez & Roser, 1995). Characters, then, are a conduit through which readers enter, move through, and are affected by narratives.

Students Grow in Their Awareness of Character

When literary characters are multidimensional, understanding those characters becomes a multidimensional task. For example, if the major character in a simple picturebook is a boy who finds a dog, the only character features a child reader *can* attend to are the boy's approximate age, appearance, observable actions, and what the illustrator may explicitly reveal. These surface features are the only available clues to character. Later, as readers encounter books that have characters who are more rounded, interesting, and complex, they are provided more evidence of the character's traits, motivations, intentions, beliefs, and feelings. The lost dog may now actually belong to an owner who has abused it, and whether or not to return the dog is an ethical dilemma for the boy who finds it (as in Phyllis Naylor's *Shiloh* [1989]). The boy gains dimension (and surprises the reader) because he chooses to hide the dog and lie to his parents rather than return it to the abusive owner. These internal facets of character are revealed as events unfold. E.M. Forster (1927) describes this as the novelist exposing "the inner as well as the outer life" (p. 74).

Discerning the complexity of characters is critically important to participating in the artistry, as well as the richest understanding, of most stories. Further, in complex narratives, characters—affected by events as well as their relationships with other characters—may develop and change. Readers' ability and willingness to understand character change within a story may mark a significant step in their development as literary meaning makers.

Our own work has shown that students' understanding of character shifts across grades, and these shifts are marked by more penetrating insights (Martinez, Keehn, Roser, Harmon, & O'Neal, 2002). To see how students talk about a character at different ages and grades, we read Cynthia Rylant's short story "Slower Than the Rest" (1988) to approximately 300 students in grades 1–8. Rylant's story is an allegorical tale of Leo, who is placed in special education because he is "slower than the rest." Leo feels isolated and alone until he finds the turtle Charlie, who is also "slow." It is when Leo decides to talk about Charlie during fire prevention week that Leo gains wings. In his passion for Charlie and other slow creatures for which forest fires are "unfair," Leo causes his class to "love Charlie and hate forest fires." When Leo wins a prize for the best forest fire report, he feels "fast" for the first time.

After the reading, in individual interviews, students were asked open-ended questions designed to elicit insights into their understanding of character. From students' responses to these questions, it was determined that attention to and insights into character change across grades in discernable ways (see Table 2.1).

Students in grades 1 and 2 overwhelmingly focused on the character's external (physical) traits and actions. Although they occasionally mentioned an internal trait, our youngest respondents most frequently talked about Leo's age, gender, and appearance—even though Leo's appearance is never mentioned in the short story. First and second graders also talked readily about Leo's actions. For example, one student observed, "Leo took the turtle to school." Another correctly noted, "He picked the turtle off the highway."

Attention to physical attributes was considerably less among older students. Third graders talked less about Leo's physical traits than did the students in grades 1 and 2. In grades 6–8, no students mentioned Leo's physical features.

Similarly, beyond third grade, the students talked less about a character's actions and behaviors. Instead, they talked about character traits or qualities. In third grade, almost half the students talked about Leo's traits (e.g., "He's kind because he helped that turtle.") or interests (e.g., "He likes turtles."). In grades 4 and 5, another shift occurred: Far more students talked about Leo's feelings (e.g., "He's a boy who doesn't feel part of a group. He's an outsider.") In grades 7 and 8, students inferred facets of Leo's character and

TABLE 2.1   Focus of Students' Responses

Grade	External Character Traits	Example	Internal Character Traits	Example
1–2	• appearance • gender • actions	He's a boy.	• interests • traits	Leo likes turtles.
3–4	• actions	Leo took the turtle to school.	• interests • traits • feelings	He's kind because he helped that turtle.
5–6			• interests • traits • feelings	He's a smart boy because what he said about his project was good.
7–8			• traits • feelings • relationships	He's slow and doesn't have friends, and the turtle becomes his friend.

attempted to verify their judgments by drawing from the story evidence (e.g., "He had low self-esteem [because] he wasn't as fast as others. He could do what they did but slower. When he finally did something, he felt proud of what he accomplished").

Across grade levels, though, few students talked about character relationships—and this may have been a function of the story itself—in which the strongest positive relationship was between a child and an animal. Only in grades 6–8 did we observe an increased number of students talking about character relationships. For example, one eighth grader observed, "He's afraid of what people think about him. He can't fight for himself. He has no friends and needs someone to pick him up."

Finally, older students seemed more ready to consider and admit to a character's change. When we invited the third through eighth graders to talk about whether the main character changed in any way, only half of the third graders believed Leo changed. When third graders did talk about character change, they generally focused on Leo's behavior (e.g., "He changed a little bit because he didn't have a turtle. Then he got a turtle and changed."). By contrast, fourth graders talked primarily about changes in Leo's feelings (e.g., "When he presented his thing about forest fires, at the beginning he was slow. But he won the medal and it made him feel happier and smarter."). Students in grades 5–8 talked most about changes in Leo's feelings (e.g., "He finally has pride in himself when he gets the award."). Among eighth graders, there was nearly complete agreement (94% of the students) that Leo had changed.

Not surprisingly perhaps, we learned that as students develop, they seem to discover and talk about characters from the outside in—from the most visible to the least visible attributes. Our research is consistent with the findings of others who have explored students' literary understanding. For example, Lehr (1991) learned that even young children may talk at length about characters and their motivations. For the kindergartners, second graders, and fourth graders in Lehr's study, talk about character motivation frequently became the pathway along which they were able to discuss story themes. Lehr concludes that students who understood the inner workings of characters are able to take that information and "generate an overarching construct for the story" (p. 52).

Graves (1989) also finds that student responses to character fall along a general developmental continuum. When he invited students in grades 1–6 to write letters about the stories they read, Graves discovered that students in primary grades simply *mention* characters in stories as they write about what happened. Students in intermediate grades give more attention to character motives as they attempt to summarize plots, perhaps seeing the close interconnection between character and plot. As students grow more sophisticated, some are even able to critique the plausibility of events, given the apparent nature of characters, and to explore the interrelationships of characters.

Although there seems to be a general continuum of character understanding along which students move, it is neither prescriptive nor unalterable. Given the right text, timing, experience, and interest, even students in kindergarten and first grade can learn to attend to the inner character, a finding confirmed by Wollman-Bonilla and Werchadlo (1995). These researchers found that nearly a quarter of first graders' responses in literature journals focused on understanding characters. The students "expressed understanding of characters' thoughts or feelings, either stated or implied in the text" (p. 564).

Students at the Same Grade Level Vary in Their Responses to Character

Investigators also find that students may go about the process of constructing literary meaning in highly individual ways. When Lawrence Sipe (1998, 2000) listened closely to the responses of four first and second graders, he found that only one student talked extensively about the feelings of story characters. When Marjorie Hancock (1993) conducted case studies analyses of four middle-grade readers, she found that one in particular had the "ability to enhance...meaning through deeper involvement with the characters" (p. 350). When Lee Galda (1982) investigated the literary responses of three fifth graders, she found that only one student focused extensively on characters' motives and emotional states. This one student, unlike the other two, saw "literature as a narrative of emotions, rather than events..., and distinguished between inner and outer reality [of characters]" (p. 14). These differences suggest that teachers must be carefully attuned to students' responses in order to see which students are primarily interested in following storylines rather than delving into the feelings, thoughts, and beliefs of the characters they meet in stories.

Applying Findings to the Classroom

Character understanding may offer a beacon through story worlds. If teachers are going to help students make use of the light, they must appreciate the importance of character understanding to literary meaning making. They must also be aware of how students grow in their understanding of character while simultaneously recognizing that even young children can begin to explore inner facets of character.

Our own research, as well as that of others, suggests that teachers can take steps to ensure that students attend to the inner workings of the characters they meet in stories. Teachers can bring character-rich literature into the classroom—books like *Amazing Grace* (Hoffman, 1991) for students in the primary grades or *Pictures of Hollis Woods* (Giff, 2002) for older students. Equally important, teachers can help students move beyond attention to plot to explore character traits, feelings, motives, and relationships as they respond to stories through talk, writing, drama, or visual representations.

REFERENCES

Emery, D.W. (1996). Helping readers comprehend stories from the characters' perspectives. *The Reading Teacher, 49,* 534–541.

Forster, E.M. (1927). *Aspects of the novel.* New York: Harcourt Brace.

Galda, L. (1982). Assuming the spectator stance: An examination of the responses of three young readers. *Research in the Teaching of English, 16*(1), 1–20.

Golden, J.M., & Guthrie, J.T. (1986). Convergence and divergence in reader response to literature. *Reading Research Quarterly, 21,* 408–421.

Graves, D.H. (1989). Research currents: When children respond to fiction. *Language Arts, 66*(7), 776–783.

Hancock, M.R. (1993). Exploring the meaning-making process through the content of literature response journals: A case study investigation. *Research in the Teaching of English, 27,* 335–368.

Langer, J.A. (1995). *Envisioning literature: Literary understanding and literature instruction.* New York: Teachers College Press; Newark, DE: International Reading Association.

Lehr, S.S. (1991). *The child's developing sense of theme: Responses to literature.* New York: Teachers College Press.

Lukens, R.J. (1999). *A critical handbook of children's literature* (6th ed.). New York: Longman.

Martinez, M.G., Keehn, S., Roser, N.L., Harmon, J.M., & O'Neal, S. (2002). An exploration of children's understanding of character in grades 1–8. In D.L. Schallert, C.M. Fairbanks, J. Worthy, B. Maloch, & J.V. Hoffman (Eds.), *Fifty-first yearbook of the National Reading Conference* (pp. 310–320). Oak Creek, WI: National Reading Conference.

Martinez, M.G., & Roser, N.L. (1995). The books make a difference in story talk. In N.L. Roser & M.G. Martinez (Eds.), *Book talk and beyond: Children and teachers respond to literature* (pp. 32–41). Newark, DE: International Reading Association.

Nikolajeva, M. (2002). *The rhetoric of character in children's literature.* Lanham, MD: Scarecrow.

Sipe, L.R. (1998). Individual literary response styles of first and second graders. In T. Shanahan & F.V. Rodriguez-Brown (Eds.), *Forty-seventh yearbook of the National Reading Conference* (pp. 76–89). Chicago: National Reading Conference.

Sipe, L.R. (2000). The construction of literary understanding by first and second graders in oral responses to picture storybook read alouds. *Reading Research Quarterly, 35,* 252–275.

Wollman-Bonilla, J.E., & Werchadlo, B. (1995). Literature response journals in a first-grade classroom. *Language Arts, 72,* 562–570.

LITERATURE CITED

Giff, P.R. (2002). *Pictures of Hollis Woods.* New York: Random House.

Hoffman, M. (1991). *Amazing Grace.* Ill. C. Binch. New York: Dial.

Naylor, P.R. (1991). *Shiloh.* New York: Atheneum.

Rylant, C. (1988). Slower than the rest. In *Every living thing* (pp. 1–7). New York: Aladdin.

Part II

Creating

Characters

3

Hey, Character,
Where Did You Come From?

Katherine Paterson

Katherine Paterson knows that characters come from anywhere—an image that won't go away, a snippet of text, a word dropped at just the right time. In this chapter, she gives insights into the creation of Jip, Put, Lyddie, and Robbie—only a few of her memorable characters.

WHERE A CHARACTER COMES FROM IS OFTEN A mystery—even to the writer. The whole writing of my book *Jip, His Story* (Paterson, 1996) involved puzzling questions. All I had when I began was the image of a child falling off the rear of a wagon—a child no one comes back to look for.

How could such a thing happen? I have four children, and I can imagine either of my sons rolling off the back of almost anything, but I can't imagine not eventually noticing, nor, having noticed, not searching heaven and hell to find him. Yet, I was going to write about a child deliberately left

What a Character! Character Study as a Guide to Literary Meaning Making in Grades K–8 edited by Nancy L. Roser and Miriam G. Martinez, with Junko Yokota and Sharon O'Neal. Published by the International Reading Association. Chapter 3 copyright 2005 by Katherine Paterson.

behind on a country road. I had a few clues to what the story would be about because the wagon indicated pre-automobile days. Then, I made the deliberate choice to set the story in Vermont, USA, because I live in Vermont and it is easier to do historical research where you live.

My next puzzling question was, What would happen to a 19th-century boy abandoned among the Vermont hill farms? Some kindly couple might take him in and raise him as their own (Happy ending!), but what kind of a plot would that be? Having written *Lyddie* (Paterson, 1991) a few years earlier, I was familiar with the "poor farms" of Vermont history. Poor farms were conceived as a compassionate and economical way to take care of a community's homeless people. I decided Jip would go to a poor farm. Then I researched the farms of the mid-19th century.

In my research materials I met Putnam Nelson, one of the few characters in any of my books modeled after an actual person. I was reading *History of Hartford, Vermont* (Tucker, 1889) when, in a section telling about the town's poor farm, I came across a paragraph about a resident named Putnam Proctor Wilson. Wilson was one of two people who were mentally ill for whom the town built wooden cages. "These men," says the unnamed writer,

> were raving crazy most of the time, and there caged up like wild beasts in narrow filthy cells, [I] often saw them and their pitiable condition, was impressed with the conviction that the inhuman treatment to which they were subjected, was sufficient of itself to make lunatics of all men. Poor old Put. [*sic*] had some rational moments and was always pleased to see children to whom he would sing the old song, "Friendship to every willing mind" [*sic*], etc., as often as requested. (as cited in Tucker, 1889, p. 308)

Chills went up and down my spine. How could such a man be?—a man seen so dangerous by the authorities that he is confined to a cage and yet, in those times when he is lucid, children come to hear him sing? These children (Where did *they* come from?) were somehow not afraid. They knew Putnam well enough to know that he would sing an old favorite and, like an indulgent grandparent, that he would never tire of singing it for them.

Children often ask me if I put real people in my books and I usually say, "No. Characters in books have to be believable, and real people aren't believable." Still, I was determined to put Putnam Nelson into the book. But would any reader believe him? A psychiatrist friend spent hours reading 19th-century medical texts, searching for a diagnosis. His conclusion was something like this: I totally believe that such a man really lived, but I can't give you a 20th-century diagnosis. Our ways of looking at mental illness have changed radically, and, perhaps, for all we know, the illnesses themselves have changed.

Ironically, although many readers, young and old, have asked me for a diagnosis of the character Put's illness, no one has told me that he was unbelievable. The character they question for believability is Jip. He's too good to be true, I'm often told. That comment makes me sad. It means the questioner has never met someone who is pure in heart, and there are such people in the world. I've known several myself.

However, Robbie Hewitt in *Preacher's Boy* (Paterson, 1999) is not one of them. In the book, Robbie's favorite author is Mark Twain. It does not take a great leap, then, to see where Robbie had his beginnings. When I began to write *Preacher's Boy*, the United States was in the middle of millennia madness. What, I wondered, was happening at the turn of the last century? I read memoirs of that time and went through so many newspapers on microfiche that my eyes blurred and my head pounded. And what I found, sadly, was that many of the problems facing people in 1899 had not gone away in the past 100 years of civilization's halting march. War, poverty, homelessness, ignorance, and all the attendant prejudices still flourish. The marvelous utilization of electricity, the telegraph, the telephone, even the automobile, have not made the world a better or safer place.

I put Robbie into the midst of that imperfect, but hope-filled setting and gave him something every child needs but too few possess: a pair of wise and loving parents. I decided Robbie's father would be a preacher, and so played against stereotypes. A good father is rare in today's fiction, but a wise and loving Christian minister is practically an endangered species. I am the daughter of a minister and my husband is the son and grandson of ministers, as well as being a minister himself. We have four children, all of whom grew up as children of a minister, but *Preacher's Boy* is entirely a work of fiction. Any resemblance to actual persons living or dead is purely coincidental.

But Robbie has to grow. When I first started writing fiction, I developed a slogan to guide me: *Something's got to happen; someone's got to change.* And, of course, the person who has to change in *Preacher's Boy* is Robbie. So along with giving Robbie Tom Sawyer–like adventures, I gave him a brother who is mentally handicapped—a brother that Robbie had to learn to both love and respect.

I have just finished writing my 14th novel. Believe me, it never gets any easier. The day I mailed it to Virginia Buckley, who has been my editor now for 30 years, I said to my dear friend (who is also edited by Virginia), "Well, I'm sure there is plenty wrong with the book, but if Virginia doesn't love these *children*, I'll have to find another editor." It was an empty threat. Besides, Virginia did love the children. But this gives you some idea of how fiercely I love my characters.

Many years ago, I was taking part in a book discussion on *The Great Gilly Hopkins* (Paterson, 1978) with a group of inmates at the Chittenden Correctional Center in Burlington, Vermont. The leader stopped and asked the 20 some men and women earnestly discussing the book how many of them had been foster children. Every single participant raised a hand. Afterward, a tall young man brought his book to me for an autograph. I asked him his name. "No," he said, "I want you to sign it for my daughter. Her name is Angel." Angel is the name of the 11-year-old central character in *The Same Stuff as Stars* (Paterson, 2003).

REFERENCE

Tucker, W.H. (1889). *History of Hartford, Vermont, 1761–1889*. Burlington, VT: Free Press Association.

LITERATURE CITED

Paterson, K. (1978). *The great Gilly Hopkins*. New York: HarperCollins.
Paterson, K. (1991). *Lyddie*. New York: Lodestar/Dutton.
Paterson, K. (1996). *Jip, his story*. New York: Lodestar/Dutton.
Paterson, K. (1999). *Preacher's boy*. New York: Clarion.
Paterson, K. (2003). *The same stuff as stars*. New York: Clarion.

4

Finding My Own Stories, My Own Characters

Deborah Wiles

Deborah Wiles believes characters come from "the stuff of our lives." She explains how she imbues her characters with the qualities and feelings of her own life. Then she shows how, as she works with students, she encourages them to find their own stories— because their personal stories "determine their own characters, and the characters they create."

"OH, MISS EUUUUULA! CAN YOU COME OUT and play?"

In *Love, Ruby Lavender* (Wiles, 2001), 9-year-old Ruby stands in front of Miss Eula's house at the end of each long summer afternoon and calls to her grandmother to come and play with her. Miss Eula always comes to the door and welcomes Ruby inside the Pink Palace, where there is Orange Crush to drink and peanuts to parch and a world on which to ruminate—a Southern world full of stolen chickens, overflowing gardens, staunch enemies, steadfast friends, whispered dreams, terrible tragedies, and a bushel-basket full of hope.

What a Character! Character Study as a Guide to Literary Meaning Making in Grades K–8 edited by Nancy L. Roser and Miriam G. Martinez, with Junko Yokota and Sharon O'Neal. Copyright 2005 by the International Reading Association.

I love Ruby Lavender. She is me, in her overalls and bare feet, her 9-year-old soul reeling from the loss of a beloved grandfather, her heart harboring a secret that will free her once she speaks of it, and her whole life revolving around her relationship with her wacky grandmother, Miss Eula.

Miss Eula is me, too, fanning her face with an old straw hat, championing the underdog and lost causes, understanding that the loss of a lifetime is also a confirmation that life does go on. And, I am Ruby's mortal enemy, Melba Jane, who wears frilly dresses and tappy shoes and curls her hair into a mass of catfish guts cascading around her shoulders, whose vanity gets the best of her, and yet who has a heart that comes to terms with grief and loss and loneliness, that learns how to integrate and transcend those hard feelings and come into a more peaceful place.

I am Dove. I am Aunt Tot. I am Miss Mattie. All of my characters are me. In *Love, Ruby Lavender*, these characters chronicle my own journey through loss and grief, through the minefields of anger and hopelessness, and into the welcoming arms of friendship and love.

If this way of looking at character seems "heavy," it is. But take heart— I don't write thinking, "I will create characters who feel grief and anger (and delight and giddiness), expressing these feelings in their actions." In fact, it is only after I have written a story that I discover its deep themes. I visit the same questions in all my work: What is justice, forgiveness, kinship, love? What are the consequences of our actions and how do they inform our lives? I can look at a story as I finish it and recognize that I'm revisiting these questions. I say, "Oh, you again," and smile.

My students do this too. Whether they are fourth graders or 40-year-olds, they write about their questions. They write about the issues that touch them, the questions that wrestle with their hearts. In his book *How to Write: Advice and Reflections* (1995), Pulitzer Prize–winning author Richard Rhodes writes, "Story is the primary vehicle human beings use to structure knowledge and experience" (p. 197).

Yes, that's it. We tell our stories. We dance them, sing them, paint them, draw them, write them. "Guess what happened to me today," is one way to tell your story. Putting your life into fiction is another. I write fiction that comes directly out of my life experiences. When I teach, I want my students to truly understand that they, too, have the world to write about, that they can create characters who come directly from the stuff of their lives. I try to show them how to do this. I start by sharing some of my story and showing students how the characters in *Love, Ruby Lavender* come directly from the real-life characters I grew up with, as well as from my own heart and experiences, and, ultimately, from my own questions.

Turning Personal Essay Into Fiction

I was born in Alabama and grew up in an Air Force family, moving frequently all my young life. My parents were from Mississippi, so we spent summers in Mississippi surrounded by honeysuckle and heat, baking powder biscuits and general stores, dust and lemon drops, the Methodist hymnal, and a cemetery full of long-ago family. I was fascinated by the smallest details of life in Mississippi—another country, it seemed—and by the eccentric characters who walked across the stage of my life there, who said "I'm not one to gossip, BUT..." and "Bless your heart!" and "Come love my neck!" and "Over my dead body!"

I loved Mississippi. Mississippi was home. My family spent summers in the tiny town of Louin, which became Halleluia in *Love, Ruby Lavender*. I wanted to share this small town in all its glory and grime. As a young writer who was trying to find her voice, I tried to find something to say. I discovered the art of the personal essay in the library when I stumbled across E.B. White's *One Man's Meat* (1941). That led to my reading other writers who were chronicling their lives, sharing their worlds and worldviews. I studied essays, reading them as a writer, trying to figure out how they were written and what made them work. Then I began to imitate them. This has turned out to be my method of learning how to write, and also my method of teaching writing: I use model after wonderful model to learn, to teach, to understand.

I tried to master the personal essay and came to love personal narrative writing. Today, it is by far the most frequent kind of writing I teach. Students come to understand that they have stories to tell. We *all* want to share our stories; it is part of the human experience. How can we access our stories? How can we best share them?

In 1985 I discovered Cynthia Rylant's picturebook *When I Was Young in the Mountains* (1982). It begins,

> When I was young in the mountains, grandfather came home covered with the black dust of a coal mine. Only his lips were clean, and he used them to kiss the top of my head. (n.p.)

I was completely bowled over. This was it. This was what I had been trying to touch. I began to collect picturebooks that chronicled a life-and-times experience—there were oodles of them. I studied them and tried to write my own. I gathered dozens of rejections from children's book publishers; I didn't know how to tell my story, how to access it. What *was* my story? Where was I from? I began to make lists. This was a key.

Making Creative Lists

I discovered George Ella Lyon's (1999) poem "Where I'm From" and it opened a world for me. It begins,

> I am from clothespins and Clorox
> and carbon tetrachloride,
> The dirt under the back porch,
> (black, glistening, it tasted like beets). (p. 3)

I began to list all the stuff of my life—the food (sweet tea, fried okra, stewed tomatoes), the geography (backyard sandbox, tree fort in the sweet gum, knothole in the sugar maple), the history (civil rights movement, Cuban missile crisis, the Beatles), the people (my crazy maiden aunts, wacky grandmother, the little brother who drove me crazy), the places (Mississippi, Hawaii, general stores, schools, military air bases), and on and on—the language, the joys, the sorrows, the holidays and traditions. Look at all I had to write about! It was right there in front of me on my lists.

I have students do this exercise to tell me where they are from. I provide a list of categories (or sometimes we come up with the categories together). I make sure to include feelings such as happy, sad, scared, and mad, and senses such as smells, tastes, touches, sounds, and sights. I also read picturebook after picturebook to them and I ask them to listen, to read, as writers: Where is the author from? How does she tell her story? What techniques does she use?

I have a collection of slice-of-life picturebooks that are wonderful windows into the authors' lives—and into character. Students see that people are always telling their stories—always—and that their personal stories are their histories, their biographies. It's important for students to find ways to tell their stories. The stuff of their lives and how they interpret it, how they respond to it, determines not only their character, but the characters they create.

Let me give you an example of how this works for me as a writer, as a chronicler of my life and my stories.

Infusing Characters With Feeling

In *Love, Ruby Lavender*, which began as a picturebook called *We All Be Jovie and That's the Truth*, I tried to capture my love for a people and a place. I adored my grandmother (who really was named Miss Eula). I wanted to share the feeling I had when I woke up in Mississippi, with the day—the summer—stretching out ahead of me. I had made my lists, remember. Now, with my lists in front of me, I asked myself, How did it *feel*? I began to tell a story with a feeling, and I coupled that feeling with details of Mississippi and with the language of joy:

> I wake up feelin' like the bubbles in an RC Cola—
> All fizzed up and ready to pop!
> The sun salts my eyes and I blink.
> A mockingbird salutes me—Hiya, Dixie!
> I drizzle clovered honey onto buttered biscuits
> And they float down my throat in a happy daze.
> Thwack! Thwack! Granny's pink flip-flops
> Smack her hard little heels, right on down the hallway.
> The screen door slaps shut and there's Annie Mae,
> Smelling like purple grapes on a hot day.
> She totes a mess of baby butterbeans for me to shell
> You know, those beans that taste like shirt cardboard?

Turning Voice Into Character

In the manuscript I go on to describe a day in the life of a young girl in Mississippi, a story based on my real life. A grandmother is in the story. Moon pies, the washateria, the cemetery, and wallpaper roses are in the story. It was my first attempt at fiction, and it caught the eye of editor Liz Van Doren at Harcourt. It never did turn into a saleable manuscript, but it taught me that I had a voice, that I could create a character—many characters—based on my own life. Encouraged, I went back to my lists and poured over them, added to them. Soon another story suggested itself. I plucked my larger-than-life grandmother off the list and began: "Miss Eula was a shining star; she had a poet's heart."

It wasn't long before Miss Eula had a granddaughter named Ruby Garnet Lavender—three colors I loved and that were on my list. Now what? Something had to happen. I consulted my lists. Chickens. My Aunt Beth raised chickens. What did I know about chickens? Not much, but they intrigued me. My eye fell on the three maiden aunts—Ivy, Bemmie, and Bess. Hmmmm...I remembered how they scared me when I was a little girl; they were old and wrinkly and had long, bony fingers, beaky noses, scratchy voices. They were like chickens, weren't they? Yes.

With the sweep of a pen, I created three chickens named Ivy, Bemmie, and Bess. I had them make a dramatic entrance, for my three aunts always made dramatic entrances. I decided that Bess loved to eat, that Bemmie always got into trouble, that Ivy was peaceful and sweet—just like my aunts. I had characters. I had character traits. Now these characters could interact with one another. What did they care about? How did they feel about one another? I didn't know, but I would find out as I let them talk with one another, let things happen to them, as I made it all up based on my life lists.

Miss Eula would leave Ruby and go to Hawaii. I took this event directly from my life. (My father had made a home movie called *Miss Eula Goes to Hawaii*, which was on my list.) When Miss Eula went to Hawaii, Ruby would be bereft (already I was beginning to write about loss and grief, although I didn't see it).

As Ruby and her grandmother began to speak to each other on the page, they became real to me. How could I show their solidarity, their delight in one another? I had them liberate those chickens in the first pages, thereby introducing all the characters. I had them burst onto the stage, look at one another, meet one another, react to one another. They became characters in their own right.

The Crucial Role of the Antagonist

When Liz read the first draft of what would become *Love, Ruby Lavender*, she wisely asked, "Are there any other children in this town?" Well...yeah. OK. Liz nudged me in the right direction: "Ruby needs someone to push against." Melba Jane was born. She is so integral to the story—there is no story without Melba, there is no plot without opposition. At the time I had no clue how to create a character who was Ruby's nemesis, but by then I trusted my list, so I turned to it again. There, smiling at me with his beady little eyes and that look that said, "I'm telling Mom!" was my brother Mike.

I tell my students that Mike tortured me when we were kids. He is a year younger than I am, and he always wanted to do what I did, have what I had, go where I went—and he told on me all the time. He had an angelic smile that said, "I'm so sweet, don't you just *love* me?" but he was a little demon! Oh, I was so angry with Mike when we were young, and he was so jealous of me. I always tell my students that, as writers, they can get revenge against those who did them wrong, and I tell them, "I turned my brother into a 9-year-old girl."

All the qualities that my brother possessed I moved into Melba Jane: She came to life immediately. By remembering how much I had disliked my brother at one time, I was able to make Ruby's reaction to Melba Jane powerful, even visceral. I knew *just* how Ruby felt about Melba. And, since my own heart beats in each of my characters, I also knew just how Melba felt about Ruby—it was the same anger, and I could access it with both characters.

Giving Characters Depth

I tell students that they can use the disappointments, sorrows, and rages of their lives to infuse their characters with emotion and depth—for that's where character depth comes from: the willingness to "go there," to tap the fear you felt, the sweetness you knew, the anger, the joy, all of it.

I give my characters defining characteristics, in order to make each of them distinct and memorable. Some characteristics I make up because they please me, and some come directly from memories, from my list. Ruby's left overall strap keeps slipping off her shoulder, and she is always pushing her red hair out of her face. She says, "Good garden of peas!" when she is surprised or frustrated. I show her steadfastness, her hotheadedness, her determination by listening to her and being true to her feelings, to her heart. How would she react to Melba Jane? To Miss Eula? To her mother?

Lesser characters are important, too, and deserve their own space on the stage. Aunt Tot is a terrible cook, but she doesn't know it. This trait comes directly from my memories of visiting my Aunt Mitt (who, in her day, was a tremendous cook but in her eighties, would serve stale coconut cake and warm root beer, smiling proudly all the while). Evelyn Lavender, Ruby's mother, is the county extension agent (extension agents were on my list). She wears her hair in a long braid (suggestive of my hippie-like days), and offers a sense of order and practicality to Ruby's world, as does Miss Mattie, who runs the general store (which comes from my memories of Mr. Jeff Simmons's store in Louin).

The Stuff of Character

So you see, the stuff of story is threaded all through a life. The stuff of character is already there, too, and students can access it in many ways; writing lists is just one method. If students start with a "one from column A, one from column B" approach when they create characters, it soon grows into an organic process. I have learned to lean into characters: to imbue them with the qualities of others and of myself and to watch them take those qualities and be true to themselves, to change, to grow. My characters always surprise me. And yet, as I finish their stories, I discover that there is no surprise at all; I am simply writing, once again, about my questions—about justice, forgiveness, kinship, and love. And I am writing about what I know: I am writing about my world, my life, my heart.

REFERENCES

Lyon, G.E. (1999). *Where I'm from: Where poems come from.* Spring, TX: Absey.

Rhodes, R. (1995). *How to write: Advice and reflections.* New York: William Morrow.

White, E.B. (1941). *One man's meat.* New York: HarperCollins.

LITERATURE CITED

Rylant, C. (1982). *When I was young in the mountains.* Ill. D. Goode. New York: Dutton.

Wiles, D. (2001). *Love, Ruby Lavender.* San Diego, CA: Harcourt Gulliver.

5

Character Is the Engine

Kate DiCamillo

The creator of the characters India Opal Buloni, Gloria Dump, and Despereaux, Kate DiCamillo shows that "there is salvation in stories with characters who are real to us." When asked what the best way to make stories is, DiCamillo likes to say, "Start with a good character, and the rest will take care of itself."

"Scarlett O'Hara was not beautiful, but men seldom realized it when caught by her charm as the Tarleton twins were." (Mitchell, 1936, p. 3)

THAT SENTENCE IS, I FIGURE, AS GOOD A PLACE AS any to start a talk about character. I was 9 years old when I met Scarlett O'Hara. It was a rainy Saturday morning in Florida during hurricane season. I had read all of my library books, and I was waiting for my mother to take me to the library so that I could check out more.

"Hurry," I told her. She was sitting at the dining room table grading papers. "I don't have anything to read."

"Find something to do," my mother said, without looking up at me.

What a Character! Character Study as a Guide to Literary Meaning Making in Grades K–8 edited by Nancy L. Roser and Miriam G. Martinez, with Junko Yokota and Sharon O'Neal. Copyright 2005 by the International Reading Association.

"That's what I'm telling you, I don't have anything to do. I really, really need a book. I'm bored." I paced back and forth in front of her. I cracked my knuckles.

"Do not tell me that you are bored," said my mother with her teeth gritted. "Find something to do. Now."

The something I found to do was to sit down next to the sleeping dog and pull back her eyelid to make sure that she was really, genuinely sleeping and not just faking it. Beneath her eyelid, there was another piece of skin, a membranous curtain that did not move. I poked it. I tried to peel it back. It wouldn't budge. The dog chuffed a small protest. Her feet twitched. She was dreaming, running somewhere.

"For God's sake," said my mother, again without looking up, "leave the dog alone."

I got up and wandered into the living room. I stared at the book-lined shelves. What torture it was—when I so desperately wanted, needed, was dying for a book—to be faced with *these* books, the living room books, the adult books.

Their sins were many: They had no pictures. The type was small. And they were brown. All of them, everywhere. Brown spine. Brown cover. The simple act of opening one seemed to release a brown miasma in the air. The books smelled like mildew. They smelled like rainy, boring Saturday mornings.

I sighed.

From the dining room, my mother shouted, "I'll give you something to sigh about."

I sighed again; and then, as a way of intensifying my suffering, I reached out and took down from the shelf the fattest, the brownest, the most boring-looking book. I opened it. Mildew. The rich, deep smell of decaying paper. And written on the flyleaf in faded blue ink: "From Honey to Tootie, who is brave, too. April 3, 1937." How in the world, I wondered, could anybody with a name like Tootie be brave? I rolled my eyes.

I flipped to the last page: 1,037. I took the book to the dining room and sat on the floor next to the dog. I leaned over and peeled back her eyelid again. That other, dark curtain was still there. Her feet were still twitching. What was she dreaming about?

"I mean it," said my mother. "Leave. The dog. Alone. Find. Something. To do."

"Who was Tootie?" I asked.

"Who?"

"Tootie."

"I have no idea," said my mother.

"It says in this book that she was brave."

"Hmmmm," said my mother. "Really."

"I'm going to read this book. It has 1,037 pages."

"Good," said my mother. "That's excellent. *That's* brave."

I opened the book. Chapter one. "Scarlett O'Hara was not beautiful...."

It was 1973. I was in the dining room, sitting on the floor. The carpet was yellow, sculptured shag. It was raining outside and dark as night, even though it was 10 o'clock in the morning. My mother was grading papers. The dog was sleeping beside me, her flank rising and falling.

That was the world that I was in...and then I was gone from it, pulled into a story that I didn't totally understand, pulled there by a character who was complicated and troublesome and very, very real.

I did as my mother suggested. I found something to do: I disappeared into *Gone With the Wind*. Over the next month, nothing existed for me except that book.

"Law," said Ida Belle Collins, our next-door neighbor, "Look at her carrying that book around with her everywhere she goes. Bigger than her and likely to squash her to death if she drops it."

"Not really meant for you, my dear," said Mrs. Mumphy, the school librarian. But she let me go on reading.

"What's it about?" asked my brother, bending over to look at the book.

"Um," I said, struggling for an answer that would satisfy him, "The Civil War?"

"Oh," he said. He nodded. "The Civil War, the war between the states." And he straightened up and started reeling off figures and numbers and battles and generals.

"You know who the real heroine of that book is, don't you?" asked my fourth-grade teacher, Mrs. Landau.

I sensed a trick question. I was a nimble child, quick on my feet, adept at discerning what answer an adult wanted and then giving it to them. "Melanie?" I replied, after some careful, adult-like cogitation.

"Yes," said Mrs. Landau, "exactly. Remember that. Melanie is the good one. She is the true heroine."

I did not tell Mrs. Landau that if the book had been about Melanie Wilkes and Melanie Wilkes alone, I would have long since stopped reading. Pure, unmitigated good doesn't make for a compelling story. But Scarlett O'Hara lying, cheating, stealing—there was a story.

There was a character.

For me, both as a reader and as a writer, character *is* story. Character is the engine, the powerful, complex, whirring, humming, intricate thing that pulls me forward when I'm reading and that pulls the story forward when I'm writing. To find the answer to why that is, why character is so powerful, I turn to E.M. Forster (1927):

> We cannot understand each other, except in a rough and ready way, we cannot reveal ourselves, even when we want to, what we call intimacy is only a makeshift; perfect knowledge is an illusion. But in the novel, we can know people perfectly and apart from the pleasure of reading, we can find here a compensation for their dimness in life. In this direction, fiction is truer than history, because it goes beyond the evidence, and each of us knows from his own experience that there is something beyond the evidence.... [Characters in novels] are people whose secrets lives are visible or might be visible: we are people whose secret lives are invisible. And that is why novels, even when they are about wicked people, can solace us; they suggest a more comprehensible and thus a more manageable human race, they give us the illusion of perspicacity and power. (pp. 98–99)

In that Florida dining room in 1973, my mother sat grading papers, unknowable to me. My father had left the family four years before and it was impossible, really, for anyone to say exactly why. I knew nothing beyond the evidence. I knew only that he was gone. And beside me on the floor, the dog slept, her secret life hidden behind the membrane curtain of her eye.

In all our relationships with other living beings that curtain exists. It is merciful as it separates us, to some degree, from their pain. But it separates us, too, from their hearts, from the true knowing of another. In good, character-based fiction, the curtain is removed, the veil lifted. And that, as Forster points out, is empowering. It is empowering because understanding the other sheds light, somehow, on our own dark hearts.

In *Gone With the Wind*, Scarlett O'Hara comes back to Tara and finds her mother dead, her father insane, and the house destroyed. This, it seems, is the basic, elemental fear of childhood; and it has the force and power of a fairy tale. Because Scarlett's heart (troubled and dark though it may be) was visible to me, I was empowered. I was 9 years old, but I was dealing, still, with the loss of my father. I was faced, as all children are, with the daunting prospect of surviving in an uncertain world.

I am not making a case for *Gone With the Wind* being great literature. I am saying that Scarlett is a great character. I am saying that there is salvation in stories with characters who are real to us. Those characters can lead us through darkness, to the other side, to light, to survival, to understanding.

As a writer, too, it is in character that I find my salvation. When I go into schools and talk about writing, one of the first questions I am asked is, How do you do it? How do you make up stories?

Look, I say, I'll show you. We'll make up a story together. And I give the kids some character names: Susie LaTouche, Franco Swiper, Gerald Pinker. Then I tell them three things about each of these characters. I give each character a physical detail: Susie LaTouche has a tattoo of a winged horse on her left bicep. Franco Swiper is missing his pinky finger. Gerald Pinker combs his hair straight down so that the bangs cover his eyes.

I give each character an emotional detail: Susie LaTouche has a deep and profound fear of flying. Franco Swiper cries every time he sees a picture of his Granny Eileena Rose. Gerald Pinker regrets that he never told his brother Lamott that he loved him.

And finally, I give each character a prop. In her purse, Susie LaTouche has a postcard from Spain signed, "Love, Alberto." Franco Swiper never leaves home without a screwdriver. Gerald Pinker wears bright white tennis shoes.

Then I ask the students to write a diary entry for Susie LaTouche, a news release about Franco Swiper, a letter from Gerald Pinker to his brother Lamott. From these small exercises arise the most incredible, wonderful, amazing, imaginative stories.

Start with a character, and the story takes care of itself. Or, as Flannery O'Connor (1969) said, "If you start with a real personality, a real character, then something is bound to happen" (p. 106). Character *is* the engine.

But I know what you are going to say: "Yes, but where do the characters *come* from?" People ask this question of writers all the time. They ask with suspicion (as in, "You're not writing about me and my unhealthy relationship with Ted, are you?"). They ask with wonder (as in, "How does a little girl like you make up those big old characters?"). They ask the question for practical purposes (as in, "I, too, would like to make up some characters. Where do I start?"). And they ask with love and longing (as in, "I miss those people. Where did they come from? I want to go to that place, too.").

But alas, no matter how they ask the question, no matter what they mean by it, my answer is always the same: I don't know.

And I really, truly don't.

But, I get tired of saying "I don't know" all the time. And I get the feeling that people get tired of hearing me saying it. Worse, I get the very distinct feeling that people think I am being crafty, that I am guarding trade secrets or purposefully playing dumb.

In the spirit of honesty, I have taken a close look at some of my characters. I have tried to figure out where they come from. I have tried to trace them back to their origins.

In a story called "Bee Hugs" (DiCamillo, 2001a), a middle-aged Vietnam veteran who dresses up as a bee passes out biscuit-and-honey samples for Captain Bob's Bee-licious Biscuit restaurant. Where did this character come from? The answer is a busy intersection in Jacksonville, Florida. I saw a man waiting to cross the street who was wearing the bottom half of a bear costume and holding a big bear head under his left arm. He looked tired and lonely—and way too old to be dressed up like a bear. His haggard face stayed in my mind, and when I sat down to write, that face, with all its questions and despair, shone before me. The bear mutated into a big, old bee, and the story was off and running.

India Opal Buloni, the narrator of *Because of Winn-Dixie* (DiCamillo, 2000), made an appearance during a long, hard winter. One night before I fell asleep, in my mind I heard a little girl's voice with a southern accent say, "I have a dog named Winn-Dixie." I sat down the next morning and started to write; and Opal, it turned out, had a lot more to say. She was a character born from listening, a character born from a single, strange, late-night sentence.

When I worked at a bookstore, I loved to rifle through the lost and found box. I never knew what would turn up. One day, under the usual jumble of gloves and scarves and one-armed baby dolls, I discovered a picture of three kids posing with the Easter bunny. Off to the far right, almost cut out of the picture, but not quite, was a hard-bitten woman smoking a cigarette, looking bored and disgusted. "Look at you," I whispered to the picture, "smoking with the Easter bunny." The next morning when I sat down to write, I saw that bored, defiant, hurting face. How did somebody like that end up waiting in line to get her picture taken with the Easter bunny? I wrote a story to find out—"And Mothers Wonder Why Their Babies Cry" (DiCamillo, 2003).

I saw the midget Celestine, the main character of my short story "Nova" (unpublished) one day when I was driving home from work. She was standing on the side of the road with her hands on her hips, staring at a Chevy Nova that had steam rising out of its raised hood. I said out loud as I went past her, "Don't worry, I'll write it all down." And I tried to—in a story that tells how important that Nova was to Celestine.

Another character came from a photograph, this one a picture that one of my best friends from college showed me. In the snapshot, my friend is 10 years old, sitting on a gold bedspread, and wearing white knee socks.

"Where was this taken?" I asked her.

"That," she said, "was taken in a hotel called The Kentucky Star. It was the hotel where my parents' marriage ended. Really, as far as I was concerned, it was the hotel where the whole world ended."

So I wrote a story called "Leverage" (unpublished) about the end of the world. A little girl named Norma witnesses the dissolution of her parents' marriage in a hotel room in Kentucky. In the story, there was a secondary character named Rob whose father was the maintenance man at the hotel. When I finished writing "Leverage," Rob wouldn't go away. I couldn't figure out what he wanted. Until a tiger came along. And Rob's story turned into *The Tiger Rising*, a novel about a boy and a tiger and a girl named Sistine Bailey (DiCamillo, 2001b).

So, there are some answers about where characters come from, I guess. Though it seems to me that the mystery, the I-don't-know, of where characters come from is still firmly in place. Why that photograph? Why that person? Why that voice?

I don't know. But I do know that when I read back over these answers, the same phrases keep popping out at me:

I saw.

I listened.

I looked.

I heard.

I sat down.

I wrote.

And finally, this phrase, perhaps the most important of them all:

I wrote to find out.

Characters, when you write about them, work the same magic as they do when you read about them: They remove the veil and help you to understand the heart of another; thereby helping you to understand your own heart.

In a wonderful essay titled "Better and Sicker," author Lorrie Moore (1994) says that there are no easy answers, that "Most things literary are stubborn as colds; they resist all formulas—a chemist's, a wet nurse's, a magician's. Finally, there is no formula outside the sick devotion to the work" (p. 190). Moore goes on to quote poet William Carlos Williams: "Catch an eyeful, catch an earful and don't drop what you've caught" (p. 190).

In other words, look, listen, and then sit down and try to capture it. But underlying all the looking and listening and trying to hold on, there should be—there must be—curiosity, amazement, a sense of wonder.

When I was a junior in college, I decided that I would be a writer. I went and visited my father specifically to deliver this portentous news. I sat at his kitchen table and said my piece, something about how I felt myself called to a life of higher art and suffering; and then, looking off into the distance, bravely facing my tortured future, I recited a poem by Berryman that begins this way, "Life, friends, is boring. We must not say so" (Berryman, 1982, p. 16).

I recited this poem in its entirety, hoping to impress my father with my resolve, my world-weariness, my intention to go on and create art in spite of the fact that the world was such a grim and dull place.

When I was done, my father cleared his throat and said, "You don't really believe that, do you?"

"What?"

"That life is boring?"

I shrugged.

"You can't be a writer if you believe that," he said. He was genuinely dismayed. "Look," he said. "You can't be bored. If you want to be a writer, you have to be *amazed*, always, constantly, forever amazed."

"Whatever," I said. And I shrugged my shoulders again.

But over my desk now, 17 years after that conversation, there hangs a little sign that says "Make like Kathy Plinkett on the way to the pencil sharpener." Why? Because Kathy Plinkett knew how to be amazed.

You probably don't know Kathy Plinkett (pseudonym). She was my best friend in grade school. And in the fifth grade, when we were finally together in the same classroom, Kathy spent most of the year sharpening her pencil. Kathy's desk was at the back of the room and by walking up to the front, to the pencil sharpener, she got to stare at everybody in the classroom.

And stare she did: Her mouth was open; her eyes were dreamy and intent. It was evident that Kathy Plinkett was amazed, delighted, transported by the variety and wonder of human nature. She stared to see what people were wearing. She noted the wax in their ears and the dirt under their nails and the bandages on their fingers. She ogled what they were reading, what they were writing, the jewelry they were wearing. She took note of frayed socks and bitten nails and bruises and haircuts. She stopped to listen to conversations. Kathy's forays to the pencil sharpener and back were field trips, sociological studies, inquiries into human nature, small celebrations of its eccentricities.

"Lord God," shouted Mrs. Funnel, our fifth-grade teacher, "how many times a day do you have to sharpen that pencil?" Or, "Sweet, suffering Lucinda, if you're going to sharpen your pencil, then sharpen it and sit back down and quit eyeballing people."

Whenever Mrs. Funnel yelled, Kathy picked up the pace, but she did not stop staring.

"The writer," wrote Flannery O'Connor (1969), "should never be ashamed of staring. There is nothing that doesn't require his attention" (p. 84). I believe this advice is essential to the writer. Hone your sense of wonder. Look. Listen. Marvel. And the characters will come to you. As Lorrie Moore (1994) says,

> It is crucial to keep ourselves, as a species, interested in ourselves. When that goes, we tip into the void, we harden to rock, we blow away and disappear. Art has been given to us to keep us interested and engaged... so that we can attach to this life, a life that might, otherwise, be an unbearable one. (p. 184)

That is what Scarlett O'Hara did for me as I sat on the floor of the dining room, the sleeping dog beside me. She engaged me, made me interested in myself. She revealed her heart to me and, by doing so, nailed me firmly to the earth. She made my sometimes unbearable life more bearable, more comprehensible.

When we write, when we summon characters out of the mist and on to the printed page, we are connecting with ourselves and with each other. Good characters deepen the mystery of existence. At the same time, they shed light on that mystery. This is why characters in books are so powerful, so necessary.

Let us all—as readers, as writers, and as human beings—make like Kathy Plinkett on the way to the pencil sharpener and be perpetually amazed by the characters, real and imagined, who inhabit it, who reveal their hearts to us, who keep us so firmly here.

REFERENCES

Berryman, J. (1982). Dream song 14. *The dream songs*. New York: Noonday Press.

Forster, E.M. (1927). *Aspects of the novel*. New York: Harcourt Brace.

Moore, L. (1994). Better and sicker. In J. Heffron (Ed.), *The best writing on writing* (pp. 182–190). Cincinnati, OH: Story Press.

O'Connor, F. (1969). *Mystery and manners: Occasional prose*. New York: Farrar Straus Giroux.

LITERATURE CITED

DiCamillo, K. (2000). *Because of Winn-Dixie*. Cambridge, MA: Candlewick.

DiCamillo, K. (2001a). Bee hugs. *Minnesota Monthly, 35*, 40–41.

DiCamillo, K. (2001b). *The tiger rising*. New York: Candlewick.

DiCamillo, K. (2003, Fall). And mothers wonder why their babies cry. *Water-Stone Review, 6*(1), 116–129.

Mitchell, M. (1936). *Gone with the wind*. New York: Macmillan.

6

The Power of Small Moments

Kimberly Willis Holt

Drawing from her own stories as well as stories by others, Kimberly Willis Holt shows how authors reveal characters through "small moments."

AFTER WATCHING THE TELEVISION MOVIE OF my novel *My Louisiana Sky* (Holt, 1998b), my friend Sug called me. "I loved the movie," she said, "but I kept waiting for Granny to open the porch screen door and empty her coffee cup into the yard." Sug missed that moment in the book that gave her a glimpse into Granny's no-nonsense personality and country ways.

Large important decisions made by characters during the plot are not the only way writers help readers grow to understand characters. Small moments also build characters as real as life. Many times characters unfold gently through a gesture, a bit of dialogue, or even an observation. These small moments may be subtle, but don't underestimate their strength.

What a Character! Character Study as a Guide to Literary Meaning Making in Grades K–8 edited by Nancy L. Roser and Miriam G. Martinez, with Junko Yokota and Sharon O'Neal. Copyright 2005 by the International Reading Association.

In *Prairie Songs* (1985) author Pam Conrad demonstrates how a single moment can reveal character. The main character, Louisa, and her family meet the new doctor and his beautiful wife who have just arrived at their Nebraska prairie. Shortly after introductions, Louisa's mother serves milk to the doctor's wife, Mrs. Berryman. In that brief time, Louisa compares her mother to the doctor's wife:

> I followed her gaze to my mother, suddenly shocked by the contrast. Was Momma really that plain? Plain as a walnut. Her hair was wound up out of sight, holding none of the promise of those wheat-colored treasures pinned behind Mrs. Berryman's delicate ears. Momma's face seemed heavy, her skin creased into fine folds like the sleeves of her blouse rolled up over her elbows. (p. 14)

Louisa longs for something different and more exciting than the life she's known. This yearning unfolds throughout the story, but readers see an early glimpse of this in Louisa's comparison of her mother and Mrs. Berryman. Later in the story readers witness Louisa's growth and admiration for her mother's strength opposed to Emmeline Berryman's fragility. After the doctor and his wife lose their baby, Emmeline retreats within and loses a part of herself. Louisa's mother feels her own stress from the experience, a reminder of having recently lost a child of her own, yet she deals with the hardship in a completely different way from Emmeline:

> She scooped the eggs into the bowl and walked over to one of the pots that was full of water, ready to overflow. She carried it to the door and opened it, letting in a gush of air. She flung the water away from the house, and as she did so, she let out an earsplitting scream, long and loud and awful, that must have skittered for miles over the prairie. She was smiling as she turned to us and closed the door. "There," she said, straightening her collar and setting the pot back down in a puddle beneath the never-ending drip. (p. 117)

In *When Zachary Beaver Came to Town* (Holt, 1999), I could have written the character Scarlett Stalling as a stereotyped, self-centered, junior high school beauty, but I wanted her to have a heart and to eventually realize Toby's feelings for her—even if she couldn't return them. I tried to convey this in a scene when Scarlett returns to Toby his mother's pearl necklace:

> Scarlett tucks a strand of hair behind her ear and tilts her head in a way that makes me melt. "Toby Wilson, you are the nicest boy in

Antler." She walks out of the kitchen and out of the café, her sandals slapping the linoleum floor. (p. 183)

Patricia MacLachlan tells a spare, but powerful, story in *Sarah, Plain and Tall* (1985). At the beginning of the book, we understand that the motherless children have a loving, affectionate father. MacLachlan accomplishes this with few words:

> Papa put his arms around me and put his nose in my hair.
> "Nice soapy smell, that stew," he said.
> I laughed. "That's my hair."
> Caleb came over and threw his arms around Papa's neck and hung down as Papa swung him back and forth, and the dogs sat up. (pp. 6–7)

Jolene, the main character in *Mister and Me* (Holt, 1998a), is sassy and gutsy. These characteristics are magnified when Jolene cuts into jigsaw pieces the velvet that Leroy, her future father, buys for her mother. Later in the story I reveal Jolene's vulnerable side when she leaves the Valentine's dance with Leroy:

> Then Leroy did something that shook me to the core. Something I had never heard him do before. He whistled. He whistled a tune like the ones I remembered my daddy whistling years before. I slid my hand into his, and he suddenly stopped whistling. Car engines started and filled the night air like a band warming up before a show. Then Leroy tightened his grip around my hand and went back to whistling that song. (p. 67)

Until that moment, Jolene has kept an emotional distance from Leroy even though she feels a void not having a father. Leroy's whistling reminds Jolene of her father and her desire to fill that void. When she slides her hand into Leroy's, she opens her heart to him. It is a mere sliver in time, but it changes her life dramatically.

When Leshaya in Han Nolan's *Born Blue* (2001) is accused of stealing from her foster family, she makes such a good case in defending herself that I believe her until the next chapter, when she says,

> I looked into the mirror and told myself to be strong. I had to be stronger than them all ganging up on me. I thought 'bout them things I took. Didn't know why I took them 'cept they was pretty. (p. 120)

Leshaya's self-assessment makes the reader understand that she lied, not only because she didn't want her foster family to know she stole from them, but also because she saw her denial as a way of standing up to them. The reader gets a sense that she believes people have been against her in the past and her actions are a result of that belief. This scene, combined with her convincing denial earlier, also makes readers realize that she cannot be trusted. This small moment unveils one of Leshaya's flaws and gives us insight into her background, making her character "real."

In Richard Peck's *A Long Way From Chicago* (1998), Joey defies his fear of being beaten up by Ernie Cowgill when he hears his sister scream in the kitchen. Joey's love for his sister outweighs his fear. His ability to rise above that fear defines his protective side.

Though fleeting, these moments will stay with me forever and, as a result, so will the characters.

Occasionally a moment betrays a character and makes me reject a story; like trying to jam the wrong puzzle piece into an open spot, the moment doesn't fit the character. Once I read a book that takes place in the early 20th century in which the main character's mother is quite modern thinking. The author did a fine job convincing me of the plausability of this by showing the mother in defining situations, including smoking in front of men to prove she is tough enough to accompany them on a rugged journey. But later, when the mother is appalled at the suggestion that she and her daughter wear pants because they will be riding horses every day of the trip, I lost my belief in the character as well as the story. I just couldn't reconcile the mother's earlier modern thinking and actions with her strong negative reaction to wearing pants. A mere moment can make a character real, or it can destroy the character. A moment is powerful.

It's no wonder that I am drawn to small moments as a way of revealing character. Sometimes a small moment in my own life inspires a character. When I was 9, my mother and I rode to my grandmother's house in the Louisiana piney woods. We passed a lady walking on the side of the road. Because something about her looked scary to me, I mentioned the woman to my mom. She explained that the lady was mentally retarded and that her husband was as well. She told me they had a lot of children. Although I never saw that lady again, I thought of her often and, as I grew up, I wondered about what had happened to her children. That tiny moment played over and over in my mind until eventually the woman on the road inspired Corrina in *My Louisiana Sky* (Holt, 1998b).

Traces of my childhood slip into much of my writing. When I was in third grade, my mother enrolled me in dancing lessons. The day of the first class, we arrived early and I waited in the car with my mother. I felt a mixture of excitement and insecurity. Most of the girls I would be in class with had been taking lessons since they were three. I dreamed of twirling on my toes and of finally accomplishing a perfect cartwheel. The only skill I felt confident about was a somersault. I could do a mean somersault. I'd practiced across the living room shag carpet for months.

While my mother thumbed through a copy of *Redbook* magazine, waiting for class to begin, I watched a group of girls my age in black leotards and pink tights gather in a corner of the teacher's yard. They were, no doubt, my future classmates, and I wanted terribly to be standing outside the car in their circle. My mother glanced up from her magazine and noticed me looking at them. "You can get out of the car if you want," she said, probably assuming that I would walk over and introduce myself. Instead, I opened the car door, squatted in the start position and proceeded to somersault my way across the grass.

"What a showoff!" one girl exclaimed. The others giggled.

Embarrassed and confused that my perfect somersaults didn't impress them, I rushed back into the safety of our car. "What did you expect?" my mother asked, shaking her head.

As painful as that incident was to me, I revisited it when I wrote about Racine's first dance class experience in *Dancing in Cadillac Light* (Holt, 2001). I changed it some, though:

> Racine looked longingly at the girls, then asked, "Can I wait over there?"
>
> "Go ahead," Momma said.
>
> "You don't have to stay, Momma," Racine said. "I'll get in okay."
>
> "I do have to. I need to pay Lynette. Besides, it's too far to walk all the way home to have to turn back around."
>
> I'd have bet anything Racine was going to twist her butt, walking over to that snobby group, but no, she plumb surprised me. Racine did six one-handed cartwheels across Miss Logan's yard until she landed with both arms straight up smack in front of those girls.
>
> "What a show-off!" Frannie said.
>
> Curtie Lou stepped forward. "Yeah, Racine Lambert, what are you doing here?"
>
> My hands curled into fists. The last time I'd fought was in second grade, when I'd socked Randy Harper in the mouth for tripping me in class. But when I started to charge toward those prissy girls, Momma snapped her fingers. "Jaynell, let it be."

Racine planted her hands on her hips. "I'm taking dancing lessons now. I'm in your class."

The girls exchanged looks. Frannie tightened her ponytail. "But we have a recital in a few months. We've been practicing since September. How are you going to know the steps?"

"Yeah," Curtie Lou said, "you're going to make us look like fools."

"I'm a fast learner." Racine spun around, then headed back to us. I was almost proud of her. She sounded so tough. That's why I was surprised when she reached us with wet eyes.

"What did you expect, showing off like that?" Momma said when Racine plopped down next to us on the curb.

Racine closed her eyes tight like she was trying to keep tears locked up. "I just want to dance." (pp. 125–126)

In this brief scene, I show the traits of both Racine and the narrator. Racine is a showoff, but sensitive enough to be hurt by the girls' remarks. Jaynell thinks her sister Racine is prissy, but still wants to defend her when someone causes her pain.

I also use glimpses of real life to add details to a story. I walk daily for my health, but these neighborhood tromps serve as treasure hunts for details, too. Once I passed a group of young children walking in a procession, wearing upside-down plant pots on top of their heads. The image amused me and I quickly recognized it as something spoiled, bratty Tara might do (that would reveal her bossy side). That moment became a part of *When Zachary Beaver Came to Town* (Holt, 1999):

> Before I step through the gate, Tara and three other little kids march past me in a line. Upside-down plastic plant pots perch on top of their heads. Tara, the leader of the pack, has about seven vacation Bible school ribbons pinned to her shirt. Moist wisps of hair cling to her sunburned face.
>
> She walks up to me and says, "We're having a parade, and I'm the mayor. And they're the Shiners." (p. 100)

Sometimes I fret over the tiniest image: Will the reader pick up on what I'm trying to show about this character? When Mrs. Cruz in *Keeper of the Night* (Holt, 2003) offers to visit Isabel's brother in the mental hospital, Isabel tells her the hospital is picky about visitors: "'Oh,'" [Mrs. Cruz] says, staring down at her feet. I'm not sure she understands, so I add, "'I mean I just got to see him today for the first time'" (p. 277).

By having Mrs. Cruz stare down at her feet, I wanted to show her feeling of inadequacy. And I wanted Isabel's perceptiveness to shine when she explains why Mrs. Cruz won't be able to visit her brother. Can brief descriptions accomplish that kind of insight into characters? I think so.

Most of the mail I get from readers mentions their favorite scenes, most often major plot-points in the story. Of course I'm pleased whenever people share their enjoyment with something I have written. Occasionally, though, a reader expresses how much he or she likes a scene that is not a major plot point, such as the one in *My Louisiana Sky* (Holt, 1998b) in which Tiger's mother is peeling potatoes after she has spent weeks in bed, grieving for Granny.

Letters from readers that discuss small moments are rare, and I treasure them dearly. Because I know, without ever meeting that reader, that we are kindred souls, bonded by our appreciation for characters revealed through the smallest of moments.

LITERATURE CITED

Conrad, P. (1985). *Prairie songs.* New York: Harper & Row.

Holt, K.W. (1998a). *Mister and me.* New York: Putnam.

Holt, K.W. (1998b). *My Louisiana sky.* New York: Holt.

Holt, K.W. (1999). *When Zachary Beaver came to town.* New York: Holt.

Holt, K.W. (2001). *Dancing in Cadillac light.* New York: Putnam.

Holt, K.W. (2003). *Keeper of the night.* New York: Holt.

MacLachlan, P. (1985). *Sarah, plain and tall.* New York: Harper & Row.

Nolan, H. (2001). *Born blue.* San Diego, CA: Harcourt.

Peck, R. (1998). *A long way from Chicago.* New York: Dial.

The Shades of Character

Franny Billingsley

Franny Billingsley writes that her plot comes first and that she "backs into" the creation of characters. But it is when character intersects with plot that "character springs to life." And once a character has needs, motives, and places to go, that character may surprise you—just as Corinna does in *The Folk Keeper*.

THERE ARE A HUNDRED PLACES TO BEGIN A NOVEL, which means there are a hundred places to begin developing a character. My novels spring from story—from the nugget of a plot idea—and so my task is to develop a character who will serve the needs of my plot. I back into character, so to speak. Other writers, such as Lois Lowry (2001), begin with character. As Lowry says,

> I always go about the creation of a character, first. Then I set a series of events in motion—starting, usually, with one precipitating incident. (A soldier calls, "Halte!" A girl, mourning her mother, stands and walks away from the body. A puppy is abandoned in an alley.) I move the character through those events, and the character responds *the way*

What a Character! Character Study as a Guide to Literary Meaning Making in Grades K–8 edited by Nancy L. Roser and Miriam G. Martinez, with Junko Yokota and Sharon O'Neal. Copyright 2005 by the International Reading Association.

that character would. Each response triggers new events—and the character again responds *the way that character would.* (p. 4, emphasis in original)

Lowry starts with character, while I start with plot, but what is true for us both is that character springs to life as it intersects with plot. Lowry's character responds "the way that character would," which triggers new plot events. My plot forces my character to act in certain ways, which in turn triggers new plot events.

In his book *Story* (1997), Robert McKee makes an interesting connection between plot and character:

Medieval scholarship devised another ingenious conceit: the *Mind Worm.* Suppose a creature had the power to burrow into the brain and come to know an individual completely—dreams, fears, strength, weakness. Suppose that this Mind Worm also had the power to cause events in the world. It could then create a specific happening geared to the unique nature of that person that would trigger a one-of-a-kind adventure, a quest that would force him to use himself to the limit, to live to his deepest and fullest. Whether a tragedy or fulfillment, this question would reveal his humanity absolutely. (p. 374)

I love the idea that the character's journey is unique to her, that it's the only journey that would test this particular character. And although it makes intuitive sense to design the journey to fit the character, my process doesn't allow that. I have to work backward and design the character to fit the event. I have to ask myself, what kind of character will this event test to the limit?

My biggest struggle is finding the true heart of my plot, which means I have to find the true heart of my character. To explain: Although I start with the nugget of a plot idea—I know the central story problem—I know neither how my protagonist becomes embroiled in the problem nor how she extricates herself. And as it turns out, I can only solve those problems by coming to understand my character more deeply. It's the old chicken-and-egg question: Which comes first, plot or character? Didn't I just finish saying that I start with plot? Am I now saying that I start with character? My process is murky, susceptible not to rational explanation but rather to illumination— illumination through example. So come with me, if you will, on a journey through the creation of my second novel, *The Folk Keeper* (1999). The way is dark, but if you will follow, I will carry the lantern.

The novel was inspired by the selkie stories, the stories of those creatures who swim in the sea in the form of seals, but who can, by shedding their sealskins, walk the land as human beings. If, however, their sealskin should be lost or stolen while they're in their human form, they can never return to the sea. Perhaps the best known of the selkie stories—in this country, at least—is the story of the fisherman who falls in love with a selkie maiden and steals her sealskin so that she must remain on land and become his wife. In a bittersweet twist, one of their children finds the sealskin and, without understanding what it is, shows it to the selkie woman. The selkie woman then returns to the sea, leaving her human family behind.

Those children have always haunted me: What must it be like to be half-selkie, half-human? And so I began *The Folk Keeper* by modeling my protagonist, Corinna, on those children. Corinna knows nothing of her true heritage; she has been brought up in an orphanage. She thinks she's a human and she looks like a human, but there are mysterious things about Corinna that she herself cannot explain (for example, she always knows what time it is and her hair grows two inches every night). Corinna eventually comes to live with a family on a rocky island, and it is there, surrounded by water, that she comes to understand who she truly is. She then has to make a decision: Is she more of a selkie and will she live a life mostly in the sea? Or, is she more of a human being, and will she live a life mostly on land?

I began, then, with the idea for the major plot complication—half-human girl discovers her heritage and has to decide who, or what, she truly is—but I knew neither how she was going to discover the truth nor what her decision would be. It is difficult to begin a novel knowing so little about the mechanics of the plot, and so my first drafts relied almost exclusively on mystery—for doesn't every reader love a mystery? I set out to establish a mysterious connection between Corinna and the sea. I portrayed her always thinking and dreaming about the sea, soaking her feet in saltwater and the like. Surely (I thought), the mystery will so fascinate my readers that they will keep on reading until they reach the explanation. But mystery can grow tedious, as mine did, if a plot is static, as mine was. The problem was that Corinna was passive. There was mystery, but the mystery was always acting on her (that is, she responded to her inexplicable dreams and longings by mooning over the sea), rather than acting on the mystery herself (that is, taking action to solve the mystery). I found myself unable to dream up a series of events that would plausibly lead her to self-discovery and, eventually, a decision about where she belongs.

I despaired of my plot, and I also despaired of Corinna's fate as a memorable character. She was, frankly, boring. Passive. Sometimes, I tried to cudgel her into being interesting (spunky, feisty, colorful) by putting strong words in her mouth, but because they came from me rather than from Corinna, she always sounded artificial and stiff—and bratty. When you understand a character's motives, you may find them agreeably disagreeable, but when you do not understand the motives, you tire of the character. You find them just plain disagreeable. That was the case with Corinna.

I began what was to become *The Folk Keeper* in the spring of 1993, and as late as February 1997, I was writing my editor, the late Jean Karl, letters that said things such as, "Right now I'm wrestling with my first-person narrator's voice—I haven't really captured her yet, and that's something I'm less confident of being able to do through sheer persistence."

Jean responded,

> Maybe you should not shape her up too much. Characters should not run wild and move off in all sorts of directions that keep a plot from working. But they need to be themselves and do what they feel comfortable doing. Good characters come out of the subconscious and they live when they are allowed to be themselves. If you manipulate them too much they become puppets and not real people.

This threw me into greater despair. The subconscious! Just where *is* that, anyway? *What* is it? I had no directions how to get there, no map. I could only keep plugging away, and when I had a draft that was just a shade less mortifying than the previous drafts, I sent it off to Jean.

Jean's response was a masterpiece of delicacy and insight, and of her many wonderful questions and comments, there was one comment that stood out the most. "The basic problem is just what Corinna wants for herself.... What does she want before she finds out [about her selkie heritage]?"

At once I realized that she had put her finger on the missing in-gredient, on the reason that Corinna was so passive. If the character really wants something, she is going to *do* something to try to get it. And that generates narrative energy. If a character doesn't want anything, she is just going to sit around soaking her feet in saltwater, and the novel will likely be boring.

Yes, I would give Corinna something she really wanted, and further-more, I would elevate it to the level of an obsession. And it was then that the Folk came into the book.

How did the idea of the Folk come to me? I cannot say. It seemed to be one of those comic-book lightbulb moments, but surely the idea had been percolating in that mysterious, uncharted subconscious for a long while. No, I cannot say where they came from, the Folk, those mysterious creatures living in the dark underground caverns. The Folk, ravenous and unpredictable, able to destroy the food supply of a community when they get angry. The Folk, so dangerous that there must be an entire class of humans dedicated to keeping the Folk as happy as possible. These humans are the Folk Keepers; they must sit with the Folk in those dark underground places to placate them, propitiate them. They risk injury, and even death.

This was the job I gave to Corinna, the job I made her want to perform more than anything else. It was Corinna's obsessive drive to be a Folk Keeper that provided the combustion for the story, gave it punch and vitality.

I realized at once, however, that I had to explain why Corinna would want to perform the dangerous job of being a Folk Keeper. I had already decided to have her grow up in an orphanage. Maybe her experience there could provide a motive. Perhaps her upbringing had been neglectful, even abusive. What if she were given all the most menial of tasks—washing the soiled linens, scrubbing the flagstones? What if she were disenfranchised, marginalized? It would stand to reason, then, that what Corinna would want more than anything else is power. And when she realized that she could acquire a measure of power by becoming a Folk Keeper (this crucial role in society), she made that into her life goal.

Ah! Now I was getting somewhere.

Once I came to understand all this—once I understood what Corinna wanted and, furthermore, understood why she wanted what she wanted—then Corinna began to spring to life. I experienced what Lois Lowry describes when she says,

> It's much too glib, too falsely self-deprecating, to say that the character takes over. I don't lose control. I have, after all, created the character. What he does, or she does, is entirely dependent upon me. But it happens in a subliminal way and sometimes takes me by surprise. I want it to. I love those surprises, wait for them, yearn for them. (p. 5)

Yes, Corinna said what I needed her to say, but she began to speak in ways that were organic to her, in ways that surprised me. This, then, is what Jean Karl meant when she said that good characters come from the subconscious. Once I understood Corinna, her need and motive and history, then she could begin to act on her own.

Plot intersects with character; character intersects with plot. They are, in my experience, inextricably linked. Once you have the glimmerings of one, you can back into the other. Your character may then begin to speak on the page in a way that has little to do with your conscious mind, but arises rather from the subconscious workings of a Mind Worm.

REFERENCES

Lowry, L. (2001, April). *The remembered gate and the unopened door*. Paper presented at Sutherland Lecture, Chicago Public Library. Retrieved January 11, 2005, from http://www.loislowry.com/speeches.html

McKee, R. (1997). *Story*. New York: HarperCollins.

LITERATURE CITED

Billingsley, F. (1999). *The Folk Keeper*. New York: Atheneum.

8

Characters Crossing the Line

Edward Bloor

Edward Bloor's multiple characters are, he claims, all aspects of himself. He inhabits his characters as he writes, calls them "upstairs" and "downstairs" characters, and makes certain they stay true to themselves. If impertinent characters insist on conflicting with the plot, then the plot must be shaped to accommodate them. Bloor also says that characters "cross the line" and come to reside in readers' lives.

MY NOVELS HAVE LOTS OF CHARACTERS. *Crusader* (Bloor, 1999), for example, has over 50 speaking parts. Reexamination of these characters proved something that I had vaguely suspected: They are all me—from the soccer playing boys in *Tangerine* (Bloor, 1997) to the mall denizens in *Crusader*, to the educational charlatans in *Story Time* (Bloor, 2004). Consider that I

- played soccer from the time I was 8 right into college.
- worked in four different malls in south Florida.
- currently work in educational publishing, promulgating testing materials.

What a Character! Character Study as a Guide to Literary Meaning Making in Grades K–8 edited by Nancy L. Roser and Miriam G. Martinez, with Junko Yokota and Sharon O'Neal. Copyright 2005 by the International Reading Association.

The boys, the girls, the old, the young, the good, and the despicable, I am all of them. Externally, the characters may be based on someone I know—a student I once had, one of my daughter's friends—but their thoughts, their agendas, are all mine. The characters become real to me during the year or so that it takes to write their stories. Then, some of them become real for others, often in ways I had not anticipated.

The heroes of my first two young adult novels—Paul Fisher of *Tangerine* and Roberta Ritter of *Crusader*—are basic old-fashioned protagonists, first-person narrators. Paul and Roberta are like the young narrators in many Dickens novels in that they describe what is happening and also are deeply involved in what is happening. They look at our complex society from the point of view of young people who are trying, with difficulty, to enter it. Paul and Roberta embody the themes of their novels, both of which are about survival; for example:

- A tangerine is a delicate fruit that is grown by grafting it on to the rootstock of a rough lemon tree. In *Tangerine*, Paul Fisher is a handicapped child, delicate in a way; he survives because he is grafted on to the tough kids of the War Eagles soccer team. He embodies the theme of surviving by adapting.
- In *Crusader*, Roberta survives because she becomes a crusader—in the crusading journalist sense of the word. She shines a light into the dark corners of her world, finding pieces of the truth and putting them together to solve her mother's long-unsolved murder. She embodies the theme of surviving by finding and facing reality.

Paul and Roberta were my main focus while I was planning these two novels. All the other characters, major and minor, came along purely to support them. I don't call them *major* and *minor*, though. I love Masterpiece Theatre productions such as *Upstairs, Downstairs*, and English manor house movies such as *The Remains of the Day* (Ivory, 1993) and *Gosford Park* (Altman, 2001). It is from these sources that I derived the terms *upstairs* and *downstairs* characters. Upstairs characters carry the major themes of my novels; they get to go to the interesting places and to act in the big scenes. Downstairs characters are simply there to work. They must get the main characters from point A to point B. They take care of the novel's business.

And yet, this upstairs/downstairs arrangement is not as rigid a system as it may sound. Some characters flatly refuse to stay downstairs. They have the impertinence to come up and say, "This scene could be a lot better. We could be added to it. We could make new and unexpected and unplanned-for things happen." Of course, they are absolutely right, and they wind up not only taking part in the scenes but also sometimes stealing them.

A character takes on a life—a physical description, a set of behaviors, an outlook. It's a life that, once begun, cannot be compromised by contrivances, by actions that the character would not do. A character has an imperative: to be true to himself or herself. If that imperative conflicts with the desires of the plot, then it is the plot that has to change. Because—and this is my core belief about characterization—when we presume to create a character, we are dealing with a powerful force, a phenomenon that is potentially wonderful and potentially dangerous to a reader.

I believe that characters can and do leave the page, crossing the line into real life where they influence people's lives in real ways. I tell student audiences that a book is just paper and ink until they pick it up. Then a kind of alchemy occurs, especially among young adult readers who are actively engaged in trying different personas. They connect very powerfully with books and with characters. Readers are particularly vulnerable to this phenomena at times of high stress and psychological ebbs. I believe that a book (this also holds true for a movie) at the right time can have a real impact for good; and the same book at the wrong time can have a real impact for bad.

There have been times when fictional characters have literally changed my life. During a junior year abroad, I was a lonely foreigner in London. I went to a movie theater and saw Robert Altman's *MASH* (1970). It was a celebration of jaunty, fun-loving American guys—the kind of people I had not been around in months. An alchemy occurred for me during that movie. At a time when I was feeling low and separate, I encountered these fictional characters, and I became one of them. I emerged from the theater as a jaunty American guy, and I stayed that way for the rest of my time in London.

The following year, I was back at my college in New York feeling at a dead end, as college seniors often do. It was a depressing time. I remembered something from my assigned reading that year. It was a scene from Dostoyevsky's *The Brothers Karamazov* (1880/1992) in which Zossima the Monk was at a dead end, too, and very depressed. Then he had an insight, a revelation that gave him the power to change his life overnight, to change his direction completely. By sitting and rereading that scene, I had that insight right along with him. I changed my life and my direction that night based on a character's experience in a novel.

An example of a novel's negative impact happened in the same city a few years later. Mark David Chapman sat outside John Lennon's New York City apartment reading J.D. Salinger's *The Catcher in the Rye* (1991), a prototype novel for the young protagonist looking for an identity. Chapman had an insight as well, an evil one that led him to murder Lennon and that changed many lives for the worse.

I know this "crossing the line" phenomenon happens to a lot of readers and film goers. I receive letters from students who describe the experience. Students often focus on a minor character, one who somehow touched a nerve and became real for them; for example, they may focus on Samir Samad, a strictly "downstairs" character in *Crusader*. Samir is only there to play off the Christian–Muslim rivalry in the book, reflecting back on the religious differences that begat the actual Crusades. Samir was in place waiting when an Arab American teenager from Atlanta read the book. She wrote me a letter describing how, like Samir, she had been ostracized in a mostly Christian community in the United States. She felt that people looked on her as a threat, as a potential terrorist. Her letter was written on September 10 and postmarked on September 11, 2001. I can't imagine how much worse her life became after that. I can only hope she found more characters to read about who were going through the same types of things, who gave her helpful insights, and who helped her move through her pain.

Like this girl, the kids who sit in today's classrooms seem more burdened by life's baggage than ever before. Authors, teachers, and librarians all need to be aware of the forces gnawing at young readers' lives. They need to consider the potential power of the characters they assign them to read about, because fictional characters do cross the line; they do affect real lives— for better or for worse.

LITERATURE CITED

Bloor, E. (1997). *Tangerine.* San Diego, CA: Harcourt.
Bloor, E. (1999). *Crusader.* San Diego, CA: Harcourt.
Bloor, E. (2004). *Story time.* San Diego, CA: Harcourt.
Dostoyevsky, F. (1992). *The Brothers Karamozov.* Cambridge, UK: Cambridge University Press. (Original work published 1880)
Salinger, J.D. (1991). *The catcher in the rye.* New York: Little Brown.

AUDIOVISUAL MEDIA CITED

Altman, R. (Director). (1970). *MASH* [Motion picture]. Los Angeles: Twentieth Century Fox.

Altman, R. (Producer/Director). (2001). *Gosford Park* [Motion picture]. Los Angeles: USA Films.

Hawkesworth, J., & Whitney, J. (Producers). (1971–1975). *Upstairs, downstairs* [Television series/Masterpiece Theatre, U.S.]. London: Sagitta Productions.

Ivory, J. (Director). (1993). *The remains of the day* [Motion picture]. Los Angeles: Columbia Pictures.

9

The Poet as Creator of Character

Nikki Grimes

Nikki Grimes highlights some of the characters
featured in her poetry, discusses how those characters
came into being through the creation of character
sketches, and shows how a character may develop
across a collection of poetry.

You oughta meet Danitra Brown,
the most splendiferous girl in town.
I oughta know, 'cause she's my friend.

She's not afraid to take a dare.
If something's hard, she doesn't care.
She'll try her best, no matter what.

She doesn't mind what people say.
She always does things her own way.
Her spirit's old, my mom once said.

I only know I like her best
'cause she sticks out from all the rest.
She's only she—Danitra Brown. (Grimes, 1994, n.p.)

What a Character! Character Study as a Guide to Literary Meaning Making in Grades K–8 edited by
Nancy L. Roser and Miriam G. Martinez, with Junko Yokota and Sharon O'Neal. Copyright 2005
by the International Reading Association. Copyright on all of the poetry in this chapter is held by Nikki
Grimes. See the reference list at the end of the chapter for publication information. All rights reserved.

EET DANITRA BROWN (Grimes, 1994) WAS THE first story I told through poetry. I could tell you that this style of storytelling was planned from the very beginning, that it was intentional. But, in fact, *Meet Danitra Brown* was a happy accident, the necessary invention of someone struggling to tell a story, a story that seemed to want to be a collection of poems. And so I went with it. I let the story pull me where it wanted to go. *Meet Danitra Brown*, a story of best friends, was the result.

The work began, as many of my books do, with a pair of character sketches. My character sketches are not fancy. They usually consist of several free-flowing paragraphs that outline a character's personality (shy), age, likes (the color blue), sports (soccer), physical distinctions (gangly, blue-black skin, coke-bottle glasses), and general background (only child, lives in big city, raised by single parent). Of course, voice is essential, too, and I do have a voice in mind for each character, which I try to capture in a single line of dialogue. I include the dialogue in the sketch for future reference. Often, that line ends up somewhere in the story.

My one guideline when creating a collection is that each poem must stand on its own. Therefore, I approach the crafting of each poem separately in regard to shape, form (free verse, haiku, sonnet), and rhythm. The unity of the collection is not its form, but its subject, and each poem is designed to explore one subject.

Often a critical element in a sketch becomes an individual poem. Take, for instance, the fact that Danitra loves the color purple. That detail, referenced in the rough character sketch, forms the basis of a poem that helps to flesh out the character:

Once you've met my friend Danitra, you can spot her miles away.
She's the only girl around here who wears purple every day
Whether summer's almost over or spring rains are pouring down,
if you see a girl in purple, it must be Danitra Brown.

Purple socks and jeans and sneakers, purple ribbons for her hair.
Purple shirts and slacks and sweater, even purple underwear!
Purple dresses, shorts, and sandals, purple coat and purple gloves.
There's just no mistake about it: Purple's what Danitra loves.

Purple is okay, I guess. I have worn it once or twice.
But there's nothing wrong with yellow. Red and blue are also nice.
So one day I asked Danitra if once in a while, for fun,
She would wear another color, just to surprise everyone.

But her mom has told her stories about queens in Timbuktu
and it seems they all wore purple—never red or green, or blue.
Now, she might just be a princess. After all, who's to say?
So, just in case, she'll dress in purple each and every day. (n.p.)

You might question whether a collection of poems can effectively draw
a character. But that's not a question that concerns me because I travel the
United States extensively visiting schools and, as I do, students frequently
ask, "When was the last time you saw Danitra?" or, "Do you and Danitra
keep in touch?" When I tell them that Danitra is merely a child of my
imagination, they can hardly believe it. Since the publication of *Danitra
Brown Leaves Town* (Grimes, 2001a), children have been able to revisit
their friend.

My Man Blue (Grimes, 1999) is another book that owes its life to a pair
of character sketches. Here again, each telling element in the sketch becomes
a poem. In this instance, the poem grows out of a simple physical description
of the character. As with any story, this one begins with an introduction to
Blue, the central character. The speaker is Damon, the boy whom Blue
befriends.

His leathery skin's
Like indigo ink
This rugged dude
Who some folk think
Looks fierce in clothes
Of midnight black.
Then there's his teeth:
One gold, three cracked.
And I suppose
The shades could go.
He wears them night
And day, I know.
Still, underneath
This shell, Blue hides
A harmless
Gentle-giant side. (n.p.)

As the story progresses, poems provide the history of Blue and Damon—of
how they meet and how they initially perceive each other:

My mom and me moved here without his help.
So why's this "Blue" guy stop us on the street?

His welcome is on Mom's account, I bet.
I circle, look him up and down and let
Him know his grin's not winning points with me.
My flashing eyes warn "Do not trespass here,"
'Cause in this family *I'm* the only man.
He nods. He understands. So I ease up.
Mom sees me eyeing Blue and lets me know
He's her old friend. It's safe to say hello.
She says they both grew up here way back when.
I mumble, "Well, it's news to me!" But then
I throw my shoulders back and take my stance.
He seems alright. I might give him a chance. (n.p.)

In poem after poem, the characters are fleshed out and, as they are, the reader learns how they relate to one another. You get a glimpse of the skeletons in their closets, a peek into the background stories of who they are, and what makes them tick. You learn about the characters' weaknesses as well as their strengths. A few well-chosen words is all it takes.

    A bully
kicks me in the knee.
That bully's name
is Tiffany.
    I fume
but don't return the blow.
Guys don't hit girls
Blue says, and so
    I grab
her wrists 'til she
calms down while
    Laughing
jeering kids stand 'round
and shout "You wimp!" But
they're all wrong.
    It's guys
who *don't* hit girls
Who're strong. (n.p.)

Soon, a relationship develops between Damon and Blue. They begin to invest time in one another. Before they know it, they become bound by shared experience, by moments of joy and moments of fear. Trust begins to loom large. And how does the reader know that? Because each poem spells out the interaction between the characters and the impact each has upon the other.

> My favorite ball skipped off the curb
> And some dumb kid disguised as me
> Ran blindly after it then heard
> A tire's skid and spied a rig.
> My stubborn feet refused to fly
> But Blue reached out and grabbed my belt
> And set me on the sidewalk while
> The rig reduced my ball to dust.
> Blue took my hand and marched me home
> Then disappeared without a word.
> At times I think Blue's actually
> Some gold-toothed angel, guarding me. (n.p.)

Bit by bit, emotional walls come down, replaced by the brick and mortar of friendship:

> His hands
> are a rough sculpture
> of thick fingers
> & thumbs tipped
> with work-proud
> callouses, his badges
> of tough, honest labor
> down on the docks.
> His hands
> are strong stories.
> He tells them
> sometimes when
> I let him hold mine. (n.p.)

By the time the story arcs, Damon, who once eyed Blue with suspicion, has learned to lean on him. As the story ends, Damon dreams of becoming like the man he has learned to admire:

> One day
> I'll be like Blue
> Not fierce
> In black leather
> Or built like
> A heavyweight

Boxing machine
But like that
Other Blue I've seen
The one who
Says he cares
And shows it.
The one who
Flashes gold
Every time he smiles.

My Man Blue is a work of fiction, but the character Blue is loosely based on a real gentleman of the same name who I knew in my teens. I'm happy to mine my personal history from time to time, if only to dig up images that bring a smile to the lips. The poem "Yo Te Amo" is a case in point. It is part of *A Dime a Dozen* (Grimes, 1998), a collection of poems about my family and my early dreams of becoming a writer. "Yo Te Amo" is about my mother, and every time I read it, it makes me smile:

Maybe there's some
scientific reason
she gets the urge to hug
whenever we're
jammed together
in the rush-hour huddle.

Thank God, she knows better
than to cuddle—in public.
Instead, while the train
Screeches to the next station
she leans down
to whisper in my ear
Yo te amo con
todo mi corazón.
If no one else can hear
I figure it's okay
    to smile.
Don't ask me
who she learned
that expression from
but someone
must've told my mom
that Spanish is
the language of love
    'cause

she's been speaking
mushy Puerto Rican
   to me
    for years. (pp. 22–23)

Stepping Out With Grandma Mac (Grimes, 2001b) is another collection drawn from life. One of its characters is based on my grandmother. The unnamed speaker is her 10-year-old granddaughter. I might have been inclined to create a collection of poems about a purely fictional grandmother were it not for the fact that my real one was such an original character. No make-believe grandmother could ever hope to compete.

At three I missed
The grandma in my mind,
The one who'd bounce me
On her knee, and read
Jack and the Beanstalk
While I flipped the pages.
The grandma who'd
Bake oatmeal cookies,
Take me to the zoo,
And spoil me with
Too much ice cream.
Of course,
Grandma lived miles away
Back then.

Now I'm ten
And too big to sit on
Anybody's knee.
Besides, the only bounce
My grandma has
Is in her high-heeled step
When she strides
Down the street, gathering
Men's glances.

She bakes, but only pies
At Christmas,
Hates the zoo,
And refuses to stuff me
With sweets.
Still, she's more adventurous,
Than most grandmas

I know. And she never
Makes me guess
What's on her mind
Which is fine by me.
As for baking
Oatmeal cookies
And the rest,
Let's just say
Grandma Mac
Is a late bloomer. ("Stepping Out," pp. 26–27)

Stepping Out With Grandma Mac traces the development between a sassy young girl and her complex grandmother. The poems not only paint a picture, but also reveal two distinct personalities:

On Sundays
I know
Stepping out
With Grandma Mac
Means wearing my best,
So when I show up
In a nicely pressed
White dress, with
Matching shoes and purse,
A lecture is not
What I expect. Except
It's after Labor Day
And according to Grandma Mac,
Wearing white is now
Officially a sin.
"Who cares?" I ask,
Wondering what Bible
She's been reading.
"I care," she insists.
"White is for summer,
Not for fall."
This is not what I call
A reasonable explanation.
And it's exactly these
Fancy ideas of hers
Rubbing off on me
That give other kids
The notion

I think I'm better
Than everyone else
On the block—
Like being a kid
Around here
Isn't tough enough
Already! ("Stepping Out," pp. 26–27)

Poems like this are meant to make the reader laugh. But there's more here than initially meets the eye. Beyond the verbal tug of war, there's a tug of heart. Two people bound by love are learning to communicate. The girl makes the first move. She has less to lose, less to risk than her grandmother who has invested decades in building emotional walls around herself:

When I visit Grandma Mac
She usually snaps at me
To wipe my feet
On the welcome mat
So I don't dirty her rug.
There are no hugs,
No "Come here, sugar."
Just "Well, are you
Coming in or not?"
Her cold words
Used to make me shiver
Though never enough
To chase me away.
Then, after a while,
I'd notice how a light
Switches on in her eyes
Every time she sees me.
And I'd catch her
Sneaking money inside
My purse or pocket
So I could find it later
    Like buried treasure.
And, more than once,
I saw her eyes
Bathe me with pride.
So I figure
Grandma's chilly words
Aren't brick walls
Made to keep me out.

They're more like picket fences
With gaps wide enough
For me to squeeze through—
All I have to do
Is try. ("Fences," pp. 20–21)

As the story arcs, it is the grandmother's turn to put her love on full display. Never one to speak the words, she finds a warm, quiet way to spell out her feelings on a wintry afternoon in December:

It's Christmas Eve.
Grandma and me
Huddle together outside
Of Radio City Music Hall
Bent on seeing
The Rockettes
Kick up their heels
No matter how long
We have to stand out
In the snow. Today
The sun is like some
Chilled slice of lemon,
Dripping cool light on us
While our faces freeze.
We march in place
And stomp our feet
Against the cold,
Waiting in a line
That zigzags
Down the street
And takes half an hour
To reach the ticket booth.
I would mind more
Except that Grandma
Who normally
Avoids touching
Grabs my hand,
Sticks it in
The warm well
Of her pocket
And holds it there
What seems like
Forever. ("Radio City," pp. 36–37)

When is a poem more than a poem? When it tells a story. Poetry is a great way to tell a story. But monologues aren't bad, either! That's the style of storytelling I chose for *Talkin' About Bessie: The Story of Aviator Elizabeth Coleman* (Grimes, 2002). Whenever poets or storytellers face the tyranny of the blank page, they do so armed with a lifetime of experience. One of the experiences that most influenced my approach to *Talkin' About Bessie* was my background in theater. My days of working with Barbara Ann Teer, founder and director of the National Black Theatre in the late 1960s and early 1970s, come in handy every time I sit down to sketch out a character. My study of theater has given me an understanding of an actor's approach to character. As an actor, you spend hours breaking down a scripted character into separate components in order to understand her. I find that approach useful when I'm searching for the right words to put into my character's mouth. I refer back to the small components in my notes about who she is, where she lives, how people in her environment express themselves, etc., and then I climb into her skin and "speak" on the page. Bessie required that I climb into the skins of 20 different characters, but the process was the same for each. It is that background, and my later experiments in Readers Theatre, that gave me the format of *Talkin' About Bessie*. The inspiration, though, came from another source.

Over the years, I have suffered the loss of many loved ones. I've witnessed many burials, sat at many funerals, and attended many memorials. It's the memorials that have been the most telling. At most memorials, a variety of people come forward to say something about the departed, focusing on the aspect of the person they knew best. In a matter of moments, you realize there's more to this person than you suspected. You learn about aspects never before revealed to you, and you walk away with a fuller portrait of the person than you walked in with. You may even have the sense that you hardly knew the person at all. The memory of one such memorial service was the seed for *Talkin' About Bessie*.

> Somewhere on the South Side of Chicago, in a private parlor, twenty souls gather to mourn the death of Bessie Coleman and share their memories of her. Many more had come to the house earlier that evening, but they are long gone. The grandfather clock reads 12:01 A.M., but no one seems to notice that one day has just slipped quietly in to another.
>
> Bessie eyes the gathering of family, friends, and acquaintances from her place in the photo on the mantel behind them.

"Hello, Mama," she whispers. Susan Coleman snaps her head around toward the mantel. She listens for a moment, but there is only silence. Finally, she shakes her head, and turns her attention to her ex-husband, George, who has started to speak. (n.p.)

The moment I hit upon that concept of a memorial service, I knew it was the right one for the story. I have always liked working in multiple voices, but Bessie's story seemed to especially call for it. One of those voices was that of her grade-school teacher. Hear what she had to say about Bessie:

> When it came to knowledge, Bessie was a miser,
> hoarding facts and figures like gold coins she was
> saving up to spend on something special.
>
> I'd watch her sometimes,
> poring over her lessons,
> lips pursed in concentration.
> Often, when the subject turned to math,
> she'd glance up at me and, I'd swear,
> she'd get a sort of greedy look in her eyes.
> But maybe it was just my imagination.
>
> I did not imagine her persistence, though.
> Come rain or shine, if work allowed,
> Bessie would attend the hot-in-summer,
> cold-in-winter, one-room Colored schoolhouse
> where I taught in Waxahachie.
> Not even the four-mile walk it took to get there
> discouraged her from making her way to class.
>
> Still, bright as she was, I worried that her fine mind
> would soon be sacrificed to a life spent picking cotton
> or working in the mills, like so many others had before.
>
> But, after each harvest, she'd return to class,
> determined as ever to snatch up and pocket
> every tidbit of knowledge I could offer.
> "Teacher," she'd say, "one day, I'm going
> to amount to something."
>
> > Bless God! I need not have
> > fretted in the least. (n.p.)

Stubborn she was, and proud. Bessie may well have been forced by Jim Crow laws to ride in the Colored car of the train she rode North, but in her spirit, Bessie considered herself as the equal of anyone, black or white.

And always had. Her laundry customer knew the truth of that, and it is this character I use to tell this part of Bessie's story, to throw light on this aspect of Bessie's personality.

Bessie Coleman? She was a nice-enough girl.
Polite in her way, I suppose. Goodness knows,
I couldn't complain about her work.

My laundry was spotless, perfectly pressed, always delivered
in a timely manner each Saturday, even though my family occupied
a mansion in west Waxahachie, 'bout five miles from the Coloreds.

Bessie had to walk the distance, I believe, but she managed it.
Still, there was somethin' disturbin' about her. I think
it was her eyes. She'd never look *down*, you know?

She'd come to the back door, like they were supposed to in those days.
But when I opened it, there this Colored girl would be standin',
lookin' me straight in the eye, like we were just any two people
meetin' on a street in town. You know, like we were equals.

It was odd, I don't mind tellin' you. (n.p.)

Elizabeth Coleman was a very complicated woman. As I sorted through the biographical material I found on her, I discovered a warrior woman with chinks in her armor, and I decided early on that my portrait of her would be of the warts-and-all variety, as in this poem:

Ain't nobody mentioned how crafty Bessie could be.
Not mean-spirited, mind you. Just sly. I saw that side of her,
out in the fields, whenever we were workin' cotton.

Bessie despised pickin' cotton, couldn't even stand the smell,
and she'd show it by laggin' way behind. Once, I even caught her
hitchin' a ride on the back of another picker's sack.

Her mama also caught her at it. 'Course, Mrs. Coleman
let Bessie off scot-free, seein' as how Bessie was the one
who kept the family records and tallied the bales of cotton
the Colemans picked each day, making sure the foreman
paid them their due—and, sometimes, more.

It was an open secret: now and then, as bales was bein' weighed,
Bessie'd "accidently" leave her foot lightly restin' on the scales,
then press down if the foreman chanced to look the other way.

Yessir! You might could say
Bessie bore some watchin'. (n.p.)

Say what you like about Bessie, it was clear that she was driven by a desire to leave her mark on the world, to make her life count. What that life would be, she wasn't certain. It took her a while to figure it out, and it's good for readers to know that, because a person might have a tendency to panic about not knowing what she wants to do with her life. In the end, it was her brother, John Coleman, who inadvertently showed her the way.

> World War One left me with nightmares, and a fondness far drink,
> though neitha gave me an excuse far teasin' my sister.
> Still, I goaded Bessie 'bout goin' to
> the Burnham School of Beauty Culture,
> and bein' overeager to avoid
> hiring herself out as a domestic.
> But she just shrugged. Said she'd had enough
> Of that kinda work back home.
>
> She got a jab buffin men's nails at
> a high-class barbershop an The Stroll,
> where I'd drop in to swap war stories
> and talk politics with her customers.
> I'd point out that she was still a "common laborer"
> after a lifetime of tellin' anyone who'd listen
> that she'd amount to somethin' "big" someday.
>
> She'd worked in the shop five years
> when I wandered in one afternoon,
> blabbin' 'bout airplanes and French women
> who had *real* careers as pilots.
> I turned to Bessie and joked,
> "You Negro women ain't never goin' ta fly.
> Not like those women I saw in France."
>
> The barbershop rocked with laughter.
> Then I heard this *snap* that was so familiar.
> It was that steel-trap mind of Bessie's.
> "That's it," she said. "You just called it far me!"
> She gave up her manicurin' job that very day.
>
> > That's when I knew, by whatever miracle
> > was required, Bessie would learn to fly. (n.p.)

Through the course of the book, I looked at Bessie's life from the point of view of several of her sisters and brothers, and through the eyes of teachers, news reporters, friends, and fans. Each highlighted an aspect of Bessie's life. Of course, Bessie was God's creation, not mine. She was a petite powerhouse whom I plucked from the yellowing pages of history. My task was to make her, and her particular piece of history, breathe again. By telling her story from the diverse viewpoints of those who knew her, I hoped to create a three-dimensional portrait of her as a person—warts and all.

As I was writing *Talkin' About Bessie*, I read every article and book about Bessie I could find, and I studied old newspaper clippings on microfiche. I studied flight instruction manuals till I was blue in the face, and pored over dozens of photographs and pen-and-ink etchings of old planes. I researched the late 19th and early 20th centuries and dug up and presented whatever facts about Bessie I could find. But facts are only part of a life story. Feelings matter, too. And so I climbed into Bessie's skin and tried to feel her passion for flight, a passion that gave her life focus and meaning, a passion she shared with the world.

The final monologue of the book is written in Bessie's own voice:

I'll never forget that first time in France.
My knees wobbled when I climbed into the cockpit.
The mechanic cranked the propeller for me, and soon
a fine spray of engine oil misted my goggles,
baptizing me for take off.
I taxied down the runway, praying.

But flying at Checkerboard Field in Chicago was the best.
My family and friends were there in the stands,
cheering me on as I sliced through the air.
Oh, Mama! I wish you' could've been in the plane
to feel that magnificent machine shudder
with the sheer joy of leaving the ground.

I climbed over a thousand feet that day,
did a snap roll that sent the blood rushing
to my head so fast I thought my eyes would explode.
My seat belt felt like a magnet, pulling on my spine.
I can still feel my hand gripping the joystick,
how my muscles ached from struggling
to hold the plane center. But I didn't mind.

To rest, even for a moment,
weightless and silent, on a cushion of cloud,
near enough the sun to scoop up a handful of yellow
was a privilege more than worth the price of pain.

In the end, I count myself twice blessed:
first, to have experienced the joy of flight;
and, second, to have shared it with others of my race.
I'll say this and no more:

> You have never lived
> until you have flown! (n.p.)

So it is that Bessie becomes the last, and the most important character in her own story. This introduction to her life is made all the richer for the many points of view, or cast of characters, revealed one poem at a time. To think each poem began with a character sketch!

LITERATURE CITED

Grimes, N. (1994). *Meet Danitra Brown*. Ill. F. Cooper. New York: HarperCollins.

Grimes, N. (1998). Yo Te Amo. In *A dime a dozen*. New York: Dial.

Grimes, N. (1999). *My man Blue*. Ill. J. Lagarrigue. New York: Dial.

Grimes, N. (2001a). *Danitra Brown leaves town*. Ill. F. Cooper. New York: Amistad.

Grimes, N. (2001b). *Stepping out with Grandma Mac*. New York: Orchard.

Grimes, N. (2002). *Talkin' about Bessie: The story of aviator Elizabeth Coleman*. Ill. E. B. Lewis. New York: Orchard.

Part III

Supporting
Children's
Understanding
OF
Characters

10

Students Write Their Understanding of Characters— and Their Understanding Soars

Marjorie R. Hancock

Marjorie Hancock offers readers three research-based, practical ways to reflect on and extend students' understanding of character: the literature response journal, the character journal, and the keypal journal.

S WE TRAVEL THE LANDSCAPE OF QUALITY children's literature, we encounter memorable, endearing characters who claim our hearts, engage our minds and spirits, and leave indelible tracks. Who can deny the staying power of the characters in the literature we love best? Perhaps less evident is the power of characters to gently shape potential for our own being. For example, who could ask for a

What a Character! Character Study as a Guide to Literary Meaning Making in Grades K–8 edited by Nancy L. Roser and Miriam G. Martinez, with Junko Yokota and Sharon O'Neal. Copyright 2005 by the International Reading Association.

better model of friendship than India Opal Buloni in Kate DiCamillo's *Because of Winn-Dixie* (2000)? And who but Crispin, Avi's young 14th-century hero in *Crispin: The Cross of Lead* (2002), could take readers on a quest that results in such unexpected relationships and understandings? Effective readers learn early on that holding tight to a character's hand makes reading an aesthetic, fulfilling, "growing" experience. Characters make great traveling companions as they invite reader engagement in the impending book journey. Comprehension soars as the growing relationship between reader and character encourages a hand-in-hand journey through the unfolding literary episode.

When students connect with characters, they learn that they are not alone in a complicated world. Just like they do, characters feel alone and isolated, battle bullies and foes, search for and cement friendships, seek personal identities, and both examine and celebrate their diversity. Travel with Rodzina (Cushman, 2003) on the orphan train, and you may never be quite so timid again (at least not without thinking of her trials during an arduous journey); work beside Tree-ear as he strives to gain the acceptance of master potter Min in *A Single Shard* (Park, 2001), and your understanding of dedication, gifts, and sacrifice deepens.

Sadly, not all readers build this companionship and affinity with book characters (Galda, 1982; Hancock, 1993a). Too often, their fleeting connections and spontaneous thoughts remain untapped or undocumented as the plot propels them through the text.

Time to reflect and to respond to literature is critical to building strong and lasting relationships between the reader and the text (Rosenblatt, 1978). One of the most natural ways to consider literature is through its characters, and one of the best ways to consider these reading journey "companions" is to write. The strength of written response lies in its ability to capture readers' thoughts along the way, rather than waiting until the "journey" is complete. Written responses to literature can be drawn from class discussion, can provide impetus for revisiting books, and can plant seeds that grow into more extensive writing. Written response, particularly to book characters, acknowledges readers' individuality and sense making. Ultimately, written response inspires readers to *become* the characters, to walk in their brave or brazen or mysterious shoes, to experience and recall similar joys and pain, and to grow in understanding of the created life.

Three written response formats are particularly effective for working with students, empowering them to react, interact, connect, identify, empathize, and strategize with characters:

1. response journal
2. character journal
3. keypal journal

The **response journal**, both prompted and spontaneous, encourages active reflection on characters' choices and actions, providing potential for readers and writers to construct and unveil unique understandings of character. The **character journal** (Hancock, 1993b) contributes a further dimension by inviting readers to live for a time within the story, documenting thoughts in the first-person voices of selected characters. Finally, the **keypal journal** provides an e-mail platform for discussing characters with other readers digesting the same literary work.

Written response encourages students to attain a higher involvement with the literature, to sustain personal interest in the outcome of the story, to assume an engaged spectator stance, and to maintain a growing understanding of characters of different cultures, genders, ages, and times. Sharing the fate of characters encourages the student to challenge or clarify his or her own beliefs and choices resulting in insights into one's own self. Partners discuss characters with one another via e-mail as a developing understanding of character grows through interactive verbal online discussion.

As students write about characters in any of these formats, they build character alliances as they more closely monitor a character's actions and may become character advocates as growing understandings of personal dilemmas, decision making, and moral values unfold. All three of the journals showcase the ways in which the individual reader and the literary characters interact. A relationship between reader and character forms, leading to comprehension and a sense of companionship (Hancock, 2004). Character companionship means walking in the shoes of the character—experiencing life's hurdles, feeling emotions, making decisions, and experiencing the consequences of those decisions with the character. As an active participant in a book, a student experiences enhanced enjoyment and understanding of literature.

The Response Journal: Reacting to Character

The response journal is the most focused of the three formats. Using simple prompts, teachers draw students into considering a specific literary character. Even generic prompts can spark interest in characters and lead to deep reflection on characters' inner workings and decisions. Initially, teachers might try the following simple prompts to invite students into character reflection:

- In what ways does (character) remind you of someone you know?
- In what ways does (character) remind you of another character you've met in a book?
- How would you feel if you were (character) in this situation?
- What do you think will happen to (character)?
- If you were (character), what would you do in this situation?
- What advice would you give (character) at this point in the story?
- Why do you believe (character) did or did not make the right choice?

As students respond to the prompts in written form, they recall and express their own related experiences, pose and solve problems, make logical predictions, give advice, and judge choices. The potential of prompted responses to provide initial guidelines for character interaction in early experiences with character journal response should not be underestimated. The prompts not only cause students to focus on a specific character, but also provide a framework for thinking about and understanding characters in general.

Gradually, as students mature in their character responses, they gain more independence in sharing viewpoints in their response journals, they become spontaneous responders. They no longer need prompts to direct or inspire their insights into characters as the process has become internalized.

At the intermediate level (grades 4–8), students' written responses reveal three types of character response: character introspection, character identification, and character assessment (Hancock, 1993a). **Character introspection** is insight into the feelings and thoughts of a character and the motives for a behavior. **Character identification** is bonding with a character. The student directly addresses the character or gives advice that reveals an emotional connection to the character. **Character assessment** is judging the actions and values of a character by measuring them against one's

FIGURE 10.1   Three Types of Character Response: Student Samples

---

Character Introspection

Oh, the burns. The pain Billie Jo and her mother must have endured. I am able to handle much of anything. However, when they spoke of burns, my stomach turned. The idea of Billie Jo feeling the physical pain, but worse yet, the emotional pain that lies ahead in her life. The idea of losing your mother and feeling it is your fault is a lot for a young girl to handle.

Character Identification

Billie Jo is forgiving her father and I think I am too. I liked when she said, "Hard times are about losing spirit and hope and what happens when dreams dry up." I agree with her. There have been times when I felt like I could not handle anymore. I felt like I was giving up hope. Billie Jo, I have realized that we both have to always have faith and hope.

Character Assessment

I cannot believe that Billie Jo just hopped a train west. Has she really thought through this and is it the best thing for her to do? Personally, I don't think that I could have left like that. I feel if she comes back, her father will try to understand her more and not think of her as a burden in his life.

I am so glad that Billie Jo decided to call her father and go home to him. They need each other. Now Billie Jo may be able to work with her hands so that one day she may play the piano beautifully just like her mother had intended her to do.

---

own personal standards. Evaluative statements and specific likes and dislikes appear in the writing, and high-level responses often reflect perception of character growth or change.

Figure 10.1 illustrates the three types of character response. (The entries are drawn from students' actual responses to Karen Hesse's character Billie Jo who, in *Out of the Dust* [1997], suffers severe burns in a tragic kerosene accident that results in her mother's death.)

Astute teachers perceive their students' levels of character understanding by the developmental level of written response revealed in journal entries. By modeling the three types of responses, you encourage students to interact with characters at a deep level. Giving consistent, encouraging feedback with directive—but not demanding—comments helps students fulfill their potential while not interfering with the character companionship they are achieving independently. (Table 10.1 provides examples of books for early

TABLE 10.1   Suggested Literature for the Three Written Response Formats

Prompted Response Journals (Grades 3–5)

Creech, S. (2002). *Ruby Holler.* New York: HarperCollins.

Gardiner, J. (1980). *Stone Fox.* New York: HarperCollins.

Haas, J. (2001). *Runaway Radish.* Ill. M. Apple. New York: Greenwillow.

Lowry, L. (1989). *Number the stars.* Boston: Houghton Mifflin.

Naylor, P.R. (1991). *Shiloh.* New York: Macmillan.

Park, B. (1995). *Mick Harte was here.* New York: Random House.

Wells, R. (2002). *Wingwalker.* Ill. B. Selznick. New York: Hyperion.

Wiles, D. (2001). *Love, Ruby Lavender.* New York: Harcourt.

Spontaneous Response Journals (Grades 5–8)

Avi. (1990). *The true confessions of Charlotte Doyle.* New York: Orchard Books.

Cushman, K. (1994). *Catherine, called Birdy.* Boston: Clarion.

Fleischman, P. (1997). *Seedfolks.* New York: HarperCollins.

Holm, J. (2001). *Boston Jane.* New York: HarperCollins.

Holt, K. (2001). *Dancing in Cadillac light.* New York: Putnam.

Paulsen, G. (1987). *Hatchet.* New York: Delacorte.

Salisbury, G. (1994). *Under the blood-red sun.* New York: Delacorte.

Weaver, W. (2001). *Memory boy.* New York: HarperCollins.

Character Journals (Grades 5–8)

Bauer, M.D. (1994). *A question of trust.* New York: Scholastic.

Clements, A. (2002). *A week in the woods.* New York: Simon & Schuster.

DeFelice, C. (1998). *The ghost of fossil glen.* New York: Farrar Straus Giroux

Hill, K. (1990). *Toughboy and Sister.* New York: Macmillan.

Hobbs, W. (1989). *Bearstone.* New York: Atheneum.

Mikaelsen, B. (1993). *Sparrow hawk red.* New York: Hyperion.

Pearsall, S. (2002). *trouble don't last.* New York: Knopf.

Spinelli, J. (1990). *Maniac Magee.* New York: HarperCollins.

Keypal Journals (Grades 5–8)

Giff, P.R. (2001). *All the way home.* New York: Delacorte.

Hesse, K. (1999). *just Juice.* Ill. R.A. Parker. New York: Scholastic.

Hill, K. (2000). *The year of Miss Agnes.* New York: Atheneum.

Holt, K.W. (1998). *My Louisiana sky.* New York: Henry Holt.

Lynch, C. (2000). *Gold dust.* New York: HarperCollins.

Sachar, L. (1998). *Holes.* New York: Farrar Straus Giroux.

Taylor, M. (1990). *Mississippi bridge.* New York: Bantam.

Williams, V.B. (2001). *Amber was brave, Essie was smart.* New York: Greenwillow.

response experiences [prompted response] and developing independence [spontaneous response] through quality titles specifically selected for character development.)

The Character Journal: Exploring Character Mind and Heart

The magic of the character journal (Hancock, 1993b) lies in the invitation to become the character. By taking on the character's voice and revealing his or her thoughts and feelings in first person, students respond to the unfolding events of the book. The first-person writing stance deepens student understanding of genders, cultures, and historical periods. Writing from "inside" another develops empathy and allows students to "try on" a new identity.

To be effective, character journals must be used with literature that allows students to connect deeply with a character so that students can maintain the character's voice and perspective across chapters; for example, students "become" John Barron as he faces a flash flood in the Wyoming wilderness in *The Haymeadow* (Paulsen, 1994) or take up Lyddie's hardship and challenges in *Lyddie* (Paterson, 1991) as the 19th century, New England mill-worker struggles to save the family farm. To ensure student involvement, it is best if the age of the character is similar to the age of the student. Choose literature in which the main character evidences growing maturity, continuous questioning, and even faltering, but ultimately moves ahead and learns from experience. In addition, the literature you choose should unfold through a series of decision-making episodes, blending anticipation and momentum, to ensure strong student participation. Most important, books chosen for character journals must be written in the third person so that students convert their writing to the first-person voice. This ensures originality and cultivates journal entries that brim with honesty and emotion. (Refer to Table 10.1 on page 77 for a list of suggested literature to initiate character understanding through character journals.)

Teachers should assess character journals by noting growth over time in the three character response categories. Documented evidence of growing character introspection, identification, and assessment reflected through journal responses within a single book or across several books over a longer period of time is optimal. (Teachers and students can even categorize and assess character statements through the use of a rubric that reflects specific statements of growth in understanding of character development.)

FIGURE 10.2   Character Journal Samples

A. Student Entry in Character Journal

I was very sad when my Papa died. It was really hard for me to lose someone I so dearly love. I must tell Mama that she cannot marry my persistent uncle. I will be so mad if she does and may never talk to her again.... I remember lying on the ground; I feel the earth's heartbeat. I cry because I miss my father. It was he who loved and valued the land, the same land that is being stolen away from my family. I fear I will never hear the earth again and I hold my breath as if it is my last.

B. Teacher Response in Character Journal

My Dear Esperanza,

I know how incredibly difficult it is for you to journey from wealth to poverty. The teasing and mocking by those around you make it even more difficult. You may need to stop thinking that this is just a temporary situation, Esperanza. The sooner you accept life's challenges, the sooner you will learn what is truly important in life. Is it the material possessions you so miss or is it the family who surrounds you that you treasure? Weigh this question as you attempt to handle the physical work and the continuing worries of your new life.

Figure 10.2a shows how one student converts third-person literature (*Esperanza Rising* by Pam Muñoz Ryan, 2000) to first-person journal entries. The student writes as Esperanza, reacting to events in the story. After several character journal entries, the classroom teacher responds by addressing the student as the character (Figure 10.2b). Getting into the character is hard work for students and can even be emotionally draining. By directly addressing the main character in a written response (e.g., Dear Esperanza,...), the teacher helps maintain the identification with the character and encourages sustaining the growing reader relationship with the character throughout the book.

Not only do first-person journal entries result in emotion-packed writing, but they also result in a deep level of engagement in literature that many students have not previously experienced. Reading in the guise of a literary character, feeling his or her emotions, and reflecting on one's own identity enriches the reading experience. Without the unique response format of the character journal, students may never experience literature in such a meaningful way.

The Keypal Journal: Electronic Correspondence About Characters

Through keypal journals, technology weaves with reader response to stimulate an ongoing correspondence between two readers as they discuss character development across cyberspace. Elementary or middle-level students use e-mail to exchange responses to a mutual literature selection with an electronic book buddy. The correspondence may occur between pairs of students within a school or across geographic boundaries. Students also have been successfully paired with university preservice teachers who provide support and encouragement during the exchange of ideas about characters (Larson, 2002; McKeon, 1999). Openly sharing ideas about a character and including thought-provoking questions related to character actions creates a deepening dialogue about the character between the correspondents.

In Figure 10.3a a sixth-grade student responds to *Bud, Not Buddy* (Curtis, 2000). Figure 10.3b is the response the student received from his keypal, a university preservice teacher. The preservice teacher carefully addresses the student's stance toward Bud and his accompanying inquiries, responding with humor and encouragement. Note how both correspondents invite response by sharing ideas and asking questions. In the e-mail ex-

FIGURE 10.3   Keypal Journal Samples

A. Student Keypal Journal Entry

Bud reminds me a lot of me, ornery and a little sarcastic, is there anyone he reminds you of? If so, who? I think Bud's idea to make rules was a good idea because it will help him survive in the situation he's in, they are really funny too. What do you think about them?... I think the man in the flyer really isn't Bud's dad. It has to be someone important to his mother so I bet it is his uncle. What do you think? I can't wait to find out what Bud will encounter in that freaky shed.

B. Response to Student Keypal Journal Entry

Bud does remind me of a few individuals who will remain nameless :-). Sounds like you have figured out Bud's survival mechanism. Rules! There were so many other choices that Bud could have made. Can you think of anything else he could have done to survive?... What made you think the man in the poster was close to Bud's mom? That shed experience was a bit much for me. Did you put your self in Bud's shoes during that part?... I'm anxious to hear your thoughts.

---

changes that follow, the keypals further enlist and challenge each other's thinking, focusing on character dilemmas, decisions, and determination. As the relationship flourished between the keypals, the novice reader built complex character understandings based on the supportive inquiry of the expert reader (Larson, 2002).

Electronic literature conversations invite readers into the conversations that surround good books and nudge understandings from different perspectives, producing a widened community of readers involved in thinking, talking, and writing about books. The wider response community moves in a rippling effect beyond the classroom community. It can be a similar grade level in the building or in the school district. It can move to a student in an adjacent school district. It can venture to a university community with e mail to preservice teachers reading the same literature. Or, in the ultimate scenario, it can even move beyond state or national borders to a global setting when literature of diverse cultures is read. Computer use also can be a great motivator for students, getting them involved without diminishing the focus on quality literature. (Literature for the keypal project in Table 10.1 on page 77 evokes similar standards for selection as the other lists—character age close to the reader's age, characters evidencing growing maturity, a plot that unfolds through a series of highly emotional events, and third-person text that assures first-person response in the keypal journal.)

Creating Lifelong Readers Through Character Relationships

Written responses to literary characters support and document active reading. Students report increased continuous, reflective reading when they respond to characters through response journals, character journals, and/or keypal journals. When they pause, capture a character connection on the page, and then reenter the text informed by a character relationship, enhanced comprehension occurs. Research (Hancock, 1993b) documents evidence of character empathy and understanding through direct statements obtained from 6th- through 8th-grade character journal entries. The internal dialogue that develops between students' written thoughts and their ongoing reading lingers long after the pencil leaves the journal page. Written response holds. Have students revisit their written thoughts with other readers and writers. Encourage them to comb the matted fur of Winn-Dixie along with Opal, collect firewood on the trail with Tree-ear in 12th-century Korea, feel the pain of Billie Jo as her fingers cautiously brush the dust-laden piano keys, and treasure the velvet-lined suitcase that Bud possessively carries on his journey to Grand Rapids.

When we become one with a character, we gain a lasting acquaintance. Reading and responding in a companionable process compels us to reflect on our lives—and can even shape a life. The essence of reading is unlocked in the literary friendships we develop on a lifelong journey through literature. Since character empathy and understanding are trademarks of a lifelong reader, encouraging written response to characters in a journal format results in comprehension that soars as the unending commitment to character involvement motivates lifelong reading.

REFERENCES

Galda, L. (1982). Assuming the spectator stance: An examination of the responses of three young readers. *Research in the Teaching of English, 16,* 1–20.

Hancock, M.R. (1993a). Exploring the meaning-making process through the content of literature response journals: A case study investigation. *Research in the Teaching of English, 27,* 335–368.

Hancock, M.R. (1993b). Character journals: Initiating involvement and identification through literature. *Journal of Reading, 37,* 42–50.

Hancock, M.R. (2004). *A celebration of literature and response: Children, books, and teachers in K–8 classrooms* (2nd ed.). Upper Saddle River, NJ: Prentice Hall/Merrill.

Larson, L.C. (2002). The keypal project: Integrating literature response and technology. *Kansas Journal of Reading, 18,* 57–62.

McKeon, C.A. (1999). The nature of children's e-mail in one classroom. *The Reading Teacher, 52,* 698–705.

Rosenblatt, L.M. (1978). *The reader, the text, the poem: The transactional theory of a literary work.* Carbondale, IL: Southern Illinois University Press.

LITERATURE CITED

Avi. (2002). *Crispin: The cross of lead.* New York: Hyperion.

Curtis, C.P. (2000). *Bud, not Buddy.* New York: Random House.

Cushman, K. (2003). *Rodzina.* New York: Clarion.

DiCamillo, K. (2000). *Because of Winn-Dixie.* Cambridge, MA: Candlewick.

Hesse, K. (1997). *Out of the dust.* New York: Scholastic.

Park, L.S. (2001). *A single shard.* New York: Clarion.

Paterson, K. (1991). *Lyddie.* New York: Dutton.

Paulsen, G. (1994). *The haymeadow.* New York: Yearling.

Ryan, P.M. (2000). *Esperanza rising.* New York: Scholastic.

11

Exploring Characters Through Drama

Lee Galda

Lee Galda offers both rationale and guidance for engaging students in dramatic activities—activities that result in a richer understanding of character and a greater appreciation of the ways in which authors craft them.

GROUP OF FIRST-GRADE STUDENTS ARE IN THE back of their classroom, clustered around a bench. They've just heard "The Three Billy Goats Gruff" told by their teacher, and they are eager to reenact it. Josie wants to be the troll, and is under the bench. Zach, Jamaal, and Yoon are the billy goats. Sing is the narrator and director, and the rest of the class is the audience, at least for now. They're talking about how they're going to dramatize the story, and the talk is about more than plot.

Josie:　I'm under the bridge hiding because I want to scare you.

Maria:　You need to talk with a big, mean voice.

What a Character! Character Study as a Guide to Literary Meaning Making in Grades K–8 edited by Nancy L. Roser and Miriam G. Martinez, with Junko Yokota and Sharon O'Neal. Copyright 2005 by the International Reading Association.

Josie:	I *will.* I am a big, mean troll.
Nate:	The goats are afraid of you.
Jamaal:	No, we're not! We're brave.
Zach:	We are gonna fool you, troll!
Jamaal:	We are really gonna fool you!

The group then talks about whether the goats are frightened of the troll or determined to trick the troll into letting them cross the bridge. They eventually decide that the goats are tricksters, partially because they have been listening to trickster tales for several weeks now.

These 5- and 6-year-olds are planning a dramatic response to a story they have heard and, at the same time, having a sophisticated discussion of character. They have gone well beyond the stage of naming characters and considering the sequence of events, and are discussing the dispositions of the characters as well as their motivation. All agree that the troll is mean. The two smaller goats, on the other hand, can be seen as frightened of the troll and thus willing to sacrifice their older, bigger brother, or they can be seen as smart and resourceful goats, figuring out a way to trick the troll into letting them cross. Both interpretations are plausible within the framework of the folk tale, and the children discuss these differing interpretations with interest and gusto. Their conversation shows that they are engaged by the story, are making inferences about the characters—even these stock characters that inhabit folklore—and know that they can portray characters' feelings and motivations with their voices and actions.

In the other wing of the building, a fifth-grade class is discussing Eve Bunting's *Fly Away Home* (1991). The students are breaking into small groups to role-play a discussion between the young protagonist and his friend. Both of them are homeless and living in the airport when the friend finds out that he can move to a new apartment. This discussion does not occur in the book; students are building on the events, characterizations, and emotions of the story to explore the thoughts, feelings, and actions of two characters. Like the first-grade students, they are both returning to and going beyond the story through dramatic activity. Story-based drama offers students the opportunity to relive the story and speculate about how and why characters act in particular ways.

Story-based drama may be a spontaneous choice of students, as it was in the first-grade classroom, or an experience planned by a teacher, as in the fifth-grade classroom. Both tap children's vast experience with dramatic play—experience that begins well before school entry and develops in school in a supportive context.

Entering the Story World Through Characters

When readers are engaged with a story, they "step into" and "move through" the story world (Langer, 1995). They enter what Benton (1983), borrowing the term from J.R.R. Tolkien (1964), calls the "secondary world" (p. 36). In this secondary world, readers "live through" events. Rosenblatt (1976, 1978) argues that this phenomenon is the foundation of a satisfying aesthetic experience. As engaged readers move through the story world, they both recall past actions and character reactions and anticipate future ones, as they fluctuate between close involvement with and detachment from the story (Benton, 1983). Engaged readers who are "lost" in a book, who have entered and are living through the story world, can subsequently think about the experiences and emotions presented in the story (Britton, 1970; Harding, 1962). Living through virtual experiences created in a secondary world allows readers to think about others and themselves, and to develop a sense of possibilities for life (Britton, 1970; Galda, 1998; Galda & Cullinan, 2002). This opportunity is often sparked by an intense connection to the characters who inhabit the secondary world of story.

Engagement with characters offers readers the opportunity to enlarge their own repertoire of experiences by living in the story world through the eyes of a character: "Empathetic insight allows the [reader] to view ways of life beyond his own range" (Harding, 1962, p. 136). Readers associate themselves with characters in at least four ways (Encisco, 1992, p. 92):

1. empathizing,
2. identifying,
3. merging, and
4. feeling close to characters.

Empathy is evidenced by "having a sense of the way another feels in a given situation." Identification involves "acknowledging similarities between reader and character." When readers merge with a character, they feel as if they "become the character or a part of the setting." Finally, some readers report that they feel close to or "with" a character.

Engaged readers almost always connect in some way with the characters they encounter:

> Readers connect with narratives, whether realistic or fantasy, by becoming involved with and caring about the characters, by being engrossed in the events of the story, by experiencing the story they are reading—by feeling as though they are there, in the story world...by being "inhaled by books." (Galda & Cullinan, 2002, p. 308)

Extending the Experience of the Story World Through Drama

Once reading is complete and the book cover closed, drama is a powerful means of extending students' connections with characters. Dramatic activities allow students to step back into the story world and move through it yet again. They take on roles, viewing the story world through the eyes of the characters. Dramatic activities allow students to pause and explore character feelings, traits, motivations, actions (and the consequences of those actions), and relationships. Acting out a character's role fosters a deep empathy with and understanding of an "other," albeit a fictional other, which may result in moral, social, or emotional growth, and a deeper understanding of oneself and the human condition (Britton, 1970; Harding, 1962; Rosenblatt, 1976). The exploration of character through drama—which motivates students to think, talk, and perhaps argue about characters as they plan their dramatic activity—can also result in a clearer understanding of the author's craft as it relates to character development and the unity of character and action.

The Social Nature of Drama

Not only does drama enable readers to re-create or revisit the story world, but also it allows them to do so in the company of others (Edmiston, 1993). When a reader engages with a character while reading, it is a solitary act, but when a reader engages with a character while participating in a group dramatic activity, that reader moves into a "public shared world of the text in which [one] can walk around and interact with other people in role" (Edmiston, 1993, p. 256). Drama, then, is not only an opportunity to discuss and reengage with characters, but also a means by which students make public their private understandings. This sharing enhances their own and others' understanding of story.

The social nature of literature-based dramatic activity requires discussion among the dramatists—discussion that often begins with a retelling of the main events in the order in which they occur, identifying the characters, and reflecting on what the characters are like. Thus, planning for drama provides a meaningful opportunity for both recall and exploratory talk about character. Even the most spontaneous dramatic responses are usually preceded by at least a brief discussion.

Planning for Drama and Encouraging Spontaneity

Dramatic activity in response to story is marked by spontaneity. In class-rooms where drama is encouraged, students often immediately move into interpretation of the story through drama. A few props (such as a bench to represent the bridge) and a brief discussion, and students are ready to perform. But even spontaneous drama does not occur without careful planning on the part of the teacher.

First, teachers who encourage drama select their books carefully. Many teachers introduce drama activities with simple stories that can be enacted without much planning. Folklore is often a good choice even though there is not much character development in classic folk tales. In folk tales, characters are rather flat—exemplifying only one or two traits (such as kindness and evil)—and the plot is straightforward. Folk tales, then, are a perfect springboard for making inferences about character motives and for elaborating on character actions. The framework or bare bones of the folk tale plot is easy to follow, so students can be encouraged to think and talk about character feelings and motives, to add meat to the bones of the story. Thus the Billy Goats Gruff become either lucky or clever, and the motives of Goldilocks's actions are debated. Just why did she go into the three bears' house? Was she nosey? Curious? Disobedient? When she ate the porridge was she simply hungry or was she greedy? The story shifts, depending on how a student personifies Goldilocks.

As students grow in their understanding of complex characters, any engaging story with well-developed characters can serve as a basis for drama. (A list of suggested literature appears in Table 11.1.) When they connect with the characters they read about, students easily move to take on personas in

TABLE 11.1   Suggested Titles for Literature-Based Dramatic Activity: Books
With Characters Students Care About

Ada, A.F. (1993). *My name is Maria Isabel.* New York: Atheneum.

Avi. (1997). *Poppy.* New York: HarperCollins.

Cameron, A. (1996). *The stories Julian tells.* New York: Random House.

Clements, A. (1996). *Frindle.* New York: Simon & Schuster.

Creech, S. (2002). *Ruby Holler.* New York: Joanna Cotler.

Creech, S. (2003). *Granny Torrelli makes soup.* New York: Joanna Cotler.

Curtis, C.P. (1995). *The Watsons go to Birmingham—1963.* New York: Delacorte.

DiCamillo, K. (2000). *Because of Winn-Dixie.* Cambridge, MA: Candlewick.

Fleischman, P. (1986). *The whipping boy.* New York: Greenwillow.

Gantos, J. (1999). *Jack on the tracks: Four seasons of fifth grade.* New York: Farrar Straus Giroux.

Gerstein, M. (2003). *The man who walked between the towers.* Brookfield, CN: Roaring Brook Press.

Greenfield, E. (1992). *Koya DeLaney and the good girl blues.* New York: Scholastic.

Grimes, N. (2002). *My man blue.* Ill. J. Lagarrigue. New York: Puffin.

Havill, J. (2003). *Jamaica's blue marker.* Ill. A.S. O'Brien. Boston: Houghton Mifflin.

Henkes, K. (1991). *Chrysanthemum.* New York: Greenwillow.

Henkes, K. (1996). *Lilly's purple plastic purse.* New York: Greenwillow.

Hill, K. (2002). *The year of Miss Agnes.* New York: Aladdin.

Johnson, D. (1992). *The best bug to be.* New York: Atheneum.

Lowry, L. (1984). *Anastasia Krupnik.* New York: Yearling.

Namioka, L. (1994). *Yang the Youngest and his terrible ear.* New York: Yearling.

Naylor, P.R. (1991). *Shiloh.* New York: Atheneum.

Paterson, K. (1977). *Bridge to Terabithia.* New York: HarperCollins.

Polacco, P. (1998). *Thank you, Mr. Falker.* New York: Philomel.

Williams, V. (2001). *Amber was brave, Essie was smart.* New York: Greenwillow.

---

dramatic activity. Students are likely to talk about compelling characters, often discussing them as though they are real human beings—people who they know well. This talk can be channeled into planning for drama.

When students are beginning to engage in dramatic activity, they need support. Teachers often engage the whole class in a planning discussion, talking both about the process they are using and the book that students will dramatize. Ms. Pearson, a third-grade teacher, does just this when she introduces her students to their first literature-based dramatic activity. In the following example Ms. Pearson has just read aloud the last chapter of

Sharon Creech's *Granny Torrelli Makes Soup* (2003), and her students respond to the book:

Ms. Pearson: I can tell by your comments that you really enjoyed the characters! It seems that many of you have someone like Granny Torrelli in your life. I did, too, when I was about your age, and it was wonderful to be able to talk to her about things that I didn't talk to anyone else about.

Students: [Random comments of general agreement.]

Ms. Pearson: Since we were really involved in this book, let's re-create some of the scenes that we especially enjoyed. We've done a lot of writing and talking about the story, and now we're going to do some acting. Acting out scenes is another way we can share our responses to the story.

Cameron: How will we do that? What do you want us to do?

Ms. Pearson: I'll tell you in a few minutes, but first I want to list some adjectives that describe the characters.

[Ms. Pearson writes the names of the characters on chart paper and students call out descriptors. As students give suggestions, she asks for evidence to support their ideas. Soon the page is filled with character descriptions.]

Once Ms. Pearson has students engaged, she tells them about the dramatic activity process and assigns them to small groups to work in. These groups are heterogeneous in terms of reading ability. Ms. Pearson has carefully assigned to each group students who are complementary in their abilities. Someone in each group is a good group leader; someone else has demonstrated good insights into the characters. Someone else reads with great fluency and expression; another student is good with details. Ms. Pearson balances each group for optimum success and considers using cooperative learning group roles, but decides that she doesn't need to for this particular activity. Ms. Pearson then discusses the steps she wants students to follow and displays the steps on a chart for the groups to refer to (see Table 11.2).

Students begin rereading and Ms. Pearson sets the timer for a couple of minutes. When it rings, students move on to the next step: discussing the scenes and taking notes. When the timer rings again, students begin to discuss character motives (step 3). Each group enacts a scene in step 4, and follows up with a discussion of what went well and what needs improvement

TABLE 11.2   Ms. Pearson's Dramatic Activity Steps for Students

1. **Reread** aloud the scene you are assigned.
2. **Discuss what** the characters are doing and make notes about the sequence of things.
3. **Discuss why** the characters are doing what they are doing.
4. **Assign roles** for an initial practice, including the role of audience.
5. **Re-create** the scene.
6. **Evaluate** the success of the drama.
7. **Discuss and improve** the drama and reassign roles.

Ground Rules:
• Stay in character (don't be yourself).
• Talk to others using their role names.
• Think about what is working and what is not.

(steps 6 and 7). Ms. Pearson talks with the class about what they find easy and difficult in the activity, reminding them that they don't have to be perfect and that tomorrow they will have more time to work on their scenes before they present them.

When the groups act out their scenes the next day, the whole class discusses the characters' personalities as the groups have presented them. The class also considers how some of the characters change during the course of the story, and how the characters change in their feelings toward one another. Finally, Ms. Pearson enriches the dramatic activity with the creation of a character timeline, on which students draw the changes in characters according to pivotal events.

Using Dramatic Activity to Explore the Author's Craft

Story-based drama can also be used in classrooms as a reoccurring response option for students. Teachers can make dramatic activity a formal assignment when they want students to closely consider character traits and motives. Over time, teachers can move students from re-creating scenes to inventing new ones.

As students learn to use drama to step back into the world of story, they also learn about literature. In addition to giving close and careful thought to characters, students explore what the author does to create characters. Like the students in Ms. Pearson's classroom, they consider not only what a character is like or how a character might react, but also *how they know* these things about a character. If, for example, they describe Granny Torrelli as kind, they can list the things that Granny does or says that make them think she is kind.

Discussion of character as a precursor to dramatic activity offers the perfect opportunity for talking with students about how authors create characters. Talk about what a character looks like and how students know this information. Explore what a character says and does and how the character's words and actions allow readers to build a picture of the character. Look at how the characters talk to one another and discuss how their talk reveals characteristics and dispositions. Consider how characters act toward one another and how each interaction allows readers to know a little more about them. All of these character explorations naturally lead back to the story, as students search for evidence to support their interpretations of the characters.

More sophisticated readers can use these planning discussions to consider how the attributes, attitudes, and actions of a character influence what happens, and how the events of the story precipitate subsequent character development. In discussions like this, students learn a lot about the author's craft.

Interpreting and Improvising Story Scenes

There are many types of dramatic activity, among them mime, puppetry, invented dialogue, interpretation, improvisation, role-playing, and full-fledged dramatic staging. Some lend themselves to re-creation of what occurs in a story; others allow students to go beyond the information given and create something new. In dramatic interpretation, students reenact the story as it was told. Rarely do they deviate from the plot and characterizations of the text, except to infer motives and ways of demonstrating characteristics. Another kind of dramatic activity is improvisation, also known as role-playing. In improvisation, students create new scenes that are not in the original story, based on what they know about the characters.

Stewig (1983) points out the differences between interpretation and improvisation: Interpretation is successful if it is an accurate re-creation of the author's text; improvisation asks students to extend or expand the text. Both interpretation and improvisation ask students to think about characters and then build on what they know about them to create a dramatic performance. Improvisation also requires students to go beyond what they know, imagining a character's response to a new situation. Well-placed questions help students to set up alternate scenes to improvise. For example, if, during an interpretation, students decided that the Billy Goats Gruff are tricksters, the teacher might help them prepare for improvisation by asking, "What do you think the three Billy Goats Gruff said to one another when they were planning to trick the troll?" Then students could expand on the story, acting out a conversation that did not take place in the narrative but that reveals the characters' motivations.

Improvisation often takes the form of going beyond the story's ending. Dramatizing what happens *after* the biggest billy goat joins his brothers in the grassy meadow extends the story beyond the folkloric "snip, snap, snout, this tale is told out" ending. After reading Katherine Paterson's *The Great Gilly Hopkins* (1978), students could consider the meeting of Mamie Trotter, William Ernest, Gilly, and Gilly's grandmother after Gilly has lived with her grandmother for a few months. The possibilities for extending stories with improvisation are almost endless, if you select books wisely. See Table 11.3 for extension ideas.

The Prerequisite of Dramatic Activity: Pleasure

Although improvisation does not tie students as closely to the original text as interpretation does, improvisation cannot be successful unless it is firmly rooted in the text. Whether students are interpreting or improvising a story, they still begin by taking pleasure in reading or listening to a story. Enjoyment is paramount. Why would anyone want to dramatize a story they didn't like or spend time with characters they don't care about?

When you finish reading a story, it's a good idea to open up the floor for discussion, asking for student responses to and interpretations of the story, and urging students to listen to and respond to one another's ideas. Listen closely to their discussion. If it is passionate, then it may be a good time to suggest a dramatic activity. As discussion continues, questions about character qualities, motivations, and relationships can help focus students on what they will need to think about and discuss further if they are to have a successful dramatic experience. Graphic organizers—such as character maps in which characters and their attributes are positioned around a circle, with their feelings about one another written on the line connecting them— help remind students of what the class has discussed once they break into

TABLE 11.3   Suggested Literature-Based Improvisation Activities

Title	Description and Grade Level
The Tale of Despereaux (DiCamillo, 2003)	This novel ends with the small mouse, Despereaux, reunited with his beloved Princess Pea. Students may invent future scenes between the Princess and Despereaux or Mig and her father; deliberations on mouse etiquette among the mouse community; conversations between Roscuro and other rats; or conversations between Roscuro and Despereaux. The possibilities are endless. (Grades 2–4)
The Day of Ahmed's Secret (Heide & Gilliland, 1990)	In this story, a young boy in Cairo, Egypt, performs his daily work while holding a secret that he is eager to share with his family. When he gets home he is finally able to share his secret: He can write his name. The story ends with him demonstrating this to his family. Students can think about who some of the family members might be (by looking at the illustration) and what they might say. They may improvise the scene just after Ahmed tells his secret. (Grades K–1)
The Giver (Lowry, 1999)	The ending of this novel is open to several interpretations. One interpretation is that Jonas and Gabe make it to Elsewhere and that Elsewhere is a place. Students can improvise a scene in which Jonas and Gabe are found outside on the sled, a scene in which Jonas returns to the Community, or a scene in which the Community discovers that Jonas is gone. (Grades 5–8)
The Other Side (Woodson, 2001)	Two young girls, one black and one white, sit on a fence that separates their yards; they eventually become tentative friends even though no one else wants them to. Older students can role-play these characters in both historical and contemporary settings and improvise dialogue that reveals the girls' strength of character, as well as the influence of society on their actions and convictions. (Grades K–6)

planning groups. When the conversation slows, you can arrange students in groups and ask them to follow the steps to interpret or to improvise a scene (refer to Table 11.2 on page 90). As students grow comfortable, they often begin to spontaneously engage in dramatic play about stories (Hickman, 1981).

Enriching the Language Arts With Dramatic Activity

Literature-based dramatic activity encompasses many aspects of language arts. Students either read or listen to a story. They respond to the story in various ways, including through writing and discussion. As students discuss their perceptions of the secondary world, they return to the text to find evidence for their perceptions. Once engaged in creating a dramatic enactment, students talk with each other to plan, and to present and support their opinions. They also reread and, in many cases, write down important points. When performing, students use oral language in a new, more formal fashion, taking on the language patterns of the characters they represent, and of the authors who created them. They also have the opportunity to be the audience for others, learning to watch and listen from a supportive yet critical stance, and to give useful feedback to others. Above all, students engaged in drama in response to literature are considering why characters act as they do, and are trying on the persona of another, thinking and acting in a manner that is different for them.

By harnessing students' inclination to play and imagine, teachers can foster positive literary experiences that help students understand themselves and others while adding to their knowledge of how stories work. Dramatic activity extends students' opportunity to dwell within the story world, to consider life as it might be, and to do so in the company of peers. With each new book, it enhances the connections students make with story, providing a deep and rich base of experience upon which to build. Far from being a frill or time filler, exploring character through drama is a powerful tool for helping students refine their reading, writing, listening, and speaking abilities.

REFERENCES

Benton, M.G. (1983). Secondary worlds. *Journal of Research and Development in Education, 16*, 68–75.

Britton, J. (1970). *Language and learning.* New York: Penguin.

Edmiston, B. (1993). Going up the beanstalk: Discovering giant possibilities for responding to literature through drama. In K.E. Holland, R.A. Hungerford, & S.B. Ernst (Eds.), *Journeying: Children responding to literature* (pp. 250–266). Portsmouth, NH: Heinemann.

Enciso, P. (1992). Creating the story world: A case study of a young reader's engagement strategies and stances. In J. Many & C. Cox (Eds.), *Reader stance and literary understanding* (pp. 75–102). Norwood, NJ: Ablex.

Galda, L. (1998). Mirrors and windows: Reading as transformation. In T. Raphael & K. Au (Eds.), *Literature-based instruction: Reshaping the curriculum* (pp. 1–11). Norwood, MA: Christopher-Gordon.

Galda, L., & Cullinan, B.E. (2002). *Literature and the child* (5th ed.). Belmont, CA: Wadsworth.

Harding, D.W. (1962). Psychological processes in the reading of fiction. *British Journal of Aesthetics, 2,* 133–147.

Hickman, J.E. (1981). A new perspective on response to literature: Research in an elementary school setting. *Research in the Teaching of English, 15,* 343–354.

Langer, J.A. (1995). *Envisioning literature: Literary understanding and literature instruction.* New York: Teachers College Press; Newark, DE: International Reading Association.

Rosenblatt, L.M. (1976). *Literature as exploration.* New York: Noble and Noble.

Rosenblatt, L.M. (1978). *The reader, the text, the poem: The transactional theory of the literary work.* Carbondale, IL: Southern Illinois University Press.

Stewig, J.W. (1983). *Exploring language arts in the elementary classroom.* New York: Holt, Rinehart and Winston.

LITERATURE CITED

Bunting, E. (1991). *Fly away home.* Ill. R. Himler. New York: Clarion.

Creech, S. (2003). *Granny Torrelli makes soup.* New York: Joanna Cotler.

DiCamillo, K. (2003). *The tale of Despereaux.* Cambridge, MA: Candlewick.

Heide, F.P., & Gilliland, J.H. (1990). *The day of Ahmed's secret.* Ill. T. Lewin. New York: Lothrop, Lee & Shepard.

Lowry, L. (1999). *The giver.* Boston: Houghton Mifflin.

Paterson, K. (1978). *The great Gilly Hopkins.* New York: HarperCollins.

Tolkien, J.R.R. (1964). *Tree and leaf.* London: Allen & Unwin.

Woodson, J. (2001). *The other side.* Ill. E.B. Lewis. New York: Putnam.

12

Exploring Character Through Readers Theatre

Susan Keehn, Miriam G. Martinez, and Nancy L. Roser

Readers Theatre gives students the opportunity to better understand a character by stepping into that character's shoes. Susan Keehn, Miriam Martinez, and Nancy Roser make recommendations for selecting books, creating scripts, and getting started with Readers Theatre in your classroom.

O BETTER UNDERSTAND OTHER PEOPLE, WE ARE sometimes advised to "walk a mile in their shoes." When the people we want to understand are literary characters, we can "walk in their shoes" through the medium of Readers Theatre.

Readers Theatre is an interpretive reading activity in which students use their voices to bring characters to life. Unlike some forms of dramatic activity, Readers Theatre requires no memorization, sets, props, or costumes. Instead, students practice reading the script (based on a book) until their reading is fluent and expressive—revealing the feelings, reactions, and desires

What a Character! Character Study as a Guide to Literary Meaning Making in Grades K–8 edited by Nancy L. Roser and Miriam G. Martinez, with Junko Yokota and Sharon O'Neal. Copyright 2005 by the International Reading Association.

of the characters. The rehearsed script is then read for an audience—a type of performance reading (Worthy, Broaddus, & Ivey, 2001). As students perform their roles, they transform themselves through the talk, thoughts, and experiences of characters (Busching, 1981).

Because Readers Theatre requires rehearsal, and therefore rereading, it is an effective instructional intervention that improves oral reading fluency. Recent studies have documented that the practice associated with Readers Theatre does, indeed, contribute to oral reading fluency and proficiency (Briggs & Forbes, 2002; Keehn, 2001; Martinez, Roser, & Strecker, 1998/1999; Millin & Rinehart, 1999; Roser et al., 2003). Teachers and researchers also attest to the fact that students are motivated by the performance aspect of Readers Theatre. In addition, because students take on roles, Readers Theatre encourages deep insight into literary characters and helps students understand plot through the characters' perspectives. Well understood characters guide students through the nuances of plot, just as plot reveals those characters. Readers Theatre is a powerful medium for helping students in grades 1–8 gain insights into literature.

Selecting Literature for Readers Theatre

When using Readers Theatre in the classroom, whether with beginning or advanced readers, there are a number of criteria for selecting books. However, when the primary instructional goal is to foster insight into character, the single most important criterion is rounded, memorable characters.

The Character Criteria

When selecting books for Readers Theatre, there are at least three facets of character to consider: character traits, feelings, and motives.

Character traits often drive the story problem or shape its outcome. When the characters have clearly defined traits that influence story events, then the challenge for the performer is first to understand the nature of the character and second to make that nature apparent to the audience. In James Marshall's *Fox in Love* (1982), the central character is Fox: a lazy fellow who consistently seeks ways to take shortcuts. This trait, which repeatedly gets Fox into the humorous predicaments that mark the Fox series, must be clearly conveyed. Similarly, the audience needs to understand that the central character of Roger Duvoisin's *Petunia* (1966) is a proud and bossy goose—

traits that lead to chaos in the barnyard. Without first grasping character traits, the audience may find a plot difficult to follow.

Feelings are another important facet of character. When students recognize a character's feelings and the changes that occur in those feelings over time, they gain insight into the very nature of the character's struggles. Books in which characters express strong feelings or in which feelings change over the course of the story make for good Readers Theatre, especially when the aim is to help students better understand character. The feelings of Alexander, the mouse character in *Alexander and the Wind-Up Mouse* (Lionni, 1987), run a wide gamut. Early in the story Alexander is sad that humans dislike him. Then, after meeting Willy, the wind-up mouse, Alexander becomes envious because Willy is loved by humans. When the children grow tired of Willy, though, and throw him into the trash, Alexander's feelings change once again as he feels sorry for his new friend. Finally, Alexander feels excited and hopeful when he discovers a way to change Willy into a real mouse. This broad range of emotion makes *Alexander and the Wind-Up Mouse* a good story for Readers Theatre.

Readers Theatre is also a vehicle through which students examine and interpret character motive. **Motive** underlies a character's intentions and goals. It drives a character's actions. When students understand character motive and can link motive to actions, they view the story as a cohesive string of events rather than a series of unlinked actions. Books with characters who have clearly defined motives often make rich Readers Theatre scripts. *Harry and the Terrible Whatzit* (Gackenbach, 1977) is one such book. When Harry's mother descends into the dark, gloomy cellar and fails to return, Harry is determined to rescue her even if it means facing the dangers that surely await him in the cellar. Once in the cellar, though, Harry is unable to find his mother. Convinced that the terrible Whatzit has harmed his mother, Harry's worry overcomes his fear. He confronts the monster, demanding to know what has become of his mother. The intensity of Harry's motive carries him not just to the cellar but to the triumph over the Whatzit, who is, of course, intimidated by such a brave and ferocious child.

Performance Group Size

When selecting books for Readers Theatre, consider the number of groups and the size of the groups you will form. One class can be divided up into several performance groups. When appropriate, the same script can be used for all performance groups. To match the challenge of the text with the reading ability of the students, you may want to have each group work with a different script, one that best matches the children's abilities. It takes some practice to supervise three different repertory groups at one time, so begin with only one performance group. The ideal size for a Readers Theatre group is five or six students. However, when a Readers Theatre group is small, then the book you choose must have few parts. *Knots on a Counting Rope* (Martin & Archambault, 1987) is entirely a dialogue between a boy and his grandfather; a script based on this book has parts for two readers, or you could cast each character twice if you have four students. If the performance group is large, the book needs to have many characters. *Albert's Impossible Toothache* (Williams, 2003) has six characters and a narrator; its performance group could have as many as seven members. The number of parts needed for a group can be adjusted as needed; for example, one student can read two or more small roles, or a narrator's part may be divided for multiple students.

Cultural Relevancy

It is of primary importance to choose literature with which your students will connect. Many teachers who work with students from diverse backgrounds report that Readers Theatre is most successful when scripts are based on culturally relevant literature. In one fourth-grade classroom, for example, students were recent immigrants from Mexico so the stories and poetry chosen for Readers Theatre reflected that culture. Especially notable were *My Name is Jorge: On Both Sides of the River* (Medina, 1999) and *A Day's Work* (Bunting, 1994) These two books depict experiences of characters who are Mexicans in the United States. Their stories are told through dialogue. Because the students easily identified with the characters and their experiences, they related to the feelings of the characters. This understanding was reflected in students' voices when they performed (Roser et al., 2003).

Special Criteria for Selecting Picturebooks

When selecting picturebooks for Readers Theatre, you want both rich characters and an engaging story. You also need a story that contains good dialogue. A wonderfully dramatic story such as *Officer Buckle and Gloria* (Rathmann, 1995) is less than ideal for Readers Theatre because so much of its critically important story information is contained exclusively in the illustrations. Although some narration can convey important information, picturebooks containing a great deal of integral pictorial information are difficult to use in Readers Theatre. The picturebooks listed in Table 12.1 offer vivid characters and can be readily adapted for Readers Theatre.

Selecting picturebooks for beginning readers to use in Readers Theatre can be especially challenging. Not only must the book's language be within the reach of young students (Larkin, 2001), but the book must also contain sufficient dialogue. Many books for beginners have limited dialogue or none at all. Many are also not particularly character rich. Even so, there are some

TABLE 12.1   Character-Rich Picturebooks for Readers Theatre Scripts

Agee, J. (2001). *Milo's hat trick*. New York: Hyperion.
Baker, K. (2002). *Meet Mr. and Mrs. Green*. San Diego: Harcourt.
Bluthenthal, D.C. (2003). *I'm not invited?* New York: Atheneum.
Brown, M. (1993). *Arthur's pet business*. New York: Little Brown.
Brown, M. (1996). *Arthur's first sleepover*. New York: Little Brown.
Bunting, E. (1994). *A day's work*. New York: Clarion.
Champion, J. (1993). *Emily and Alice*. Ill. S. Stevenson. San Diego, CA: Harcourt.
Duvoisin, R. (1966). *Petunia*. New York: Knopf.
Gackenbach, D. (1977). *Harry and the terrible Whatzit*. New York: Clarion.
Graham, B. (1992). *Rose meets Mr. Wintergarten*. Cambridge, MA: Candlewick.
Guest, E.H. (2002). *Iris and Walter*. Ill. C. Davenier. San Diego, CA: Harcourt.
Henkes, K. (1991). *Chrysanthemum*. New York: Greenwillow.
Henkes, K. (1993). *Owen*. New York: Greenwillow.
Kellogg, S. (1976). *Much bigger than Martin*. New York: Dial.
Kvasnosky, L.M. (1999). *Zelda and Ivy and the boy next door*. Cambridge, MA: Candlewick.
Lester, H. (1999). *Hooway for Wodney Wat*. Ill. L. Munsinger. Boston: Houghton Mifflin.
Lionni L. (1969, 1987). *Alexander and the wind-up mouse*. New York: Knopf.
Martin Jr B., & Archambault, J. (1985). *The ghost-eye tree*. Ill. T. Rand. New York: Henry Holt.
Martin Jr B., & Archambault, J. (1987). *Knots on a counting rope*. Ill. T. Rand. New York: Henry Holt.
Medina, J. (1999). *My name is Jorge: On both sides of the river*. Honesdale, PA: Boyds Mills Press.
Mora, P. (1994). *Pablo's tree*. Ill. C. Lang. New York: Simon & Schuster.
Naylor, P.R. (1991a). *King of the playground*. Ill. N.L. Malone. New York: Atheneum.
Polacco, P. (1992). *Mrs. Katz and Tush*. New York: Dell.
Soto, G. (2002). *If the shoe fits*. Ill. T. Widener. New York: Putnam.
Williams, B. (2003). *Albert's impossible toothache*. Ill. D. Cushman. Cambridge, MA: Candlewick.

TABLE 12.2   Easy-to-Read Picturebooks for Readers Theatre

Alphin, E.M. (1996). *A bear for Miguel.* Ill. J. Sandin. New York: HarperCollins.
Carle, E. (1977). *The grouchy ladybug.* New York: HarperCollins.
Cole, J. (1988). *The missing tooth.* Ill. M. Hafner. New York: Random House.
Finch, M. (1999). *The little red hen and the ear of wheat.* Ill. E. Bell. Brooklyn, NY: Barefoot Books.
Fox, M. (1986). *Hattie and the fox.* Ill. P. Mullins. New York: Bradbury.
Galdone, P. (1973). *The three billy goats Gruff.* New York: Clarion.
Levinson, N.S. (2003). *Prairie friends.* Ill. S. Schuett. New York: HarperCollins.
Little, J. (2001). *Emma's yucky brother.* Ill. J. Plecas. New York: HarperTrophy.
Lobel, A. (1971). *Frog and Toad together.* New York: Harper & Row.
Marshall, E. (1982). *Fox in love.* Ill. J. Marshall. New York: Puffin.
Marshall, E. (1983). *Fox on wheels.* Ill. J. Marshall. New York: Puffin.
Rylant, C. (1992). *Henry and Mudge and the long weekend.* Ill. S. Stevenson.

easy-to-read books, such as *The Little Red Hen and the Ear of Wheat* (Finch, 1999), that present characters with traits so distinctive that they drive the story action. The picturebooks for beginning readers listed in Table 12.2 work well in Readers Theatre.

Books That Lend Themselves to Script Form

An especially important criterion for selecting a book is the ease with which the story can be turned into a script. Books with extensive dialogue are ideal candidates. When stories are predominantly narration, they take work to turn into Readers Theatre. A better choice are books in which the story is told through dialogue. Author Patricia MacLachlan, a master of dialogue, relies primarily on the talk among characters to develop her stories. Scenes from her character-driven books *Sarah, Plain and Tall* (1985), *Skylark* (1994), and *Caleb's Story* (2001) can easily be turned into Readers Theatre scripts. Select key scenes on which to base scripts. In *The Watsons Go to Birmingham—1963* (Curtis, 1995), the scene in which Byron's lips are frozen to the car mirror when he kisses his image in sub-zero weather is ideal for Readers Theatre because the scene develops primarily through dialogue, and there are parts for six readers. The chapter books listed in Table 12.3 contain numerous scenes readily adaptable for Readers Theatre scripts.

TABLE 12.3   Character-Rich Chapter Books for Readers Theatre Scripts

Ada, A.F. (1993). *My name is Maria Isabel.* New York: Atheneum.
Byars, B. (1996). *My brother, Ant.* New York: Viking.
Cameron. A. (1981). *The stories Julian tells.* New York: Knopf.
Curtis, C.P. (1995). *The Watsons go to Birmingham—1963.* New York: Delacorte.
DiCamillo, K. (2000). *Because of Winn-Dixie.* Cambridge, MA: Candlewick.
MacLachlan, P. (1985). *Sarah, plain and tall.* New York: Harper & Row.
MacLachlan, P. (1994). *Skylark.* New York: HarperCollins.
MacLachlan, P. (2001). *Caleb's story.* New York: HarperCollins.
Naylor, P.R. (1991b). *Shiloh.* New York: Atheneum.
Ryan, P.M. (2000). *Esperanza rising.* New York: Scholastic.
Soto, G. (1990). *Baseball in April.* San Diego, CA: Harcourt Brace Jovanovich.
Soto, G. (1997). *Novio boy.* San Diego, CA: Harcourt Brace.
Taylor, M.D. (1995). *The well.* New York: Dial.
Wiles, D. (2001). *Love, Ruby Lavender.* San Diego, CA: Harcourt.

Adapting Books to Script Form

Readers Theatre scripts are easily created from carefully selected stories by turning the book's dialogue into actors' lines, and cementing those lines with a narrator's voice that provides needed details of setting or intervening actions. Typically, it is unnecessary to change a story except for occasionally shortening a passage of narration to keep the script moving, or by adding brief narration to explain an important detail portrayed only in an illustration.

Generally, double-spaced scripts in 14-point font are easy for students to use. Scripts for primary grades typically range from two to four pages. Scripts for students in grades 3 and higher range from four to seven pages. Make master copies of the script with one character's name highlighted on each copy. This way, each student is following along with the entire text but knows that the highlights designate the lines he or she is to read. You may even want to insert the script pages into plastic sleeves to protect them.

Students, too, can be involved in script preparation. Model how to convert a book scene to a script using a book that is familiar to the students and that has only a few characters; then have students try adapting an appropriate book for Readers Theatre. In *What Really Matters for Struggling Readers*, Richard Allington (2001) encourages teachers to allow students "to simply plow ahead on their own and experiment with script development from stories or books of their choice" (p. 83).

Establishing Classroom Procedures
for Readers Theatre

Our experience with implementation of Readers Theatre in many elementary classrooms supports the use of a weekly cycle. We have found that students' motivation to practice is maintained when performance is imminent (Keehn, 2001; Martinez, Roser, & Strecker, 1998/1999). Following we describe the Readers Theatre routine of one first-grade teacher, Ms. Akin, who was interested in supporting her students' awareness of character using Readers Theatre.

Each Monday, Ms. Akin reads aloud the original story on which an upcoming Readers Theatre script will be based. On the first Monday she read *Fox on Stage* (Marshall, 1993). On subsequent Monday storybook read-alouds of Fox books, Ms. Akin began by asking, "What do we already know about Fox? What kind of guy is he?" She then introduced the new story, inviting the students to make predictions. Her probes focused on what might happen in the stories based on what the students knew about the nature of the various characters; for example, "Knowing that Fox is often lazy and sometimes a trickster, what do you think might happen when he takes a job at a pizza parlor?" During the read-aloud, Ms. Akin paused to encourage the students to predict story events, personal conflicts, and resolutions based on their knowledge of the characters. For example, as Ms. Akin neared the end of *Fox on Stage*, she paused to ask, "Now that Fox has completely messed up his lines in the play, how do you think he will act? Will he apologize? Will he blame somebody else? What do you think?" After the reading, Ms. Akin further promoted thinking about the character's nature by asking, "What did we discover about Fox from today's story?"

On Tuesday, Ms. Akin organized her 22 students into three repertory groups to practice reading the scripts. She had each master script highlighted according to part, such as "Narrator 1" or "Fox" or "Mother." As the students read, Ms. Akin moved among the groups, coaching for character interpretation:

"Maria, you said yesterday that Fox is 'sassy.' How might a sassy Fox sound? Try that again."

"Fox is being a smarty pants here. Let's all try that with a snooty voice."

After reading through the script, students passed the master scripts clockwise around the circle. With a different script in hand, with a new character highlighted, students rehearsed again, each with a different part. Daily practice continued for approximately 25 minutes.

Wednesday's routine replicated that of Tuesday. At the close of Wednesday's work in repertory groups, students determined who would read each role for the week's performance that would take place on Friday.

On Thursday, practice in repertory groups involved students reading only the role they would perform on Friday. Thus, a student reading a Fox script typically had practiced the part twelve to fifteen times.

On Friday the students performed before an audience. Before the performance, each student stepped forward to introduce himself or herself as a character: "I am Stephen, and I will be Fox." Enthusiastic applause followed each performance. Then, Ms. Akin offered comments and solicited compliments from the audience. She intentionally focused her comments on students' representation of the character: "I really like how Billy made his voice sound sly."

After the performances, Ms. Akin paired students in the class to be penpals to write to each other about the characters in that week's story. These letters help reveal the students' growing attention to characters' internal attributes. In her penpal letters, Mercedes initially wrote about the oral reading performances rather than the characters (e.g., "Fox had a good voice."). In later letters, Mercedes addressed character traits and her own feelings about those characters: "I do not like Fox. Becuse [because] he is triky [tricky]. I like Mom. Becuse Mom is nice. Do you like Mom? Do you like Fox?" (Keehn, 2001).

The books in Marc Brown's Arthur series were also introduced, practiced, coached, and performed in the same way. In her first letter to her penpal, Jessica focused on Francine's actions: "Francen [Francine] hit Arther [Arthur] in the mouth." Her later letters offered character analysis, and addressed relationships: "I like DW becus [because] she is a blabermath [blabbermouth] and I like Arthur becus he is a good frind [friend]."

The Implications of Readers Theatre for Character Study

To gain further insights into the students' understanding of character, we (Martinez, Keehn, Roser, Harmon, & O'Neal, 2002) conducted post-performance interviews with the students throughout the nine weeks of their Readers Theatre performances: "Talk to me about a character in this week's story." The interviews showed that first graders who initially focused on characters' physical attributes and actions began to attend to internal traits such as character motivation and character relationships.

In early interviews, Julian described only action, retelling the story: "Fox went up [on the diving board] to get his sister, but when he got up there, she wasn't there." In later interviews, Julian's comments revealed a shift to a more internal focus: "Fox thinks he's cool. He thinks he's like the handsome prince in the play, but he's not. In each story Fox gets in trouble...and that Louise [Fox's sister] is a handful!"

In his first interview, Michael discussed superficial aspects of character: "He's a boy. I can tell by his name." Later, Michael talked about character traits and his own personal attitude toward the character: "Fox is crazy because he always gets in trouble. And he's mean to his little sister," as well as "He's tricky, but I like him because he is funny."

Similarly, Amanda's interviews revealed increased awareness of internal character traits. Initially, Amanda talked about the characters according to gender ("She's a girl") and physical attributes ("He wears glasses"). Four weeks later, Jessica was discussing the character's traits: "Arthur's nice. He doesn't get in fights. He likes his friends, and he is kind to them."

Readers Theatre in Bilingual Classrooms

We (Roser et al., 2003) also investigated the benefits of Readers Theatre in a bilingual fourth-grade classroom. Like Ms. Akin, Ms. May organized Readers Theatre on a five-day cycle. Each day of the week she opened the daily two-hour language arts period by reading aloud from a culturally relevant text in English or Spanish. Regardless of the repertory group to which a student belonged, or whether the student would read in English or Spanish, all children gathered to hear the read-aloud. She routinely invited the students to comment on her reading, as well as the story. Many of the students' comments began to focus on character. In the following example, the students notice how Ms. May's interpretive reading of one of the poems in *My Name Is Jorge: On Both Sides of the River* (Medina, 1999) reveals on character. The poems in Medina's book document the experiences of an immigrant child, too often called "George" instead of "Jorge," and subtly reveal Jorge's needs, feelings, and puzzlements.

Joaquin: [You] did it a little more hard each time.

Students: [agreement]

Marta:	Said like scared.
Carmen:	A little harder first and then softer...
Raul:	...to sound like Jorge.
Marta:	Sounds like scared, like sad.
Paola:	Then stronger.
Rafael:	It was you making it sound sad.
Raul:	The words are sad, so that's why you're making your voice sound sad.

Following the read-aloud discussion, Ms. May taught a minilesson aimed at helping her students make meanings—both comprehension centered (monitoring for understanding) and literary (reading for ideas, images, and feelings). When the minilesson focused on character, she collected the children's ideas about Jorge on a chart:

- Speaks Spanish
- Mexican American
- Is a boy
- Probably has black eyes and black hair
- Skin is brown
- Just arrived from Mexico
- Shy
- He's bilingual
- He doesn't like to turn into a sneeze
- George is a funny name
- His name is Jorge, not George
- He doesn't know what a George means
- He doesn't like the way it sounds
- Jorge likes Spanish more than English

Each day, Ms. May assigned a text and its accompanying Readers Theatre script to one of her five reading groups—a script to be rehearsed until performance-ready (in five days). The scripts were selected and built from stories and poems at students' independent or instructional reading levels. So, each day one of the groups was beginning the five-day sequence, and one group was finishing it; each of the other three groups were in various steps of the rehearsal process.

She allowed approximately 20 minutes for daily rehearsal. As with the first graders, students rotated scripts so that each student practiced each part. Ms. May designed the second hour of the language arts block to provide a variety of activities, including free reading or DEAR (Drop Everything and Read) time, writing, word work, and standardized test preparation. In the final 10–15 minutes of each two-hour block, one of the five groups performed a script its members had been rehearsing for the previous four class days.

Because the instruction that accompanied the literature focused on dimensions of character study—ranging from what the story characters wanted and needed, to how others saw those characters, to what characters revealed by their own talk and actions, to the ways in which characters changed—the students grew in their awareness of characters. They described characters traits more deeply and noted character change ("They are people that maybe have problems and they solve them. Maybe at first they're sad and then they're happy."). Further, the students seemed to understand that characters are created by authors in purposeful ways ("She put in a lot of details to make Charlie interesting.").

Linking Readers Theatre to the Wider Literacy Program

You can further deepen students' understanding of characters by linking Readers Theatre to the other components of your literacy program. During read-alouds, guided reading time, and conferences with students regarding their independent reading, focus discussions on characters. Such intentional focus throughout the day deepens attention to character in Readers Theatre.

Begin with one performance group—and select low-performing students, students who lack motivation or confidence to be in it, or both. While you work with the group, the rest of the class can read independently, read with a buddy, or write in response journals. Eventually multiple groups can be engaged in Readers Theatre at the same time. You may give each group a script that matches their reading level or you may prefer to mix the groups so that students work with a range of readers. Readers Theatre has been successful in groups of both types. As students become comfortable with the routines and procedures, circulate among the groups, emphasizing the interpretation of character as students work toward fluent, accurate, and expressive reading.

A Final Word

We believe that Readers Theatre holds great potential for enhancing student awareness of the complexities of character. As students assume the role of characters, they consider what the characters are like, what they hope to achieve, how the characters feel, and how the characters grow and change with experiences. Readers Theatre is also highly motivating—even for students who struggle with reading. To ensure that students gain insight into character through Readers Theatre, teachers must carefully select the books used. By supporting students through demonstrations and discussions that help them improve their dramatic readings, students' literary understanding will continuously unfold.

REFERENCES

Allington, R.L. (2001). *What really matters for struggling readers: Designing research-based programs.* New York: Longman.

Briggs, C., & Forbes, S. (2002). Phrasing in fluency reading: Process *and* product. *Journal of Reading Recovery, Spring,* 1–9.

Busching, B. (1981). Readers' Theater: An education for language and life. *Language Arts, 58*(3), 330–338.

Keehn, S. (2001, December). *A study of Readers Theatre as a fluency intervention in first grade.* Paper presented at the annual meeting of the National Reading Conference, San Antonio, TX.

Larkin, B.R. (2001). Can we act it out? *The Reading Teacher, 54,* 478–481.

Martinez, M.G., Keehn, S., Roser, N.L., Harmon, J., & O'Neal, S. (2002). An exploration of children's understanding of character in grades 1–8. In J.V. Hoffman, D.D. Schallert, C.M. Fairbanks, J. Worthy, & B. Maloch (Eds.), *Fifty-first yearbook of the National Reading Conference* (pp. 310–320). Chicago: National Reading Conference.

Martinez, M.G., Roser, N.L., & Strecker, S.K. (1998/1999). "I never thought I could be a star": A Readers Theatre ticket to fluency. *The Reading Teacher, 52,* 326–334.

Millin, S.K., & Rinehart, S.D. (1999). Some of the benefits of Readers Theater participation for second-grade Title I students. *Reading Research and Instruction, 39,* 71–88.

Roser, N.L., May, L.A., Martinez, M.G., Keehn, S., Harmon, J.M., & O'Neal, S. (2003). Stepping into character(s): Using Readers Theatre with bilingual fourth graders. In J.R. Paratore & R.L. McCormack (Eds.), *After early intervention, then what? Teaching struggling readers in grade 3 and beyond* (pp. 40–69). Newark, DE: International Reading Association.

Worthy, J., Broaddus, K., & Ivey, G. (2001). *Pathways to independence: Reading, writing, and learning in grades 3–8*. New York: Guilford.

LITERATURE CITED

Ada, A.F. (1993). *My name is Maria Isabel*. New York: Atheneum.

Agee, J. (2001). *Milo's hat trick*. New York: Hyperion.

Alphin, E.M. (1996). *A bear for Miguel*. Ill. J. Sandin. New York: HarperCollins.

Baker, K. (2002). *Meet Mr. and Mrs. Green*. San Diego, CA: Harcourt.

Bluthenthal, D.C. (2003). *I'm not invited?* New York: Atheneum.

Brown, M. (1993). *Arthur's pet business*. New York: Little Brown.

Brown, M. (1996). *Arthur's first sleepover*. New York: Little Brown.

Bunting, E. (1994). *A day's work*. New York: Clarion.

Byars, B. (1996). *My brother, Ant*. New York: Viking.

Cameron. A. (1981). *The stories Julian tells*. New York: Knopf.

Carle, E. (1977). *The grouchy ladybug*. New York: HarperCollins.

Champion, J. (1993). *Emily and Alice*. Ill. S. Stevenson. San Diego, CA: Harcourt.

Cole, J. (1988). *The missing tooth*. Ill. M. Hafner. New York: Random House.

Curtis, C.P. (1995). *The Watsons go to Birmingham—1963*. New York: Delacorte.

DiCamillo, K. (2000). *Because of Winn-Dixie*. Cambridge, MA: Candlewick.

Duvoisin, R. (1966). *Petunia*. New York: Knopf.

Finch, M. (1999). *The little red hen and the ear of wheat*. Ill. E. Bell. Brooklyn, NY: Barefoot Books.

Fox, M. (1986). *Hattie and the fox*. Ill. P. Mullins. New York: Bradbury.

Gackenbach, D. (1977). *Harry and the terrible Whatzit*. New York: Clarion.

Galdone, P. (1973). *The three billy goats Gruff*. New York: Clarion.

Graham, B. (1992). *Rose meets Mr. Wintergarten*. Cambridge, MA: Candlewick.

Guest, E.H. (2002). *Iris and Walter*. Ill. C. Davenier. San Diego, CA: Harcourt.

Henkes, K. (1991). *Chrysanthemum*. New York: Greenwillow.

Henkes, K. (1993). *Owen*. New York: Greenwillow.

Kellogg, S. (1976). *Much bigger than Martin*. New York: Dial.

Kvasnosky, L.M. (1999). *Zelda and Ivy and the boy next door*. Cambridge, MA: Candlewick.

Lester, H. (1999). *Hooway for Wodney Wat*. Ill. L. Munsinger. Boston: Houghton Mifflin.

Levinson, N.S. (2003). *Prairie friends*. Ill. S. Schuett. New York: HarperCollins.

Lionni, L. (1987). *Alexander and the wind-up mouse*. New York: Knopf.

Little, J. (2001). *Emma's yucky brother*. Ill. J. Plecas. New York: HarperTrophy.

Lobel, A. (1971). *Frog and Toad together*. New York: Harper & Row.

MacLachlan, P. (1985). *Sarah, plain and tall*. New York: Harper & Row.

MacLachlan, P. (1994). *Skylark*. New York: HarperCollins.

MacLachlan, P. (2001). *Caleb's story*. New York: HarperCollins.

Marshall, E. (1982). *Fox in love*. Ill. J. Marshall. New York: Puffin.

Marshall, E. (1983). *Fox on wheels*. Ill. J. Marshall. New York: Puffin.

Marshall, J. (1993). *Fox on stage*. New York: Dial.

Martin Jr B., & Archambault, J. (1985). *The ghost-eye tree*. Ill. T. Rand. New York: Henry Holt.

Martin Jr B., & Archambault, J. (1987). *Knots on a counting rope*. Ill. T. Rand. New York: Henry Holt.

Medina, J. (1999). *My name is Jorge: On both sides of the river*. Honesdale, PA: Boyds Mills Press.

Mora, P. (1994). *Pablo's tree*. Ill. C. Lang. New York: Simon & Schuster.

Naylor, P.R. (1991a). *King of the playground*. Ill. N.L. Malone. New York: Atheneum.

Naylor, P.R. (1991b). *Shiloh*. New York: Atheneum.

Polacco, P. (1992). *Mrs. Katz and Tush*. New York: Dell.

Rathmann, P. (1995). *Officer Buckle and Gloria*. New York: Putnam.

Ryan, P.M. (2000). *Esperanza rising*. New York: Scholastic.

Rylant, C. (1992). *Henry and Mudge and the long weekend*. Ill. S. Stevenson. New York: Simon & Schuster.

Soto, G. (1990). *Baseball in April*. San Diego, CA: Harcourt Brace Jovanovich.

Soto, G. (1997). *Novio boy*. San Diego, CA: Harcourt Brace.

Soto, G. (2002). *If the shoe fits*. Ill. T. Widener. New York: Putnam.

Taylor, M.D. (1995). *The well*. New York: Dial.

Wiles, D. (2001). *Love, Ruby Lavender*. San Diego, CA: Harcourt.

Williams, B. (2003). *Albert's impossible toothache*. Ill. D. Cushman. Cambridge, MA: Candlewick.

13

Exploring Character Through Visual Representations

Caitlin McMunn Dooley and Beth Maloch

Caitlin Dooley and Beth Maloch show how students can visually represent their understandings of characters through drawings, metaphorical sketches, language charts, and other graphic organizers.

THE CHARACTERS WHO INHABIT THE STORIES WE read invite us to join them, to care about them, to puzzle over them, and to conspire with them. Many authors of children's and young adult literature agree that their stories develop because of characters. The best teachers encourage their students to climb inside characters—to get to know character motivations, emotions, relationships, and perspectives as part of the story world. Donald Graves (1999) calls this way of learning the "long thinking" that needs to take place in schools—deep considerations and responses to complex issues and personalities that inhabit literature, as well as

What a Character! Character Study as a Guide to Literary Meaning Making in Grades K–8 edited by Nancy L. Roser and Miriam G. Martinez, with Junko Yokota and Sharon O'Neal. Copyright 2005 by the International Reading Association.

readers' lives. Although the effects of this long thinking are not necessarily captured by multiple-choice tests, many teachers and researchers agree on the inherent value of allowing students to respond thoughtfully to literature. And many teachers go even further. They support their students' understanding by making the roles, intents, attempts, and traits of characters central, salient, and clear.

One way teachers help support and deepen students' understandings is through visual representations or reinterpretations of character. Harste and his colleagues (Berghoff, Egawa, Harste, & Hoonan, 2000; Harste, Short, & Burke, 1995) suggest that exploration of multiple sign systems—communication systems such as art, music, drama, mathematics, and language—is central to the learning process. Providing opportunities for students to communicate through a variety of sign systems enables them to think, understand, and communicate in complex ways, thus opening wide the doors of possibility for long thinking.

Providing students with occasions to engage with characters pulls them into stories and bids them to connect; these occasions generate new ideas and inspire "grand conversations"—student-initiated discussions of literary elements such as character, time, mood, layers of story meaning, and points of view (Eeds & Wells, 1989; Peterson & Eeds, 1990). They also invite elaboration and reconsideration of the text (Whitin, 1996, 2002).

In this chapter, we consider the ways visual sign systems can mediate and broaden students' ways of coming to know characters. Readers' opportunities to sketch their interpretations of stories and characters, for example, evoke different responses than what might be elicited through writing or discussion. Having students create visual representations guides and enhances their understandings of the central role character plays in stories. Crafting graphic organizers, such as language charts and semantic webs, focuses readers on descriptive language and salient features of story and characters (Barton, 1996; Roser & Hoffman, 1992; Shanahan & Shanahan, 1997). These graphic representations then become artifacts of student learning, records to return to again and again, allowing time for readers to reflect on their thinking and sometimes revise their thoughts as they read.

Visual representations include drawings and images, maps, webs, and various kinds of graphic organizers. They help students to clarify and expand their initial responses and understandings of character. Visual representations are generative: They encourage multiple interpretations, grow students' understandings, and help to focus thoughtful discussions. In this chapter, we suggest ways students can be invited to draw or sketch their understandings and interpretations, as well as ways teachers can use graphic organizers to guide, focus, and extend those understandings.

Nurturing Relationships Between Characters and Readers

When considering characters in classrooms, teachers use many different ways to foster students' literary understandings and help readers enrich and diversify their interpretations. Visual representations—illustrated, graphic, and symbolic representations or reinterpretations of characters—help to grow students' understandings of stories and literary lives. They help readers transform their understandings of literature through the roles, intents, and perspectives of characters. By providing ample time for students to engage in a variety of visual meaning-making activities (in addition to writing and discussion about characters), teachers can deepen students' understandings, appreciation, and enjoyment of literature.

Creating and Transforming Understandings of Characters

ILLUSTRATING. Creating drawings or images is a way for young children, especially those who cannot yet write their words, to begin to find their words to explain characters (Avery, 2002; Graves, 1994). The act of composing a visual representation of character can also transform more experienced readers' thoughts about that story and the characters in it (Smagorinsky, 2003). For example, if a student is just beginning to describe characters through appearances, ages, and behaviors, then his or her teacher could nourish those understandings by encouraging drawings of characters. The student might begin by illustrating simple character attributes (e.g., skin color, gender, age), and, with experience, incorporate more complex characteristics (e.g., emotions).

Illustrations do not always have to be realistic images; instead, students can create collages of words and images clipped from magazines and newspapers to describe characters, or they can design more abstract portrayals using colors, shapes, and objects to represent characters. When readers describe characters through appearances, ages, or behaviors, these understandings can be fostered and articulated through the creation of pictures.

SYMBOLIZING. As students progress to understanding how a character is part of a contextualized story, they can use symbols to represent their understanding of characters. Although not necessarily limited to character study, Sketch-to-Stretch (Short, Harste, & Burke, 1996; Whitin, 1996) can be an effective strategy. After listening to or reading a story, students quickly represent their interpretations or impressions with a symbolic sketch. Essentially, students take what they know in one sign system (language) and recast it in another (art) (Berghoff et al., 2000). Designed to move beyond simple illustrations, Sketch-to-Stretch helps students synthesize and represent their understandings. Rather than make illustrations of character, students are asked to think metaphorically about the character and story.

To introduce the strategy for use with character study, groups might begin by discussing a character's pivotal role in a story. Without over-questioning, the teacher could guide the readers to consider how a character influences a story: "What color might represent this role?" "How could relationships be represented with shapes, symbols, or signs?" As students continue talking about the character as part of the story, the teacher could seek more ideas—soliciting more than one vision—of how to illustrate a character's role: "How would you show that idea?" The teacher may also guide readers' responses back to the text: "What in the story makes you think as you do?" This to-and-fro between personal and textual meanings helps students fine-tune their personal meaning making in congruence with the story.

After talking about their ideas for sketching as a whole group, students are placed in small groups to work together, sharing and building upon each other's ideas to create a single sketch. During this work time (and it *does* take time), the teacher circulates among the murmuring groups—eavesdropping, as Whitin (2002) puts it—to informally participate in their discussions. The process culminates in a whole-group sharing of ideas. Groups present their sketches, explaining their interpretations, articulating their thoughts, and even expanding their personal understandings about the characters.

MAPPING. Another way to use illustration to foster character understanding is by mapping a character's progression throughout a story. Not the same as "story mapping," which is a way to understand the structure of a story, character mapping is more like a road map representing one (or more) character's personal, emotional, and relational experiences as he or she advances from story beginning to end. Understanding character change may be a benchmark of readers' developing literary knowledge (Martinez, Keehn, Roser, Harmon, & O'Neal, 2002).

Figure 13.1 presents a character road map created in response to Pam Muñoz Ryan's *Esperanza Rising* (2000). In this example, character mapping presents a way to represent (and to think about) changes in character feelings, experiences, and relationships across the story. The map shows Esperanza's emotional pathway throughout the story. She begins in a comfortable position as a rich man's daughter, but is quickly led to sorrow at the death of her father. Esperanza and her mother are left with only two choices— to stay or flee from Mexico. Esperanza's life choices become limited as she and her mother flee to California to seek work. Esperanza proceeds along the "Rough Road" until she meets Isabel, a friend who helps smooth her path. When Esperanza's mother gets sick, Esperanza toils along "Hardship Lane,"

FIGURE 13.1   Sample Character Map

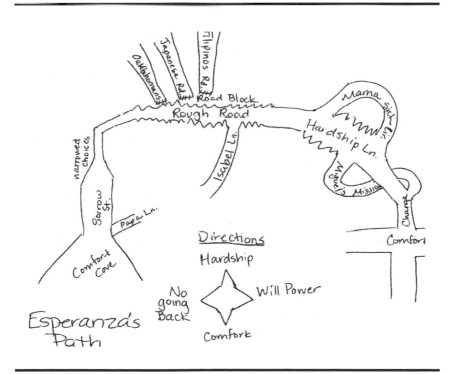

but in the end, she begins to adjust to the changes in her life, realizing that although she can never return to her Mexican home, she will survive and find pleasure in her new home with family and friends.

As with any new activity, this one will have to be modeled before students can do it independently. Also, explicit talk should take place about how this map—representing one character's experiences—is different from a traditional plot-structure map that might proceed lock-step through the action of a story. In the end, however, character mapping is a way to represent how characters move through a story much like humans move through the journey of life.

"Filling In" Understandings of Characters

GAUGING. Young readers often have difficulty understanding the emotional states and development of characters. Even as they come to know characters more deeply, they sometimes lack the vocabulary to describe their development (Barton, 1996). Students can use a variety of emotional gauges (refer to Barton's "Emotional Vocabulary Thermometer") like the gauges on a dashboard to connect with, describe, and evaluate characters. For example, the characters in A.A. Milne's classic tales of *Winnie-the-Pooh* (1926/1992) are sometimes representative of particular personalities, moods, or emotions. After reading several Pooh tales, students could work in small groups to rate the characters' emotions, moods, and personalities across stories. Students could come together to discuss their gauges, giving examples from the stories to support their views. Figure 13.2 shows several character gauges used to evaluate a variety of characters in the Milne series.

As in the examples shown, students can consider how various characters in a series think, feel, and act; therefore, they can draw more than one face on each gauge. They can gauge the characters' emotional and personality traits, arraying the characters on that trait spectrum. Students might also gauge their own emotions by drawing pointers to represent where they see themselves (refer to Figure 13.2).

Variations of this activity include using a single gauge to reexamine a character's emotions at various points in a story or using multiple gauges to show a variety of personality dimensions for one character. The character gauge activity can alert students to use specialized emotional vocabulary as they become more aware of characters' (and their own) personalities, dominant moods, and traits—prior knowledge of emotional vocabulary is not necessary for students to engage in meaningful ways with the gauging

FIGURE 13.2   Sample Character Gauges

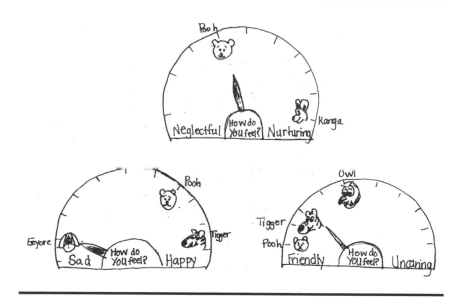

activity. Discussion of gauges also helps to deepen students' understandings of and connections with characters through a process of reflection and reinterpretation.

WEBBING. Webbing is a means of exploring and expanding students' conceptions of story characters. Webbing activities are inherently flexible because they offer a wide range of ways to graphically represent, contemplate, and connect characters (Bromley, 1990). For example, in a simple web, students write a character's name in the center circle, character actions along the lines networking out from the center, and then adjectives that describe the character or the actions in the outer circles. These adjectives might begin as physical attributes (e.g., eye color, height), but they could evolve to more complex characteristics (e.g., emotions) as students' character understandings deepen. This kind of web helps students explore the relationship between what a character *does* and who a character *is* while also providing an opportunity for students to use precise language to describe characters.

A **metaphor web** can help students further explore actions and traits of characters through the use of literary language. After reading *The Folk Keeper* (Billingsley, 1999), for example, students could create webs based on Corinna, the central character in this fantasy tale. The young orphan girl pretends to be a boy in order to become a Folk Keeper (keeper of the Evil Folk) and soon finds out that she has her own secret powers. In this web, the center is labeled "Corinna." Along the spokes that extend from the center, students write words and phrases to describe the central character. At the end of each spoke, they use the descriptions to generate a metaphor for the character. To describe Corinna, phrases along the spokes of the web could include "full of mystery" and "pretending to be someone she's not." Students might write "treasure chest" as a metaphor at the end of the spoke because Corinna is keeping a secret; she is like a locked treasure chest, full of mystery and promise. Another possible metaphor is "actress" because Corinna is trying on a role, pretending to be someone she's not.

By talking and writing together, students design their own metaphor webs, surrounding the center and spokes with representations of the complex character. Once completed, the group metaphor webs are shared with the class. As they present their own and listen to their classmates, students come to understand more deeply the complexity of character and the usefulness of metaphoric language to add dimension to the ways we can think about characters.

Whereas a metaphor web helps to deepen understanding of a particular character, a **relationship web** helps students view the interconnections of characters within a story. Students look for particular relationships between the main character(s) and other characters that support character development and plot. For instance, students could develop a relationship web for the main character in Andrea Pinkney's *Bill Pickett: Rodeo-Ridin' Cowboy* (1996). This historical biography of rodeo star Bill Pickett offers various secondary characters who are integral to Bill's success story. The relationship web might include spokes for "relationship as role models," "supportive relationships," and "doubting relationships." Students could examine what actions and words define those relationships between characters—using quotations from the story to illustrate how "doubters" destroy Bill's self-confidence or how "supporters" help Bill attain success as a rodeo star. Relationship webs help students understand how a main character is constructed and buttressed by other characters.

CHARTING. When a story has two main characters (or more), a **character perspective chart** (Shanahan & Shanahan, 1997) helps students understand how each main character builds the story. The chart is a way to represent different characters' voices and interpretations within a single story, while also teaching students the value of multiple perspectives (Emery, 1996).

In Figure 13.3, two students worked together to view Diane Stanley's *Saving Sweetness* (1996) from the perspectives of two main characters: Sweetness, the intrepid orphan escaping the orphanage, and Sheriff, the bumbling, lovable lawman. The students began by identifying the main characters. As they talked about each character, they began to see how a single story can be multiple stories, depending on the perspective taken. More complex than a simple Venn diagram comparisons of characters, character perspective charts invite students to step inside two perspectives, affording much richer interpretations of the story.

A character perspective chart can be thought of as one version of a **language chart** (Roser & Hoffman, 1992). Language charts are more flexible, however, providing opportunities for students to think, talk, and record their understandings of both stories and characters. They focus attention on particular facets of character study, create a tangible record of the language used in discussions of literature, and can be used for a variety of purposes. One way to use a language chart is to compare characters in a story or across a series of stories. To do this, the teacher creates a matrix with characters' names down the left side and column headings labeled Traits, Actions, Words, and Personality Type. Students consider a character's traits and actions presented in the stories, as well as the character's own words. Teachers use prompts such as "What is the character like?" "What did the character do in the story to make you think that way?" "Did the character say anything that makes you think that?" After the class discusses characters' traits, actions, and words, the teacher and students record their ideas on the chart. As the chart fills in with the students' insights, the teacher may ask them to look it over for patterns and to make generalizations about the characters. Figure 13.4 demonstrates how A.A. Milne's characters are revealed and reinforced by traits, actions, language, and personality.

Language charts do not have to be used only with text sets or inside literature units. Students can also examine dynamic characters within the same novel, just so long as those characters are each multidimensional and deeply engaging. Language charts create a means for "representing group-constructed meanings" (Roser & Hoffman, 1992, p. 48) as well as provide

FIGURE 13.3   Sample Character Perspective Chart

Saving Sweetness, by Diane Stanley

Character 1	Character 2
Main character: Who is the [main] character?	
Sweetness	Sheriff
Setting: Where and when does the story take place?	
Orphanage desert	Saloon Desert His house
Problem: What is the main character's problem?	
Didn't have a mother or dad and she had to scrub the floor w/ a toothbrush.	He kept on having to save her (when she was really sad)
Goal: What is the character's goal? What does he or she want to achieve?	
To get a father and a mother	He wanted Sweetness beca he had to save her and bri back to the orphanage
Attempts/Events: What does the main character do to solve the problem or get to the goal?	
She ran away. Stared at the sheriff. Asked the sheriff to adopt her.	He agrees to adopt her.
Outcome: What happened as a result of the attempt(s)?	
She got adopted. All the others got adopted.	They become a family with the other orphans!
Reaction: How does the main character feel about the outcome?	
Happy, excited!	Glad Excited
Theme: What did the author want us to think about?	
Get away from the orphanage if they're mean.	Having family.

Adapted from Shanahan, S., & Shanahan, T. (1997). Character perspective charting: Helping children develop a more complete conception of story. *The Reading Teacher, 50,* 668–677.

a record of expressions for students to return to over time, nurturing their ripening abilities to articulate thoughts and feelings.

Because language charts are filled in over time, they foster multiple opportunities for students to respond and return to texts as they read, and are especially useful for cultivating understanding of character change. Students

FIGURE 13.4   Language Chart: Winnie-the-Pooh Character Comparison

Character	Traits	Actions	Words	Personality Type
Winnie-the-Pooh	always hungry not very smart, but usually happy	looking for honey forgets his own birthday	"I guess it all comes from liking honey so much!"	Friendly
Rabbit	polite (but sometimes reluctantly so) pack-rat likes things neat and tidy	sweeping his home saves his food tried to decorate around Pooh's big bottom	"He bidged, he badged, he budged..."	Persnickety
Owl	good friend knows much from books uses big words	comes to help Pooh get out of the hole lectures Pooh about eating too much	"You are a wedged bear in a great tightness"	Wise
Eeyore	worried doubtful pessimistic	loses his tail unable to help	"It could be days, maybe weeks, even months..."	Depressed

can use a language chart to discover how character change affects the direction of a story. For example, a language chart for Karen Hesse's *Out of the Dust* (1997) might explore how several characters changed throughout the story. This chart would include the names of characters along the left margin: Billie Jo, Daddy, Ma, Mad Dog, Arley. Along the top the headings could be Traits in the Beginning, Causes for Change, and Traits in the End. More characters could be added as a story progresses, and headings for each column could be adapted to refer to other story elements guiding the investigation of change—changes in behaviors, changes in attitude, and changes in relationships. Of course, *Out of the Dust* is a uniquely rich story, with many characters developed deeply enough to be worthy of introduction.

Finding Characters Worthy of Introduction

Teachers can use many strategies to foster children's understandings of character; however, nothing is as effective as selecting literature that is appropriate and appealing to students' levels and interests. To show child readers the best of characters, it is important to seek out literature with rounded, complex characters who grapple with inner conflicts. Such characters provide rich opportunities for puzzling over, reflecting on, and representing that reflection.

By selecting character-rich literature that corresponds to students' developing understanding of characterization, providing literature-related activities, and engaging in discussions, teachers encourage students to be long thinkers—to begin to see the complex, dynamic characters as part of their own literary lives as well as a part of literature. Teachers can go a step further by broadening and extending students' interpretations through visual representations. From artistic renderings of favorite characters to metaphorical sketches to graphic organizers that elicit varying and increasingly complex understandings of character and relationships, visual representations afford unique opportunities for students to explore, interpret, and understand characters' journeys through story.

REFERENCES

Avery, C. (2002). *And with a light touch: Learning about reading, writing, and teaching with first graders* (2nd ed.). Portsmouth, NH: Heinemann.

Barton, J. (1996). Interpreting character emotions for literature comprehension. *Journal of Adolescent & Adult Literacy, 40,* 22–28.

Berghoff, B., Egawa, K., Harste, J., & Hoonan, B. (2000). *Beyond reading and writing: Inquiry, curriculum, and multiple ways of knowing.* Urbana, IL: National Council of Teachers of English.

Bromley, K.D. (1990). *Webbing with literature: Creating story maps with children's books.* Boston: Allyn & Bacon.

Eeds, M., & Wells, D. (1989). Grand conversations: An exploration of meaning construction in literature study groups. *Research in the Teaching of English, 23,* 4–29.

Emery, D.W. (1996). Helping readers comprehend stories from characters' perspectives. *The Reading Teacher, 49,* 534–541.

Graves, D.H. (1994). *A fresh look at writing.* Portsmouth, NH: Heinemann.

Graves, D.H. (1999). *Bring life into learning: Create a lasting literacy.* Portsmouth, NH: Heinemann.

Harste, J.C., Short, K.G., & Burke, C. (1995). *Creating classrooms for authors.* Portsmouth, NH: Heinemann.

Martinez, M., Keehn, S., Roser, N., Harmon, J., & O'Neal, S. (2002). An exploration of children's understanding of character in grades K–8. In D.L. Schallert, C.M.

Fairbanks, J. Worthy, B. Maloch, & J.V. Hoffman (Eds.), *Fifty-first yearbook of the National Reading Conference* (pp. 310–320). Oak Creek, WI: National Reading Conference.

Peterson, R., & Eeds, M. (1990). *Grand conversations: Literature groups in action.* New York: Scholastic.

Roser, N., & Hoffman, J.V. (1992). Language charts: A record of story time talk. *Language Arts, 69,* 44–52.

Shanahan, S., & Shanahan, T. (1997). Character perspective charting: Helping children develop a more complete conception of story. *The Reading Teacher, 50,* 668–677.

Short, K.G., Harste, J.C., & Burke, C. (1996). *Creating classrooms for authors and inquirers.* Portsmouth, NH: Heinemann.

Smagorinsky, P. (2003). If meaning is constructed, what is it made from? Toward a cultural theory of reading. *Review of Educational Research, 71,* 133–169.

Whitin, P. (1996). *Sketching stories, stretching minds: Responding visually to literature.* Portsmouth, NH: Heinemann.

Whitin, P. (2002). Leading into literature circles through sketch-to-stretch strategy. *The Reading Teacher, 55,* 444–450.

LITERATURE CITED

Billingsley, F. (1999). *The Folk Keeper.* New York: Aladdin.

Hesse, K. (1997). *Out of the dust.* New York: Scholastic.

Milne, A.A. (1992). *Winnie-the-Pooh.* New York: Penguin Puffin. (Original work published 1926)

Pinkney, A.D. (1996). *Bill Pickett: Rodeo-ridin' cowboy.* Ill. B. Pinkney. San Diego, CA: Gulliver Books.

Ryan, P.M. (2000). *Esperanza rising.* New York: Scholastic.

Stanley, D. (1996). *Saving Sweetness.* Ill. G.B. Karas. New York: Putnam.

14

Enhancing the Literature Experience Through Deep Discussions of Character

Karen Smith

Characters have the power to draw readers into story worlds. Karen Smith shows how character-rich books stimulate both the "messy" and meaningful talk of intermediate students. She shares her insights and successful strategies for creating "the deep discussions of great characters" in your own classroom through literature study groups.

CHARACTERS MATTER. THEIR LIVES AND RELATIONSHIPS draw us in as readers and keep the pages turning. If characters' lives are rich with meaning and filled with the complexities of what it means to be human, we feel compelled to hang in there, to see what the characters will do to make sense of it all. As we take the journey with them, we hope against hope that characters make the right decisions at the right

What a Character! Character Study as a Guide to Literary Meaning Making in Grades K–8 edited by Nancy L. Roser and Miriam G. Martinez, with Junko Yokota and Sharon O'Neal. Copyright 2005 by the International Reading Association.

time; we try to understand what motivates characters, and hope that we learn from their triumphs and failures.

People often say books matter because they take us to places we have never been and have not yet experienced. This is true, but even more important than place are the characters that draw us in and keep us there. Characters offer compelling views of the world. Some characters' lives mirror our own, and their stories validate us. They make us know we are not alone.

Other characters' lives are less familiar. Their experiences are much different from our own and their stories show us that there is much to be learned about the world. These characters stretch our imaginations about what is possible, what might be.

Still other characters' lives startle us. They are filled with struggles, grief, and difficulties that we never knew existed. All *great* characters' lives are compelling and complex. Whether they are familiar or strange, possible or undeserved, they lure us in. They say to us, "Come in, journey alongside us as we do our best to make sense of things." These characters' successes—or struggles to succeed—make us want and need to read.

Selecting Books With Great Characters

Great characters insist that readers understand them; they make it impossible for their readers to leave their world until we know how things worked out for them. Lyddie, in Katherine Paterson's (1991) book of the same name, understands this. This 13-year-old, mid-19th-century farm girl is forced to work to repay her family's debts. To earn money, she moves to Lowell, Massachusetts, and takes a room at a boardinghouse near the cotton mill where she gets a job. At the boardinghouse each evening, after putting in 13-hour days, Lyddie's roommate Betsy reads aloud to her from *Oliver Twist* (Dickens, 1841/2003). One day, in the midst of the noisy mill and the long hours, Lyddie finds herself feeling happy and begins to wonder why:

> The next day in the mill, the noise was just as jarring and her feet in Triphena's old boots swelled just as large, but now and again she caught herself humming. Why am I suddenly happy? What wonderful thing is about to happen to me? And then she remembered. Tonight after supper, Betsy would read to her again. She was, of course, afraid of Oliver, who was all mixed up in her mind with Charlie. But there was a delicious anticipation, like molded sugar on her tongue. She had to know what would happen to him, how his story would unfold. (p. 79)

Teachers need to select books with characters that do for students what Oliver Twist does for Lyddie. Fortunately, because of the many talented children's book authors, great characters like Oliver are plentiful. For example, How could any reader abandon Pedro in *The Composition* (Skarmeta, 2000) after experiencing his family's struggle to resist an oppressive government? Or, how could one possibly desert Opal in *Because of Winn-Dixie* (DiCamillo, 2000) as she fights to let go of what she can't have? And what about Gilly—the prototype of greatness—in *The Great Gilly Hopkins* (Paterson, 1978)? Would it be possible to leave Gilly in her quest to figure out what it means to be part of a family, and what family truly means?

Each of these great characters copes with issues and circumstances that are authentically human, and readers experience something of what it means to be human even when the literary world is far removed from their own (Peterson & Eeds, 1990). None of these characters is all good or all bad. They are human and persevere in spite of obstacles that get in their way. In the end, as so often happens in children's literature, the characters reveal courage, independence, and resourcefulness; and they offer readers a glimmer of hope.

Besides selecting books with great characters, teachers also need to select books that provide students both mirrors and windows on their world. Regardless of their gender, race, or social class, students should expect to meet protagonists who resemble themselves and share their cultural values, attitudes, and behaviors. Most students at the schools where I conduct research on children's literature are Latino. Their whole demeanor changes when their teachers read aloud from books in which the characters look, think, and act like them: They sit straighter, listen more intently, and make connections with the text as easily as they say their names. For example, when Ernestina Aragon's fifth-grade students first met Esperanza in *Esperanza Rising* (Ryan, 2000), they showed appreciation for the richness of the Spanish language that is woven throughout the fabric of the text. In particular, the girls were excited to read that Esperanza and her classmates talked about their *quinceañeras* (the presentation parties they would have when they turned 15). For one short moment, the girls in the class and the girls in the book became one. It was as if they were in cahoots with one another, talking about the dresses they would wear to their *quinceañeras*, who would escort them to the event, and how proud their families would be on that special day.

Later in the book, students' connections were more profound, especially as some of them shared firsthand the intricacies of migrant worker life. They understood that the good times Esperanza experienced with her playmates at the camp happened under a cloud of oppression that is hard to escape. Much of their talk turned to big questions about life, the kind of questions that emerge when good books are placed in students' hands: Why do some people have all the power? Is it wrong to look out for yourself even when it may cause others pain? Why do some people have less than others, even when the people with less work equally hard?

Although students need mirrors on their world, they also need books that offer new perspectives. Ana Rosa in *The Color of My Words* (Joseph, 2000), Kenny in *The Watsons Go to Birmingham—1963* (Curtis, 1995), Ji-li Jiang in *Red Scarf Girl: A Memoir of the Cultural Revolution* (Jiang, 1997), and Angel in *The Same Stuff as Stars* (Paterson, 2002) presented these fifth-grade students with knowledge, perspective, and frames of reference for particular ways of knowing that were new to them. For example, in *The Color of My Words*, the students began to understand the power of literacy and its effect on society. Through rich discussions and hard work, these students began to understand that there are many ways of living in the world.

Introducing Students to Great Characters

In *The Spying Heart: More Thoughts on Reading and Writing Books for Children* (1989), children's book author Katherine Paterson writes that characters are people, not models put together with an erector set: "You don't build people. You get to know them" (p. 92). This statement sets the tone for how to best bring books and students together in the classroom. The teacher's stance on story and character, the language used to introduce books and characters, and what students are asked to do with books all make a difference in how students see their role as readers.

When I introduce a book to children, I am introducing the people students will meet there. I talk about the characters as if they were going to walk into the room and have a live chat with the class. I ask students to get to know the characters well. I want these readers to laugh and cry with the characters, salute them for jobs well done, and challenge them for unfair deeds.

Although students need time to make sense of characters in light of their own understandings of the world, they also must learn to challenge those understandings. I often talk to students about a fault that many readers display, including me: Too often we behave like Pygmalion, recasting characters to fit our own values and agendas. Rather than recasting characters in our own image, I find it more interesting and helpful to inquire into the events or circumstances that shape or challenge characters—that puzzle us about them—and to question these moments.

Recently, in a classroom where I was conducting research, I met with a group of students who were working hard to understand why M.C. Higgins in *M.C. Higgins, the Great* (Hamilton, 1974) didn't just follow his dream and leave Sarah's Mountain. We also talked our way into a range of hypotheses for why Koly's parents in *Homeless Bird* (Whelan, 2000) didn't rescue her from her cruel mother-in-law. In time, through lots of messy talk, students learn to examine the issues important to the character, as well as the relationships among characters. In the end, students form their own opinions of why characters behave as they do. Entertaining multiple possibilities for characters' actions broadens students' perspectives, expanding their interpretative lenses, and thus stretching their understandings of the world.

Supporting Deep Discussion of Great Characters

Great characters deserve the kind of close attention we gave M.C. and Koly, but it is difficult to do this kind of exploration with a large group of students. That is why I value literature study groups (Peterson & Eeds, 1990). Literature study groups, made up of five or six students and the teacher, provide a context for an intensive exploration of a particular book.

I prefer students read the entire book before we study it as a group. During the week that students are reading, I check in with them to make sure they are keeping up with the assigned number of pages and address any questions they have. During the next week, we study: The group comes together three or four times to talk about the characters we met and discuss how and why characters think, feel, and behave as they do. We speculate on characters' motives and think about how characters are going about their lives, comparing their decisions with how we would approach things. The students learn to share perspectives. Just as they learn to consider other students' points of view, they learn to stick up for the ideals they believe to be true and fair and just (Smith, 1995).

"Messy" Discussions

Group talks about books are messy. We talk our way into ideas and we talk to sort them out. As we talk, we reflect and critique. I believe that talk, or dialogue, is the best way to make our meanings known. Because dialogue is a process of coproducing meaning, group members need one another's patience, ideas, and encouragement (Peterson & Eeds, 1990):

> Dialogue has its tough moments, when ambiguity prevails and tension mounts. After all, meaning is being examined from different perspectives.... The spirit of collaboration is tested. When the going gets tough, teachers need to remember that teaching is easy only when students are asked to become simple consumers of conventional views. Teachers who use dialogue as a means for interpreting a text must value the dynamic, ever-changing character of meaning-making that results when children are called upon to see for themselves. (p. 22)

Character Change

Sometimes to get talk going, I focus small group discussion on character change. We look at who a character is at the beginning and at the end of a story and then we explore the events and relationships that might have influenced the change. For example, I have had many great conversations with students about Wilbur in *Charlotte's Web* (White, 1952) as we worked together to uncover what events and relationships influence Wilbur's growth from a selfish little creature at the beginning of the story to a determined, selfless character at the end.

Metaphor

One group of fifth graders with whom I worked discussed their experiences of *The Color of My Words* (Joseph, 2000). In this book, 12-year-old Ana Rosa is living under a dictatorship in the Dominican Republic at a time when written words are feared and, for some, forbidden. Ana Rosa knows this, but can't keep herself from writing, even when her mother cautions her that "Writers have died here" (p. 8). At the beginning of the story, Ana Rosa and her mother are at the river washing clothes. The mother is worried about Ana Rosa and pleads with her to be patient, to not write until it's safe to do so. As the mother looks to the river, she says: "You are this river, Ana Rosa.... But you must flow softly around the rocks on your way to meet the sea. There you can do as you wish" (p. 7). Ana Rosa's passion to write, however, is greater than her mother's appeal for her not to, and she uses her words to write a political article to fight back against the government. While many in her community are proud of Ana Rosa, her mother is not. At the end of the story, Ana recounts,

> Everyone liked the article except for Mami. When she saw it, she started to cry and I knew it was because of those rocks in the river she was afraid of. The ones that I was supposed to slip softly over until I got out to that big sea, far from our Island. (p. 110)

Over the course of the book, as Ana Rosa's writing shifts from writing simple stories and poems to composing political essays, she grows in her understanding of the power of words to transform the world. Our literature study group became intrigued with the "rocks" in Ana Rosa's life. We puzzled over why she felt so compelled to write. We were scared when she decided to take a stand, yet we cheered her on. We couldn't decide if her stepfather was a "rock" or not. It is nearly impossible to have a conversation of this depth without the students viewing what is happening in the story world as an extended metaphor of their own lives—their experiences, their concerns, and their commitments to the world (Peterson & Eeds, 1990, p. 46).

The rock metaphor stayed with the group in future readings as well. After we read *The Color of My Words*, the students chose to read *Esperanza Rising*. At the first group meeting, one student talked about the rocks in Esperanza's river, referring to the symbolism from our previous study. After spending time focused on the "rocks" in Esperanza's life, one of the students pointed out that by limiting her life experiences to rocks, we were denying Esperanza her full existence. In response, the group created other symbols to acknowledge that Esperanza's life, like our own, is full of good and bad, happy and sad. We recognized that life is never one dimensional. For a final project, these students drew a river that flowed from the time they first met Esperanza at her father's ranch in Mexico until they left her at the migrant camp in California. In the river they drew objects that nurture and objects that destroy.

Exploring the Margins

In the past few years, I also have used great characters in children's literature with intermediate-grade children to explore lives of people who have been marginalized or silenced by dominant systems of meaning that operate in our society to position particular people and groups of people in particular ways. I also use children's literature to examine how people who recognize oppressive situations act collectively to contest these situations. There are many great characters in children's literature whose lives are silenced or marginalized for reasons unclear or unfair. *Sister Anne's Hands* (Lorbiecki, 2000) introduces us to an African American nun in the 1960s who faces racism in the new community and school where she is assigned to teach second grade. When students are introduced to characters like Sister Anne, they often recognize racism but do not always explore it within its larger social climate.

To examine the relevant system of domination that affects a character's life (e.g., racism, sexism, classism, or any of the multitude of "-isms"), I engage students in conversations with the book characters. I do this by inviting one group of students to take on the role of characters in the book; the rest of the class forms smaller groups and creates questions to ask the characters. I work with the students who role-play characters to develop a believable stance before they begin playing the characters. For example, when the students role play characters from *Baseball Saved Us* (Mochizuki, 1993), a story of a young Japanese American boy in an internment camp, I work with the student who plays the guard to defend his position both economically and politically. I ask why the guard accepted the job in the watchtower. Did he do it for money or out of a sense of patriotism and duty to his country? What was his position on the internment of Japanese and Japanese Americans? I do not want the character to take a politically correct stance; rather, I want students to dig deep into the underlying issues that guide their character's life.

The discussion between the characters and audience is always vivid, usually heated, and often uncomfortable. One group of students who carried out critical conversations with the characters in *Baseball Saved Us* asked questions about who went to the camps and who did not, why no one stopped the internment, and if there was resistance inside the camp. While the students who had taken on the characters could not answer these questions, they were interested in them and their questions became the seeds for future inquiries. I take notes throughout the students' conversations and then post the inquiries from these notes on chart paper so we can use them for further discussion. I help students see that the "-isms" we encounter in books and our world are not set in stone.

When students understand that unjust acts are created by humans, they also realize that humans can change them, disrupting the status quo. This is why students need to read such books as *Sí, Se Puede/Yes We Can: Janitors Strike in L.A.* (Cohn, 2002), *The Bus Ride* (Miller, 1998), and *Sweet Dried Apples: A Vietnamese Wartime Childhood* (Breckler, 1996) in which they can see how people take action on important social issues. These books offer great characters who act with courage, integrity, and hope—stretching our imaginations and providing a vision for how to make our world a better and more hopeful place.

Great characters in children's literature entertain us. They fill our lives with laughter, mystery, and wonder. But equally important, these characters validate who we are and offer us possibilities for whom we may become.

REFERENCES

Paterson, K. (1989). *The spying heart: More thoughts on reading and writing books for children.* New York: Dutton.
Peterson, R., & Eeds, M. (1990). *Grand conversations: Literature groups in action.* Richmond Hill, ON, Canada: Scholastic-TAB.
Smith, K. (1995). Bringing children and books together in the elementary classroom. *Primary Voices, 3*(2), 22–32.

LITERATURE CITED

Breckler, R. (1996). *Sweet dried apples: A Vietnamese wartime childhood.* Ill. D.K. Ray. Boston: Houghton Mifflin.
Cohn, D. (2002). *Si, si puede/Yes, we can: Janitor strike in L.A.* Ill. F. Delgado. El Paso, TX: Cinco Puntos.
Curtis, C.P. (1995). *The Watsons go to Birmingham—1963.* New York: Delacorte.
DiCamillo, K. (2000). *Because of Winn-Dixie.* Cambridge, MA: Candlewick.
Dickens, C. (2003). *Oliver Twist.* New York: Penguin. (Original work published 1841)
Hamilton, V. (1974). *M.C. Higgins, the great.* New York: Macmillan.
Jiang, J.L. (1997). *Red scarf girl: A memoir of the Cultural Revolution.* New York: HarperCollins.
Joseph, L. (2000). *The color of my words.* New York: HarperCollins.
Lorbiecki, M. (2000). *Sister Anne's hands.* Ill. W. Popp. New York: Puffin.
Miller, W. (1998). *The bus ride.* Ill. J. Ward. New York: Lee & Low.
Mochizuki, K. (1993). *Baseball saved us.* Ill. D. Lee. New York: Lee & Low.
Paterson, K. (1978). *The great Gilly Hopkins.* New York: HarperCollins.
Paterson, K. (1991). *Lyddie.* New York: Dutton.
Paterson, K. (2002). *The same stuff as stars.* New York: Clarion.
Ryan, P.M. (2000). *Esperanza rising.* New York: Scholastic.
Skarmeta, A. (2000). *The composition.* Ill. A. Ruano. Toronto, ON, Canada: Groundwood Books.
Whelan, G. (2000). *Homeless bird.* New York: HarperCollins.
White, E.B. (1952). *Charlotte's web.* New York: Harper & Row.

Part IV

The Best

OF

Character-
Rich Books

15

Looking Closely at Characters: How Illustrations Support Children's Understandings

Lawrence R. Sipe and Maria Paula Ghiso

Larry Sipe and Maria Ghiso encourage all of us to stop for illustrations, learning to "look" just as proficiently as we learn to read. When teachers become sensitized to (and more appreciative of) the images in the best of picturebooks, they can help children make satisfying discoveries that reveal characters' traits and relationships.

ILLUSTRATORS USE A VARIETY OF STRATEGIES for depicting literary characters, and readers draw on these techniques as they work to understand and connect with imaginary worlds and their inhabitants. In a well-crafted picturebook, the text and the illustrations collaboratively present the story: The words provide a cognitive frame and reveal significance and relationships that may be unclear in the pictures, while the illustrations disclose aspects of the story—such as charac-

What a Character! Character Study as a Guide to Literary Meaning Making in Grades K–8 edited by Nancy L. Roser and Miriam G. Martinez, with Junko Yokota and Sharon O'Neal. Copyright 2005 by the International Reading Association.

ter traits and descriptive elements—that the words may omit (Nodelman, 1988). In the best of picturebooks, illustrations do not merely repeat what the words describe, but join with the text in what Kiefer (1995) calls "interdependence"—the creation of a whole that is greater than the sum of its parts. As Marantz (1977) emphasizes, all the components of a picturebook are essential to the aesthetic reading experience, including not only the illustrations and words, but also the cover, endpapers, and typography. Thus, each of the parts makes its own contribution to a harmonious whole.

With help, children can learn to "read" illustrations as well as they read words—so as to experience the story as a unified aesthetic form and to respond in ways that include all picturebook features rather than privileging words over everything else. This chapter helps teachers and others who introduce books to children better understand how the details of illustrations contribute to children's literary understanding of characters and provide insights beyond those revealed in the words of a text.

It is important for all readers to learn how to look at picturebooks. When teachers themselves notice and then make a point of talking about illustrations and other visual features of picturebooks, children also learn to closely consider these features. By highlighting explicit details in illustrations and talking over what those details say about characters within the story, teachers and children experience a fuller, richer engagement with picturebooks, and this engagement becomes an integral part of the classroom culture.

In this chapter, we focus on inviting children to consider the details of illustrations and what they say about characters in the story. We begin by exploring how images of characters are suggested and elaborated through physical details like clothing or hairstyle. Specifically, we point out how careful observation of facial expressions and body language suggest characters' feelings and motivations. We show readers how to look for the position and size of character images, specifically the character's placement on a page, and the relation of a character to the illustration as a whole. We believe that when teachers are sensitized to features of illustrations, they can serve as gentle curators, helping children to "see" the relationships among characters as suggested by illustrations. We argue that book design (including front and back covers, end pages, title pages, and all other elements of a picturebook other than the words of a story and the accompanying illustrations) may also provide a wealth of character information. Finally, we demonstrate some of these heightened perspectives on the illustrator's art of character development by comparing the illustrations in two different versions of *Snow White*.

Images of Character in Picturebooks

Character traits can be constructed and inferred through artistic decisions regarding facial expression, body language, and the inclusion of details such as clothing. The aesthetic elements of line, shape, and color not only bring characters to life, but influence readers' connections with them.

Facial Expressions

Details in facial expression fill in aspects of the story often omitted by the words, and allow for the uncovering of multiple layers of character development and plot. For example, the incredibly detailed illustrations in Maurice Sendak's *Outside Over There* (1981) add depth and richness to the sparse text. Sendak's first and second "openings" (the term used for the double-page spread that contains text and illustrations in an unpaginated picturebook) offer the book's first text: "When Papa was away at sea,... and Mama in the arbor...." The illustrations do far more than disclose location; the facial expression of the mother creates a window to her state of mind. Examining this illustration prompted the following discussion in a kindergarten class:

Teacher: How do you think Mama feels right now?

Joseph: Sad!

Teacher: Why do you think she's sad?

Joseph: Because she want to go on the boat!

Teacher: Because she wants to go on the boat with who?

Joseph: With Daddy!

Teacher: With the daddy, her husband, sure! David?

David: She's sad because she couldn't go because they are taking away her house.

Teacher: They're taking away her house? Okay. And I see the baby is crying—and there is the little girl holding her and Mama is looking very, very sad.

Virginia: She's sad because she thinks her man died!

This rich conversation emanated from a careful analysis of the illustrations; the text, although sparsely eloquent, divulges only that the father is away while the mother remains at home with the children. The illustrations, however, embellish this basic information by eliciting the emotional states of the characters. The teacher explicitly asks students to consider aspects of the story that cannot be understood from the words alone. She does not ask students where the parents are, but instead poses deeper questions about the character's feelings. To answer her queries, students must look carefully at the spreads, noticing aspects of the facial expressions of the mother as well as other significant details such as the inclusion of the boat in a corner of the page.

This teacher encourages students to be explicit about the responses evoked by the illustrations, asking Joseph to explain why he believes the mother is sad. The teacher also draws students' attention to other features of the illustrations, pointing out the crying baby as evidence for their inferences. In this interchange, we can see how the teacher creates an environment for engaging with picturebooks by raising questions that emphasize the importance of illustrations, and by modeling her own observations. Within a classroom where children are prompted toward illustrations, they learn to pay attention to more than the verbal text and are able to craft their understanding of the story in response to multiple cues.

In some instances, telling facial expressions can be accomplished with a series of seemingly simple strokes of a pen or brush. As Ian Falconer demonstrates in *Olivia* (2000), even a single line can reveal volumes about a character. In the eighth opening of this book, the time arrives for the protagonist to take a nap. The text reads, "Every day Olivia is supposed to take a nap. 'It's time for your you-know-what,' her mother says." The accompanying depiction of Olivia, particularly the line of her mouth, reveals her feelings about the nap and speaks to her personality. Olivia is an energetic yet somewhat spoiled piglet who, as her facial expression on this page demonstrates, likes to get her way and most definitely does not enjoy taking a nap.

A lack of facial expression can also reveal important clues to character traits. This is evident in *Piggybook* (Browne, 1986), which chronicles the exploitation of a wife and mother by her demanding family. On one page, a sequence of images depicts the mother involved in a variety of household chores. Throughout her manual labor, her face is a blank canvas—without eyes, nose, or a mouth. This total lack of facial features is a choice by illustrator Anthony Browne that portrays the mother as a faceless laborer exploited by her family. Through their inconsiderate actions, the father and sons in *Piggybook* help create the mother's facelessness; she is a body to perform household chores rather than a person valued for her individuality.

By contrast, the piggy sons have a series of pin-points for eyes and noses, and each is dominated by a large, open oval of a mouth, suggesting a demanding nature. As the story progresses, the faces of the father and sons actually transform into pig features that denote their chauvinistic attitudes. At the end of the story, when a more equitable distribution of labor has been established by the mother, her facial features become visible, and a soft smile appears on her face.

Depictions of facial expressions can also help readers identify emotionally with characters. In Paul Galdone's version of *The Three Bears* (1985), Goldilocks is shown missing a tooth. When a teacher sharing this book with a first-grade classroom asked her students to estimate Goldilocks's age by studying the illustration, one of the students answered, "Let's make her our age!" By incorporating this important detail of young children's lives, the illustrator allows for a bond to form between text and readers because of children's strengthened visual identification with the protagonist. (Important, too, was the teacher's invitation to look closely.) This is one possible reason for Galdone's decision to depict Goldilocks with a missing tooth—to help readers identify with the character and be drawn into the imagined world of the story. By making Goldilocks about 5 or 6 years old, Galdone also gives the character innocence, setting her prior to society's "age of reason." Goldilocks then is not merely a spoiled girl who samples the property of others, but is instead endowed with a childlike innocence that excuses the self-centeredness of her actions. The urge to take something that is not yours and the feeling of getting into trouble even without malevolent intent are characteristics with which young children can identify. It is the illustration, not the words of the story, that invites these rich interpretations.

Body Language/Gestures

A character's body position is another indication of emotion and inner thought. In *Something Beautiful* (Wyeth, 1998), the protagonist is a young girl who looks past the difficult images—the "ugliness"—of her neighborhood in search of beauty. On the third opening of the text, she pauses near a homeless person. The image of a woman sleeping under a cardboard box is in the foreground, and to the left behind her, the little girl appears to be taking in the situation. Her body is facing away, as if ready to continue walking, while her head is turned to the homeless woman. The juxtaposition of the direction of her body and her head encapsulate the tension in the story as a whole: the protagonist at first does not seem to find beauty in her neighborhood, but later not only discovers it in unexpected places, but creates beauty and changes through her own actions. At the end of the picturebook, the girl promises that when she grows up, she will find a home for the woman who sleeps in the cardboard box.

For one class of kindergarten students, the image of the child looking at the homeless woman elicited powerful responses about homelessness, calling up the students' own exposures to similar images, as Kenny's talk illustrates:

Teacher: She does, she lives in that cardboard box right there on the ground. Do you think she wants to live there, Kenny?

Kenny: No, because every time when me and my mom go to the Dunkin' Donuts we see people on the ground, um, and they be sleepin' and they look like they don't have no food. And this guy is laying on the ground and came in the [Dunkin'] Donuts and he went over in the corner and then laid down in the street. It make me sad.

Clearly, this image in *Something Beautiful* revealed much about the inner thoughts of the protagonist, and provided students with a means of adding layers of response to the text.

Body positioning can also be used to depict motion or the passing of time, such as through a series of images termed "continuous narration" (Schwarcz, 1982, p. 24). The 10th opening of *Amazing Grace* (Hoffman, 1991), for example, contains a sequence of illustrations of Grace pirouetting in her room, pretending to be a ballet dancer. Each of the eight images depicts Grace at a different point in her dance, and their alignment creates a representation of the twirling and movement of the dance. The images of Grace even include the swishing of her skirt and the turning of her feet. Through this "continuous narration," the illustration captures the flow of Grace's private dance and makes more visible her energy, "grace," and determination—all essential traits of her character. In response to this illustration, a first grader commented:

Diane: It looks like a movie!

Teacher: Yes, it does. Sometimes, illustrators choose to show action by making a series of pictures like this, so it seems like the character is moving.

From the child's noticing of the illustrator's technique, the teacher creates a very brief teachable moment by extending and explaining. She takes what the child says and makes an interpretive statement about illustrations. She also makes the important point that everything in an illustration is the result of the illustrator's conscious choice. This allows other students to apply new ways of seeing to other examples.

Clothing and Hairstyle

A character's clothing or hairstyle can also help readers interpret personality and identify more closely with certain characters. In David Delamare's version of *Cinderella* (1993), one illustration presents several dancing couples, but Cinderella is at the forefront and the only character looking directly at the reader. The other characters have elaborate, mannered hairstyles, one in the shape of a duck and another resembling a rabbit. By contrast, Cinderella wears a simple, more natural hairstyle adorned with a single sparkling strand of beads. As well, Cinderella's ball gown is unpretentious and elegant, while the stepsisters' dresses have garish colors and almost vulgar patterns. This choice of clothing gestures toward the coarseness of their personalities, whereas Cinderella's attire suggests her gentle purity.

Young readers pick up on these nuances of illustrations. Tony (a first grader) responded to the illustration of the ball by asking, "Why do they all have funky hair except Cinderella?" When the teacher asked the other children for their ideas about that question, Katie posited that perhaps it was the illustrator's intent for readers to identify with Cinderella: "Probably the illustrator wants me to like Cinderella—and the other people look stupid." The children understood that through his artistic choices in depicting clothing and hairstyle, Delamare has made Cinderella a more sympathetic figure, whereas he has created emotional distance between the stepsisters and readers.

Qualities of Line

Use of line—thick or thin, jerky or smooth—is perhaps the most powerful expressive tool in the artist's arsenal. The thickness of a line may suggest the degree of refinement or delicacy of the character portrayed (Golden, 1990). For instance, Marcia Brown illustrates her classic version of *Cinderella* (1988) with dainty, frilly lines. This light touch, as opposed to a heavier line, is well-suited for Cinderella's delicate, refined role in this version of the tale.

Just as smoothly flowing lines suggest calm and serenity, the incorporation of short, cross-hatched lines can indicate a sense of motion and vibrancy. Throughout *Where the Wild Things Are* (1963), Maurice Sendak uses cross-hatching to make his characters appear energetic and active. Similarly, John Steptoe uses cross-hatching in *Mufaro's Beautiful Daughters* (1987) to meticulously define the folds of the king's garment and the muscular build of his body on the 12th opening of this noteworthy picturebook. The background of the illustration—the stone pillars and steps—is cross-hatched as well. Thus, the whole illustration pulses with life and energy, highlighting the emotionally charged meeting of Mufaro's daughter with the king.

Shapes: Curves and Angles

In addition to line, the shape of characters' bodies and the shapes of their surroundings can influence how readers feel about and interpret characters in picturebooks. Bang (1991) suggests that pointed shapes create anxiety and fear because of their association with sharp objects, while rounded shapes bring to mind a sense of well-being and security. For example, despite their gigantic proportions and their sharp teeth and claws, Sendak's Wild Things do not appear threatening to Max or to readers. The curved lines comprising their bodies and features—the waves of their hair, the scales on their bodies, and even the contours of their claws—typically create more comfort than caution.

In contrast, sharp angles and straight lines elicit a sense of danger or a high level of alertness. One of the illustrations in *Don't Fidget a Feather!* (Silverman, 1998) shows a wolf advancing on a turkey, and the scene is tinged with imminent danger through the contrasting shapes used to depict the two animals. The approaching wolf's sharp lines highlight the rigid angles of his ears, jaw, and teeth. The illustrator, S.D. Schindler, gives the wolf's fur texture with straight lines. In contrast, the turkey lying on the ground, soon to be the wolf's victim, has a rounded body outline and curved feather lines. The opposing features of these animals—the aggression of the wolf and the vulnerability of the bird—are thus emphasized by their shapes.

Position and Size of Characters

Illustrators communicate meaningful information not only through the images of characters, but also by carefully positioning them within the larger context of the page. Relative size, direction, or the framing of a character emphasize features not present in the words and provide additional potential for interpretation.

Proportion

The proportion of space commanded by a character in the illustration seems to evoke particular emotional responses in readers. A relatively small character (in comparison with the entire illustration) suggests vulnerability, loneliness, or weakness. Such is the case in *Picture This: Perception and Composition* (Bang, 1991), which contains a stylized depiction of Little Red Riding Hood. Amid four large, black rectangles that loom overhead stands a little red triangle; the size relations are used to represent Red Riding Hood's vulnerability amid the trees of the forest. James Marshall (1987) uses the same proportions in his version of *Little Red Riding Hood*. Marshall's diminutive protagonist stands in contrast to the colossal, menacing vegetation and darkness of the forest. Conversely, a character taking up a large proportion of the total illustration suggests a sense of strength, power, or menace, depending on the total context. A clear example is the cover of *Martin's Big Words*, Doreen Rappaport's (2001) account of the life of Dr. Martin Luther King, Jr. The simple yet powerful front cover is devoid of words, and is composed solely of an illustration of Dr. King's face that encompasses the entire space. In this context, the size of the image represents the real life character's significance and strength.

Framing

In many instances, picturebook illustrations are framed with lines of varying widths, bands of color, or simply with white space. When illustrations are not framed, but rather "bleed" all the way to the edges of the page, they introduce an immediacy and intensity to the reading experience. This lack of the frame suggests that the illustration is straining to join the reader's world. The transition from framed to unframed illustrations is evident across the spreads of *Where the Wild Things Are*. The white space framing the first illustration of mischievous Max grows progressively smaller as the illustrations increase in relative size until, as Max and the Wild Things start their "wild rumpus," the images expand to the edges of the page in full bleed with no words. As a result, Max's experiences with the Wild Things seem highlighted, and readers are drawn further into his imaginative actions and fictional world. The following exchange among first graders came in response to this scene:

Chrissy:	There aren't any words.
Kelvin:	Yeah, we could make up our own words.
Teacher:	What could you say for this page? [teacher shows the 13th opening, which depicts the Wild Things swinging through the trees]
Several children:	They swing like monkeys, through the air! Oooooh, oooooh, ooooh!

These students readily notice the absence of words and come up with the idea of supplying their own. The story continues and thrives without words because the illustration forms the basis of the story line, and the teacher picks up on the suggestion to add words, asking for specific examples. The energy of the Wild Things and their rumpus, emphasized by the illustrations in full bleed, is reflected in the children's spirited animal noises.

At times, illustrators choose to depict a character's body as "breaking" the frame by projecting a part of the illustration beyond the straight edge, a strategy which suggests movement, energy, or that the character is too big—either emotionally or physically—to be contained within the frame. One instance of breaking the frame occurs on the cover of *Swamp Angel* (Isaacs, 1994), a tall tale with a larger-than-life heroine. The framed cover art shows a couple at the bottom of the page looking upward; looming above them is a gigantic young woman, holding up the book's title with one hand and supporting the book's frame with the other. She is bent over to fit within the confines of the frame, and her upper back and the top of her head are not visible. This image prepares readers to predict the plot and to understand the nature of the story as a tall tale.

The following is a first-grade response to the cover:

Charles:	She's too big for the picture!
Julie:	She's bent over; she's trying to get out!
Teacher:	This is one way the illustrator shows that this girl is very, very tall.

In this instance, the teacher draws attention to the children's responses through a natural, conversational comment that amplifies the students' comments.

Placement of Character

The placement of the character on the page, and in relation to the other objects in the illustration, can communicate different feelings. Bang (1991) suggests that horizontal placement of shapes indicates calm and stability, whereas vertical placement can suggest strength or power. Diagonal placement, the most dynamic of all, implies tension, drama, and instability.

The importance of these angles of placement is evident in Charles Santore's (1996) version of *Snow White*, in which the 17th opening reveals Snow White collapsed on the floor after eating the poisoned apple. She lies diagonally on the page across the double spread, and her position is highlighted by the lines of the tiles on the floor going in the same direction. The shadow of the evil queen is cast perpendicularly across the limp body of Snow White. Even the utensils lying by Snow White's limp hand cross each other at right angles. The diagonal placement of character in this text, highlighted by the diagonal lines of objects, creates a feeling of conflict, instability, and drama, which matches the events of this tale. Teachers can help students understand how angles affect feeling by drawing a slanted line on the board. Children are able to see that the line appears as though it will fall to the horizontal, and that its unstable positioning creates a feeling of tension, drama, and expectation.

What Palette and Background Reveal About Character

Features of background and choice of palette can also reveal information about the characters and the content of the text. For example, the color palette chosen by the illustrator can indicate a range of emotions. Bang (1991) describes the traditional association of different colors with particular psychological states, a link which she consciously incorporates in her picturebook *When Sophie Gets Angry—Really, Really Angry...* (Bang, 1999). "Hot" colors like red and orange suggest heightened feelings of sensuality, anger, or joy—depending on the context. "Cool" colors like blues and greens generally indicate serenity, calm, or objectivity, again depending on context.

In *When Sophie Gets Angry—Really, Really Angry...*, Sophie's shifting emotional states are conveyed by the color palette. Her temper tantrum takes place against a vibrant red and purple background, but her returning calm is set within tones of blue and green—such as in the 12th opening where Sophie sits peacefully in a tree watching the soothing water.

In addition to the palette, the content of the background can also give readers clues about a character's feelings or reactions, and may suggest attitudes to adopt regarding the character. In *Martin's Big Words*, a single portrait of Martin Luther King appears on two successive pages, evoking different meanings in relation to the background. In the 13th opening, Dr. King's head is crisscrossed by what appears to be barbed wire or bars, suggesting a sense of imprisonment. On the next spread, the same portrait resembles a religious icon. King is presented in this image as a beloved and memorialized figure, with votive candles burning before his image. Thus, although the image of Dr. King remains constant, the changes in the backgrounds elicit very different feelings and interpretations in readers.

Illustration backgrounds can also include references to other visual images, such as paintings by other artists. This technique adds another dimension to a reader's interpretation by drawing on outside knowledge to connect with the character or to suggest particular traits. In *Olivia*, for instance, the protagonist visits an art museum. The words of the text do not explore this activity in detail, but the illustrations not only add depth to Olivia's experience but also clarify some of the text. In the 10th opening, Olivia admires her favorite picture, a detail from *Ballet Rehearsal on the Set* by Degas, and in the next opening puzzles over a detail from *Autumn Rhythm #30* by Jackson Pollock, thinking, "I could do that in about five minutes." The incorporation of these two works of art in the background of the illustration situates Olivia at the Metropolitan Museum of Art, and provides a reference when Olivia pretends to dance in a ballet and splatters her walls with paint in imitation of Pollock's work. Using concrete examples of museum pieces gives substance to Olivia's imaginative play, and allows readers who have seen such artwork to form a deeper connection with the character.

In *Sitting Ducks*, Michael Bedard (1998) includes an image reminiscent of Edward Hopper's *Nighthawks* into his tale of the unlikely friendship of an alligator and a duck bred to be eaten. The 10th opening depicts the duck coming upon the Decoy Café after escaping the safety of the alligator's house. This café correlates with Hopper's image of existential loneliness in a dark, New York street. Like the original painting, the representation of the Decoy

Café, while bright against the darkness of the night, does not appear welcoming so much as it seems glaring and impersonal. The little duck, shown gazing at the café, seems lost in the world. By incorporating an illustration based on Hopper's *Nighthawks*, Michael Bedard makes use of the sense of loneliness associated with the original image, giving additional interpretive potential. Teachers who know Hopper's painting can offer a reproduction of it to children and allow them to compare the original with Bedard's parody, pointing out that illustrators draw on the work of other artists to convey particular meanings.

Interpreting Character Relationships

Characters' interrelationships may also be represented by particular features in illustrations. The overall shape of a group of characters, for instance, can help readers interpret their interrelations within the story. In *Strong to the Hoop* (Coy, 1999), the narrator watches his brother and friends play basketball, and wishes he were old enough to join them. When he is finally included in the game, the young boy encounters many obstacles, but goes on to score the winning point. One of the last images of the book (in the 14th opening) shows the older boys hoisting the younger narrator above their shoulders. The position denotes the triumph of the narrator: It is the smallest character who occupies the illustration's focal point, the apex of the triangle created by the bodies and raised arms of his victorious teammates.

The grouping of characters also provides clues about how they relate to each other, as illustrated in the opening images of Beatrix Potter's *Peter Rabbit* (1902/1991). In her introduction of the rabbits, Potter portrays Mother Rabbit, Flopsy, Mopsy, and Cotton-tail clustered together in a solid mass. Peter, however, stands apart, facing away from his family. His placement in the illustration foreshadows the events of the story, contrasting Peter, who will shortly go exploring in Mr. McGregor's garden, with his obedient siblings. The detail was noticed by a first grader:

Nancy: Peter's turning away—he's already thinking about getting into trouble.

Teacher: He's not paying attention to his mother like Flopsy, Mopsy, and Cotton-tail, is he?

Here, the teacher validates and amplifies the child's comment by highlighting the difference between Peter and his docile sisters. It is interesting to note that this comment was made after the class had experienced several readings of Peter Rabbit, and it demonstrates that there is always something new to notice in illustrations. The position of the characters embodies the events of the text and allows readers to make predictions about Peter's personality and the action of the story.

Illustrators can also draw readers' attention to characters and spotlight particular relationships or feelings through the intensity of color in an image. In *Goin' Someplace Special* (McKissack, 2001), for example, one of the illustrations depicts a young African American girl about to enter a whites-only hotel lobby during the pre–Civil Rights era. She is surrounded by white adults, with a menacing man looming above her. The tension in the scene is heightened by the vibrant blue of the little girl's dress—the brightest hue in the image. Her dress contrasts sharply with the saturation of black on the man's suit jacket, which, because the man's arms are extended, seems to surround and threaten to engulf her. The intensity of the blue dress and its juxtaposition with the dark color of the jacket evoke the drama of the situation and the opposition of the two characters.

Interpreting Peritextual Features

The "peritext" of a picturebook refers to all the components of a picturebook that "surround" the text of the story or the accompanying illustrations (Higonnet, 1990). These components include the title page, half-title page, dedication page, copyright information, front and back covers, end pages, and the dust jacket. These elements are often used by illustrators to convey meaning, and can reveal essential clues to the characters that would be missed if readers attended only to the text.

The front and back covers of a picturebook often denote the relative importance of characters, foreshadowing actions, emotions, and thoughts. The front cover of *Piggybook*, for instance, is indicative of the relationship among the different characters. In this image, the mother is carrying the rest of the family on her back—a pun on the term "piggyback"—and throughout the book, it is indeed the mother who bears the burden of familial responsibility by carrying an unfair load of family chores. When teachers invite students to spend time looking at and thinking about the covers, often asking them to make predictions about the story, children learn that the cover is an important tool for illustrators to convey information about the main characters of a story. By ensuring that conversations about the peritext comprise a routine part of read-alouds, teachers encourage students to become accustomed to paying attention to all features of a picturebook, thus enhancing understanding and deepening students' literacy engagement.

Comparing the front and back covers can also reveal volumes about the characters in a picturebook. The front cover of *Mufaro's Beautiful Daughters*, for instance, shows the vain sister, Mayara, gazing into a mirror and primping, while the back cover depicts the hard-working sister, Nyasha (the Cinderella counterpart) laboring dutifully in the fields. These images encapsulate the central and contrasting traits of both characters, traits which affect the story action. The front and back covers provide an organizing frame for the story conflict.

Similarly, comparing two versions of *Little Red Riding Hood* demonstrates the importance of front and back cover illustrations for evoking particular responses to the text. Christopher Coady (1991) offers Red Riding Hood on the blue background of the front cover with her face partially concealed in shadows. The back cover reveals the dark silhouette of the wolf howling at the moon, its contours crisp against the darkness of the night. This is a wolf to be feared. James Marshall's (1987) *Red Riding Hood* also presents a picture of a little girl on the front cover and a wolf on the back. However, the tone of Marshall's illustrations is vastly different, foreshadowing a much lighter version of the tale. His Red Riding Hood is drawn with curved lines and soft edges in cartoon-like fashion. She wears a smile and looks content. The wolf on the back cover is not a figure anyone would fear; in fact, he appears bashful, hiding amid the trees and clutching a straw hat in front of him. This wolf does not pose a serious threat to Red Riding Hood. These two versions of the classic tale have very different endings that correlate with the pictures on the front and back covers: In Marshall's text, a hunter rescues Red Riding Hood by opening up the belly of the wolf and releasing her grandmother and her, while in the Coady text, Red Riding Hood and her grandmother perish.

The general emotional or situational context for the characters can also be suggested through variations in the endpages of a picturebook. The front endpage of *When Sophie Gets Angry—Really, Really Angry...* is brilliant red, emphasizing Sophie's anger at the beginning of the text. At the end of the story, however, Sophie's emotions have calmed, and the back endpage is a peaceful and soothing blue.

The composition of the title page can also indicate a great deal about the context for interpreting characters' actions and feelings. The title page for

The Adventures of Sparrowboy (Pinkney, 1997) resembles the cover of a comic book. Young children readily identify this similarity, as is evidenced in these observations of a group of kindergarten children:

Malik: He's in a comic.

Kaleetha: He's a superhero!

Kenny: That [the title] looks like it does in Superman!

In combination with the image of a boy, the title's slanted comic-style typeface display led these young readers to make a connection between the characters of Sparrowboy and Superman, and to enter the picturebook with an inkling of Sparrowboy's superhuman traits. The picturebook tells of the adventures of an African American boy who becomes a hero after a sparrow transfers magical powers to him, allowing him to fly and thus solve several problems that arise in the neighborhood. The heroic nature of the character was thus foreshadowed by the title page, and students readily observed and applied this information to the text as a whole. Such observations can occur because teachers convey the importance of illustrations and the peritext to their students, creating an environment in which children are invited to see, wonder, and speak about art. When children make associations like the ones above, teachers can ask for supporting evidence: "Why do you think that?" or "Why might the illustrator make that decision?" Thus, we can create a "talk zone" for working out understandings and connections with storybook characters through interpretation of visual features.

Comparing Character Representations in Two Versions of a Story

One way of drawing attention to the ways in which illustrations indicate character is to compare two illustrated versions of the same story. A classic pairing of this type is Nancy Elkholm Burkert's illustrations for *Snow-White and the Seven Dwarves* (Jarrell, 1972) and Trina Schart Hyman's illustrations for *Snow White* (Heins, 1974). The aesthetic strategies described in this chapter can be applied to images in these two texts that depict similar scenes, thus highlighting the importance of illustrations for interpreting and responding to story events. Overall, Burkert's illustrations are "cool" and objective, whereas Hyman's are "warm" and emotional. As Nodelman (1988) suggests, the artistic elements of the Burkert version deemphasize key moments of action by lessening the terror of the major events and centering illustrations on moments just prior to or after the central episodes of the story. Hyman's version, by contrast, includes continuous, intense images of the main points of the narrative that counter the detached tone of the verbal text. We will look more closely at the relationship between these two fairy tale accounts by analyzing two pairs of illustrations. This is an important exercise for teachers because it guides us in looking more carefully at our own knowledge while building skill in interpreting illustrations. This is a necessary first step in getting children to look more closely at illustrations as a source of information about storybook characters.

The first opening of both versions depicts Snow White's mother sitting at a window with its frame "of black ebony" (Heins, 1974; Jarrell, 1972). In Burkert's version, we observe her from an outsider's perspective, framed by the large expanse of the window and the gray stone wall. In this image, Snow White's mother appears as a sedate, pleasant woman. She gazes peacefully downward, perhaps at the finger she has just pricked with her embroidery needle.

In contrast, Hyman's illustration is shown from an insider's perspective, and as we look wistfully through the window alongside the Queen, a deeper connection is forged between reader and character because of the immediacy of the illustration and the shared visual perspective. But Hyman depicts Snow White's mother after she has pricked her finger, and the vibrant drops of blood stand out in stark contrast to the gleaming white snow on the windowsill. In Burkert's tranquil version, there is no blood at the scene.

The color palettes of the two stories are distinct: Burkert uses muted hues while Hyman includes dark, rich colors and contrasting tones. Hyman's strong colors create a sense of intensity and action, while the subdued tones of the Burkert version allow the reader to remain more detached from the story. As well, in the Burkert version, Snow White's mother is dressed very formally, with an elaborate headdress, whereas Hyman shows us a figure with more informal clothing and a less elegant hairstyle. These artistic choices make it easier for readers to identify emotionally with Hyman's portrayal of Snow White's mother.

Although Hyman focuses much of the story on the wicked queen, depicting her ten times, Burkert's version represents the character only twice, and in both instances with her back to readers. As Nodelman (1988) perceptively describes, Hyman's is one of the few versions of the story that objectively portray the evil queen's beauty. Often, the queen is depicted as physically repulsive, with the features of a witch, when in fact, the narrative specifies that until the arrival of Snow White, the queen was the most beautiful woman in the land. In the second opening, Hyman portrays the wicked queen as a svelte blond, who is nonetheless made to look sinister through the incorporation of other details in the illustration. The queen holds a black kitten, which she appears to be stroking pensively. The mood of the room is dark, with numerous black candles shining gloomy light on the queen and her mirror—gruesomely decorated with naked devils, menacing faces, and other ominous creatures. Within this atmosphere, the wicked queen looks straight out at the readers, drawing us into the action and into her nefarious machinations to get rid of Snow White.

This image of the queen staring out at the audience contrasts sharply with Burkert's depiction of the queen in the ninth opening, which shows her dancing gleefully, clutching the poisoned apple, her back to the readers. The queen herself does not hold center stage; rather, her books, utensils, and potions, which represent her knowledge, are in the forefront. Whereas Hyman emphasizes the Queen's sensuousness, Burkert emphasizes her devious mind. Even though this illustration contains just as many macabre images as Hyman's version, including tarot cards depicting death, a skull, various insects, poisonous plants, and a knife, the illustration does not appear as jarring or as threatening as the one in Hyman's version. This is in part due to the detached reader stance created through the absence of a connection with the evil queen, whose face readers never see. In addition, the muted colors and grainy quality of the illustrations make the image appear more subdued, despite its graphic components, and allow the reader to view the story from a more detached perspective.

The Interdependence of Text and Illustration

In a well-crafted picturebook, the illustrations and the verbal text work together to create the larger story. Illustrators use a variety of artistic techniques to help define characters, whether by focusing on the images themselves or by manipulating elements of the background or peritextual features. By carefully examining the illustrations, readers can gain a deeper understanding of character traits and story elements that are not fully explained in the words alone. Consideration of all the elements of a picturebook allows readers to integrate their knowledge into a unified aesthetic experience.

On their own, children may not examine illustrations in-depth. Rather, close "reading" of illustrations is most likely to occur within a classroom in which children are taught to look at all the features of a text. When teachers regularly share their own observations and sensitivity to illustrations, appropriately and judiciously, children begin to follow those leads, and to consider all available cues when responding to picturebooks.

To focus on the elements of illustration, we have artificially isolated features (such as shape or line), although we are aware that these features come into play simultaneously. In a similar way, in discussions with children, we find we do best by focusing on one or two of these features at a time. Further, we have found that successful teachers aim to increase children's awareness of illustrators' techniques gradually over many read-alouds and book discussion sessions, using awakening awareness to extend and refine children's literary understandings. Such ongoing attention to the intricacies of illustrations results in children's development as insightful, perceptive readers of picturebooks.

REFERENCES

Bang, M. (1991). *Picture this: Perception and composition.* Boston: Little, Brown.

Golden, J.M. (1990). *The narrative symbol in childhood literature: Explorations of the construction of text.* New York: Mouton de Gruyter.

Higonnet, M. (1990). The playground of the peritext. *Children's Literature Association Quarterly, 15,* 47–49.

Kiefer, B.Z. (1995). *The potential of picture books: From visual literacy to aesthetic understanding.* Englewood Cliffs, NJ: Prentice-Hall.

Marantz, K. (1977). The picture book as art object: A call for balanced reviewing. *The Wilson Library Bulletin,* 148–151.

Nodelman, P. (1988). *Words about pictures: The narrative art of children's picture books.* Athens: The University of Georgia Press.

Schwarcz, J. (1982). *Ways of the illustrator: Visual communication in children's literature.* Chicago: American Library Association.

LITERATURE CITED

Bang, M. (1999). *When Sophie gets angry—really, really angry...* New York: Blue Sky Press.

Bedard, M. (1998). *Sitting ducks.* New York: Putnam & Grosset.

Brown, M. (1988). *Cinderella.* New York: Simon & Schuster.

Browne, A. (1986). *Piggybook.* New York: Knopf.

Coady, C. (1991). *Red Riding Hood.* New York: Dutton Children's Books.

Coy, J. (1999). *Strong to the hoop.* Ill. L. Jean-Bart. New York: Lee & Low.

Delamare, D. (1993). *Cinderella.* New York: Green Tiger Press.

Falconer, I. (2000). *Olivia.* New York: Atheneum.

Galdone, P. (1985). *The three bears.* New York: Clarion.

Heins, P. (1974). *Snow White*. Ill. T.S. Hyman. Boston: Little, Brown.

Hoffman, M. (1991). *Amazing Grace*. Ill. C. Binch. New York: Dial.

Isaacs, A. (1994). *Swamp Angel*. Ill. P.O. Zelinsky. New York: Dutton.

Jarrell, R. (1972). *Snow-White and the seven dwarfs*. Ill. N.E. Burkert. New York: Farrar Straus Giroux.

Marshall, J. (1987). *Red Riding Hood*. New York: Dial.

McKissack, P. (2001). *Goin' someplace special*. Ill. J. Pinkney. New York: Atheneum.

Pinkney, B. (1997). *The adventures of Sparrowboy*. New York: Simon & Schuster.

Potter, B. (1991). *The tale of Peter Rabbit*. London: Frederick Warne. (Original work published 1902)

Rappaport, D. (2001). *Martin's big words: The life of Dr. Martin Luther King, Jr*. Ill. B. Collier. New York: Hyperion.

Santore, C. (1996). *Snow White*. New York: Park Lane Press.

Sendak, M. (1963). *Where the wild things are*. New York: HarperTrophy.

Sendak, M. (1981). *Outside over there*. New York: Harper & Row.

Silverman, E. (1998). *Don't fidget a feather*. Ill. S.D. Schindler. New York: Aladdin.

Steptoe, J. (1987). *Mufaro's beautiful daughters*. New York: Lothrop, Lee & Shepard.

Wyeth, S.D. (1998). *Something beautiful*. Ill. C.K. Soentpiet. New York: Bantam Doubleday Dell.

16

Bringing the Best of Characters Into Primary Classrooms

Junko Yokota and William H. Teale

Junko Yokota and William Teale introduce ways to categorize characters, provide memorable examples of characters in children's books, and suggest how teachers can nurture children's understanding of characters.

IN THE PRIMARY GRADES (kindergarten through grade 3), it is perhaps character more than any other feature that attracts children to literature. Frog and Toad, amazing Grace, Curious George, Koala Lou, Lilly with the purple plastic purse, Charlotte the spider, Martha the dog, Ira who sleeps over, the Little Red Hen, Max and Ruby, Miss Nelson, John Henry, Strega Nona, Amelia Bedelia—these and countless other characters intrigue young children. What is it about such characters that makes them interesting, endearing, or memorable? Why do some characters live beyond the confines of their books in students' minds? How can

What a Character! Character Study as a Guide to Literary Meaning Making in Grades K–8 edited by Nancy L. Roser and Miriam G. Martinez, with Junko Yokota and Sharon O'Neal. Copyright 2005 by the International Reading Association.

teachers heighten children's understanding of character, as well as deepen their engagement with literature and promote their development as lifelong readers? Examining how authors and illustrators of books appropriate for primary-grade children craft characters can help answer these questions.

The Creation of Characters in Books for Young Children

It is common to distinguish between *flat characters* and *round characters* in literature. A flat character is one-dimensional and changes little or not at all over the course of the story. A round character is complex, displaying many different aspects of his or her character and typically showing growth or development over the course of the book. Round characters are the characters who stick in readers' minds. Authors and illustrators develop round characters by imbuing them with both inner qualities and external qualities. In a book for young children, some of these qualities are conveyed through the text while others are revealed through the illustrations.

For example, a round character that is likely to have lasting appeal with young students is the pigeon who yearns to be powerful in *Don't Let the Pigeon Drive the Bus* (Willems, 2003). Because Willems created this work as a picturebook, he used both text and illustration to establish character. This pigeon wants to drive something big with four wheels, so when the bus driver steps out, the pigeon asks, pleads, reasons, cajoles, inveigles, bargains, wheedles, begs, connives, negotiates, bribes, whines, demands, and uses just about every other technique imaginable in an escalating series of tactics to convince the reader to let him drive the bus. By the end of the book, students recognize a number of characteristics that make him a fully developed, round character: He comes across as determined and clever, and it is easy to associate him with a whole range of real-life, capable young children who use all means of strategies to persuade their parents or other people to let them have their way.

Willems creates this irresistible character through the text in the phrasing and intonations of the pigeon's persuasive language; for example, "I'll tell you what,..." "Please?" "I never get to do anything," "Hey, I've got an idea," and "I'll be your best friend" show his resourcefulness at being convincing. Willems also uses the illustrations, especially the pigeon's facial and gestural features, to adeptly portray the character. The facial expressions (realized almost exclusively by the way in which the pigeon's eyes are drawn) and the body posture and movements that accompany the pigeon's various persuasive tactics and his reactions when he doesn't get his way portray the pigeon's growing frustration.

Throughout the book Willems depicts the inner qualities of persuasive determination and mighty conviction and external qualities of begging behavior and even a tantrum that give readers insight into the character, but one especially interesting example is found at the point when the pigeon finally realizes he won't get his way. Willems has him erupt in a full-fledged, two-page-spread tantrum—writhing, feathers flying, eyeballs popping, and screaming "LET ME DRIVE THE BUS!!!" in large, scratchily written, black-and-yellow uppercase letters on the strongest colored background in the entire book. Clearly, this is a pigeon capable of great emotion.

Following this is another two-page spread with muted lavender background, showing a few lingering feathers scattered along the bottom and the pigeon on the far right side, head drooped, eye lids half shaded, with a black squiggle in a speech bubble above his head. A few pages later, the book ends with an even larger four-wheeled vehicle entering the scene. The pigeon gazes up at it from the lower left hand corner with an expectant look on his face, saying merely, "Hey...." Through these techniques, Willems depicts many of the pigeon's outward actions and reactions while simultaneously providing insight into the character's determination and non-defeatist spirit.

There are scores of other round characters that provide excellent opportunities for primary-grade children to think about what makes characters tick and study how the creators of the books they read succeed in making strong characters. Like the example just cited, most books that succeed with primary grade children are picture books. However, quite a number of chapter books with strong characters are also appropriate for primary-grade classrooms. Third graders and even a considerable portion of second-grade students can read these books themselves; kindergarten and first graders can access the characters in these books through read-alouds. It is useful to consider patterns in how each of these types of books reveals character.

Combining Text and Illustration to Depict Character in Picturebooks

Most picturebooks develop characters through a combination of text and illustration. For example, Kevin Henkes masterfully balances text and illustration to reveal characters. In *Chrysanthemum* (Henkes, 1991), the central character is initially joyously pictured as a confident child who delights in her name. Early in the book, the text describes various specific ways in which she enjoys hearing and seeing her name. A change in tone is then signaled by the text, "And then she started school." When faced with the ridicule of classmates, Chrysanthemum "wilted." The accompanying illustrations show a wilted Chrysanthemum, with worried eyes and a downcast face.

It is only when a new teacher arrives (who all the children try to impress) that Chrysanthemum realizes her good fortune. The new teacher's name is Delphinium, and it turns out that she is considering naming her new baby Chrysanthemum. When Chrysanthemum "blossoms" as a result, regaining pride in her name, her visual image reinforces this change as she is illustrated in increasingly larger proportions.

Developing Picturebook Characters Primarily Through Text

Some picturebooks rely centrally on the text to develop character, especially when the key aspects of what makes the character tick are "inner" features, as in a number of William Steig's characters. Doctor De Soto, for example, is a memorable character for many primary-grade children (Steig, 1982). He resonates with children as a compassionate, principled, and clever mouse dentist. The text that Steig creates is key to understanding Doctor De Soto. Even though the De Sotos "refused to treat animals dangerous to mice, and it said so on his sign," Doctor De Soto's compassion is evident when a pitiful looking and sounding fox approaches the office and the dentist says to his wife, "That poor fox.... What shall we do?" As to his principles, Doctor De Soto states, "Once I start a job,... I finish it." And at the end of the story, the text notes that "Doctor De Soto and his assistant had outfoxed the fox," conveying the doctor's clever nature. Though Steig's excellent illustrations convey much about both the fox and Dr. De Soto, it is impossible for child readers (or even adult readers) to discern the fact that Dr. De Soto is true to his principles or such a clever character simply by reference to the pictures in this book. Rather, the text is the primary source of these particular character insights in the book.

Developing Picturebook Characters
Primarily Through Illustration

In contrast to Steig's *Doctor De Soto*, David Shannon's books about David—
No, David! (1998), *David Goes to School* (1999), and *David Gets in Trouble*
(2002)—reveal character almost exclusively through illustration. The books
contain minimal text. *No David!*, for example, has no more than five words
on any two-page spread, and all of them are commands like, "No, David!" or
"Don't play with your food!" The insights into who David is come from the
actions and detailed facial expressions Shannon creates. In *David Goes to
School*, David's facial expressions in a number of the illustrations indicate that
he often doesn't realize when he is doing something wrong, that his mis-
behavior is not an intentional act. This insight is key to understanding David
as a character. As Shannon has said, "He's sort of an accidental anarchist, and
that's a big part of his personality; he's not a mean-spirited kid, he just doesn't
think" (Drennan, 1999).

The Creation of Round Characters
in Chapter Books

Although many chapter books for younger children have delightful and
supporting illustrations in them, the pictures are not integral to the books.
Chapter books predominantly depict character through text. As with all
books, chapter book authors typically draw upon a combination of three
factors to reveal character—physical description, actions, and internal
state—but, of course, chapter book authors rely on words to do this.

Depicting Physical Traits Through
Text in Chapter Books

In *Charlotte's Web*, E.B. White (1952) clearly uses all three factors to develop
his characters. Readers learn through the text that Wilbur is a runt who is
"very small and weak" and "will never amount to anything." This physical
trait propels the entire story. Readers of the novel discover another physical
trait that has significance with respect to character behavior when Wilbur
notes that Charlotte has "awfully hairy legs," and she responds that they are
hairy for a good reason. She continues, "Furthermore, each leg of mine has

seven sections—the coax, the trochanter, the femur, the patella, the tibia, the metatarsus, and the tarsus" (p. 55). Wilbur is amazed, but when he realizes that he doesn't have that many leg sections, Charlotte assures him that he doesn't need them because he doesn't have to spin a web—something that takes a lot of "leg work." As the story unfolds, readers understand why this physical description of Charlotte and her physical ability is especially important to their understanding of the plot and the outcome of the story. If Charlotte had not been able to do such "leg work," she could not have woven words into her web—the words that attracted such widespread attention and saved Wilbur's life.

Depicting Character Actions Through Text in Chapter Books

Actions and the reasons behind those actions are key to understanding characterization in *Charlotte's Web*. Readers gain a sense of Templeton the rat's character when he begrudgingly goes off in search of magazine clippings with words for Charlotte to spin (as part of a plan to save Wilbur from the butcher block). Templeton does so only when reminded that if Wilbur were to perish, so would Templeton's food supply.

Depicting the Internal State of Characters in Chapter Books

Changes in character feelings are revealed in *Charlotte's Web* through text that describes Wilbur's sorrow, despair, and hope as he learns of his beloved friend Charlotte's imminent death. Upon hearing that Charlotte will soon die, "Wilbur threw himself down in an agony of pain and sorrow. Great sobs racked his body. He heaved and grunted with desolation. 'Charlotte,' he moaned" (p. 165). Inconsolable at the thought of her death, Wilbur is full of hope as, all winter long, Wilbur watches over Charlotte's egg sac. "For Wilbur, nothing in life was so important as this small round object—nothing else mattered" (p. 176). The birth of the babies makes Wilbur's "heart pound" as he gives a squeal. But when they fly away, he screams, "'Wait a minute!' Wilbur was frantic, Charlotte's babies were disappearing at a great rate." He cries, "Come back, children!" (pp. 178–179). "He couldn't bear to watch any more. In sorrow he sank to the ground and closed his eyes. This seemed like the end of the world, to be deserted by Charlotte's children. Wilbur cried himself to sleep" (p. 180). In the end, though, he feels hopeful again because three of the children remain with him. He trembles with joy and "Wilbur's heart brimmed with happiness" (p. 182).

The Use of Stock Characters and Round Characters

Sometimes authors and illustrators create memorable characters for young children by capitalizing on stock characters. Stock characters are types of characters that have become predictable and conventionalized because they so often appear in a genre of literature. For example, think of the wolf, the fox, or the trickster character as they typically appear in traditional literature. We mention characters such as these and the genre of traditional literature because, as scholars have pointed out, typically folktales have "little development of setting or characters" (Temple, Martinez, Yokota, & Naylor, 2002, p. 140). Thus, although most young children are drawn to folktales, the stories often do not offer rich opportunities for exploring character because they rely on stock characters (that don't need a lot of explaining) to move the story along.

The wolf is a good example. Whether in *Little Red Riding Hood* (Hyman, 1983) or *The Three Little Pigs* (Galdone, 1979), the wolf is basically unidimensional, a representation of evil who seeks merely to ingest a tasty girl, grandmother, or pig. The fox frequents traditional literature, usually as a sly character that ultimately has evil intentions. The rabbit, coyote, and spider tricksters that appear in folktale stories are clever, but typically that is the sole characteristic that distinguishes them.

It is, however, possible to use the stock character as a vehicle for developing a round character. In *The Wolf's Chicken Stew*, for example, author Keiko Kasza (1987) introduces what appears to be a typical wolf who stalks a chicken to cook in his chicken stew. But this wolf turns out to be an excellent cook who whips up "scrumptious" pancakes, doughnuts, and a cake. He is also a complete softy for the fluffy chicks who gleefully hop all over their "Uncle Wolf" and give him "a hundred kisses" for all the treats he left them. Kasza deftly depicts the wolf's body language and facial expressions to create a character with a distinct personality and, ultimately, a decidedly un-wolf-like attitude toward chickens. Readers come to realize that this is not the typical wolf character.

Or, consider the fox in *Doctor De Soto*. Steig incorporates the stock sly, deceitful fox who remains true to his character in that he plans to eat Dr. De Soto and his wife once they finish the fox's dental work. But Steig also imbues the fox with distinctive physical and internal characteristics that elevate him beyond the merely stock character: Fox is impeccably dressed and has the outer airs of a gentleman. Steig also presents the inner dialogue the fox has with himself about the morality of eating the De Sotos after they had helped him with his aching tooth, so it is clear that the fox is not singularly evil. In the end, however, the fox decides to take the low road and devour the De Sotos. But, in providing insight into the fox's reasoning and depicting the fox's ultimate humiliation through illustration and by having the fox utter his final words "frank oo berry mush" through glued together teeth, Steig has created a character that young children find interesting and memorable.

Author Helen Lester and illustrator Lynne Munsinger capitalize on another stock character: outsider/loser. In *Tacky the Penguin* (Lester, 1990), Tacky's appearance and actions are carefully crafted to make him a lovably odd character. By the time the reader has gone from the opening page through the following five double-page spreads, the character is established through the illustrations. Tacky is shown in a boldly colored Hawaiian shirt on the first right-hand page—in contrast to the conformist penguins on the left-hand page (clustered together, aligned in rows, regularly placed within the frame of the drawing, moving synchronously, and so forth). Unconventional Tacky is by himself, moving irregularly all over the pages—even causing the illustration of the splashing water to go beyond the frame of the drawing. Tacky is definitely odd, but he is also definitely Tacky, comfortable with who he is and what he does.

Tacky, Steig's fox, and Kasza's wolf all play on stereotyped images to create complex and memorable characters. So do other spunky tricksters like Flossie in *Flossie and the Fox* (McKissack, 1986) and the one-of-a-kind A. Wolf in *The True Story of the Three Little Pigs* (Scieszka, 1995). These characters emerge from stock images to live as particular characters that young children can study and appreciate for their multidimensionalism and literary merit.

Helping Young Children Learn About Character

Students are often very perceptive in understanding characters, seemingly coming to their understandings without explicit teaching. However, a significant number of children are unable to develop more than a surface understanding of character on their own; they need instruction that helps them to understand the qualities that define characters. Fortunately, there are ways that teachers can help them hone their abilities and sharpen their perceptions related to character understanding. When teachers are aware of how character is revealed, they can scaffold their students' understanding by asking questions, guiding discussion in particular directions, and offering response opportunities that facilitate student thinking about character. Three things can be especially powerful in helping students study characters more deeply: (1) description, (2) relationships with other characters, and (3) setting.

Character Revealed Through Description

Asking questions helps students think about how characters are revealed through description. For example, a teacher could ask, "What does the text tell you about the character?; What does s/he look like?; What does she do?" Students can profitably explore the question, "What does the character look like?" in a book like William Steig's *Shrek* (1990). The text says that Shrek is ugly, and the illustrations confirm that description by depicting him with red eyes and many black marks covering his green, misshapen head. But much of what the reader knows about Shrek's ugliness comes from reading the descriptive passages about how others *react* to Shrek's appearance. In fact, it is not until the end of the book that the princess he is to wed describes Shrek's physical attributes: "Your lumpy nose, your pointy head, your wicked eyes, so livid red..." (n.p.).

Addressing the question "What does a character do?" is appropriate for a book like *The Very Busy Spider* (Carle, 1984) that uses descriptive text to build and confirm a character's qualities. In such works, the illustrations do little to heighten awareness of the character's qualities; rather, they depict the plot. In *The Very Busy Spider*, various farm animals approach the spider, asking the spider to join them in activities such as eating, running, jumping, rolling, chasing. Each time, the spider does not answer but rather continues to spin her web. Readers can deduce that the spider is not companionable but is very industrious and goal-oriented; when the spider finally finishes her web, she achieves her goal by catching a fly in it. In other Carle books, the central character is given a single defining character attribute in the title of the book—lonely, hungry, grouchy—and that attribute is depicted through textual description of the character. The firefly is lonely until finding a friend; the caterpillar is hungry until metamorphosis turns it into a butterfly; the ladybug is grouchy until it is taught a lesson. Each book endorses the character quality exponentially, thus making the "very" in the title quite apt.

It is also useful to ask primary-grade students who read or listen to chapter books to state character qualities based on descriptions by probing how they arrived at those understandings: "How do you know that the character looks that way/acts that way?" Beverly Cleary creates memorable characters in her books about Ramona Quimby and her family (e.g., Cleary, 1981). Her descriptions of what Ramona thinks, feels, and does are what help readers understand the qualities that define Ramona. She begs, interrupts, sighs, complains, hopes, and wonders a lot; by considering these and other descriptions of her behaviors and thoughts, readers come to know a fully described character that comes to life in a believable way. In one situation, for example, Ramona and her older sister Beezus are told by their parents that they must prepare dinner the following night because they were so unappreciative of their current dinner. (They denigrated the "yucky" and disgusting tongue that was a cheaper cut than "regular beef.") The girls behave perfectly the next day, hoping that their parents will forgive—or forget. But their mother is both "cheerful and heartless," and the girls are expected to follow through on their punishment. In this, and other situations throughout the series of books about the Quimby family, each character is described in ways that are true to real life.

Character as Revealed Through Relationships

Often, character is revealed through characters' relationships with one another. Typically, those relationships are understood by examining various elements of dialogue and action. In some cases, the relationship portrayed is one-sided, such as the relationship between Max and his mother in *Where the Wild Things Are* (Sendak, 1963). The mother is an unseen character who is developed in relation to the behavior and response of Max, her rebellious son. She sends Max to his bedroom without his supper when he misbehaves; but when Max returns to his room from his "journey" to the land of the wild things, he finds his supper waiting for him. Readers can interpret that the character of Max's mother is both firm and loving. In addition, they can interpret that Max's character is rebellious when reacting to the punishment but also still longing for his mother when he tires of playing with the wild things.

In other cases, a relationship is predominantly focused on linked characters, such as Frog and Toad (e.g., Lobel, 1970). In books such as this, the two character names are virtually inseparable; each name used independently loses its meaning, which is created in reference to the other character. In still other instances, the character is defined by his or her relationship with many others, such as in Nikki Grimes's *Talkin' About Bessie* (2002), in which different facets of Bessie Coleman's character are revealed as she is remembered by a series of different people in her life. What is also interesting about character in this book is that it is a real character who lived; the book is a biography of aviator Elizabeth "Bessie" Coleman.

Rosemary Wells's books about siblings Max and Ruby are a good example of how two characters are understood in light of their relationship. Readers come to know Max through his actions; they come to understand Ruby through her dialogue. But it is the description of Max's actions in response to Ruby's dialogue that reveals what these two characters are really all about. Ruby is bossy and subjects Max to her rules. Max doesn't argue—in fact, he doesn't say anything. He simply disregards her edicts and does whatever he wants to do—usually in opposition to Ruby's stance. In *Bunny Party* (Wells, 2001), for example, Ruby sends out invitations to Grandma's birthday party to all of her dolls but tells Max that there is no room for extra guests. Max simply undermines her authority by replacing her dolls one by one with his stuffed animals, deceiving Ruby without confronting her. Ruby is unaware of how this has happened; she is confused as to why Rapunzel has been replaced by Jellyball Shooter Spider. Without didactic description, young children learn much about the individual characters of Max and about Ruby through their relationship, a relationship depicted through both text and illustration.

In *Dear Mrs. LaRue* (Teague, 2002), readers see a series of letters written by the dog, Ike, to his owner, Mrs. LaRue, who has sent him to dog obedience school. Mrs. LaRue's letters are never shown, but readers know she has written back because of what Ike writes in his letters. The illustrations show Ike in his obedience school setting, and the humor lies in the fact that the color illustrations show the reality of the spa-like place whereas the black and white illustrations depict Ike's grim description of a jail-like place. Ike's actions also reveal his character as he escapes from obedience school, embarks on an adventure, and eventually returns to Mrs. LaRue. Although Mrs. LaRue is pictured in the opening and closing of the book, she is largely an unseen and unheard character. Readers understand her character through her relationship with Ike as revealed through her implied correspondence with Ike.

Peggy Rathmann reveals both of the central characters in *Officer Buckle and Gloria* (1995) through their relationship with one another. Officer Buckle is the "straight man" and his dog, Gloria, the comedic one. What makes the book especially humorous is that Officer Buckle is oblivious to the antics of Gloria because they happen behind his back, but where everyone else in the book can see them. Gloria's hilarious actions are revealed through the illustrations, letting readers join the book characters in the joke played on the unassuming Officer Buckle. In fact, at the climax of the story, television cameras reveal to the public world Gloria exaggeratedly acting out of all the safety tips as Officer Buckle takes a deep bow to acknowledge what he thinks is applause for his safety tip presentation—something that had always put his audience to sleep prior to the arrival of Gloria. The relationship between Officer Buckle and Gloria is central to this story. The book opens with Officer Buckle working alone, unsuccessfully, and at one point shows Gloria also trying to work alone, but unsuccessfully. Ultimately, their relationship is repaired when they realize, "Always stick with your buddy."

Character as Revealed Through Setting

In Allen Say's *Grandfather's Journey* (1993), the historic period plays a vital part in helping readers understand the grandfather. The backdrop on every page in the first part of the book is dramatic: the ocean liner on which the grandfather immigrates to America, the landscape of the Grand Canyon, vast farm fields, and the California coastline. When the grandfather returns to Japan, he is shown inside a Japanese home, a backdrop that serves as dramatic contrast to the settings in America.

Beyond just having children look at surface differences in setting, it is helpful for them to consider how the juxtaposition of character against the setting helps the viewer to understand the character better. For example, when first arriving in the United States, Grandfather wears clothes that are too big and also look uncomfortable; the people he is surrounded by as he stands in front of the barber shop are all much taller and represent a natural part of the scene. Teachers could ask, "How might Grandfather feel in these situations?" Yet when the grandfather returns to his original homeland of Japan, he looks as if he belongs comfortably when he is shown wearing a cotton yukata that seems entirely natural within the setting of the Japanese home. Again, it is the juxtaposition of the character against his setting that speaks to the character's feelings.

Demi's book *The Empty Pot* (1990) reveals the character of Ping in relation to his setting. The book opens with a natural world shown predominantly in green. Ping is placed in contrast to his setting in numerous ways. On various pages he is shown as part of a long line of children who wait to get a seed from the Emperor, surrounded by all the plants he has grown while facing the pot with the one seed that won't grow, set apart from all the children who are joyously taking their beautiful plants to the Emperor, and walking side by side with his father who gives him support and words of wisdom. The most dramatic page on which Ping is shown in contrast to his setting is the one on which the Emperor asks him why he brought an empty pot. The Emperor stands at the lowest left corner of the double spread; Ping stands at the uppermost right corner. The rest of the page is entirely white space—the other children who were depicted with their flourishing plants on the pages immediately prior have disappeared—a design created to bring emphasis to the encounter of the Emperor and Ping. Ping's character is revealed against his setting in that readers see how conscientious he is as he tries to grow his seed, and they sense his shame in being confronted by the Emperor.

One rich chapter book example that illustrates the importance of the character in relation to setting can be found in *Charlotte's Web*. The initial paragraphs of chapter 3 clearly establish all of the book's characters in relation to their barnyard setting. The barn is described as large and very old, with the odor of hay, manure, and "perspiration of tired horses...and the wonderful sweet breath of patient cows. It had a peaceful smell" (p. 30). One way to get children to envision the setting is to ask questions like, "What does the place look like? Smell like? Feel like?" A teacher might encourage children to draw the setting, to write down a few words in "list poetry" format, and to "retell" what they remember about the setting. Getting children to become aware of understanding how characters are revealed through their setting also means making connections between setting and character. After they have described the setting, the next questions could be, "How did the setting impact what happened in the story?" The children could use their books to go back and cite specific passages to support their answers.

Engaging Students

Authors and illustrators whose characters appeal to primary-grade children use a variety of techniques to make their characters come alive. By engaging young children in discussions and other activities that get them to examine what characters look like, do, and feel; how they relate to other characters in the book; and what their settings tell about them, we deepen children's engagement with the book, thereby enhancing their comprehension and the literary experience. Even young children can consider techniques in text and in illustration like those discussed in this chapter if we lead their explorations appropriately and select quality books for them to delve into. Such explorations lead to a deeper understanding of how character in particular and literature in general works.

REFERENCES

Drennan, M. (1999, September). Back to school with David Shannon. *BookPage Online*. Retrieved March 3, 2004, from http://www.bookpage.com/9909bp/david_shannon.html

Temple, C., Martinez, M.G., Yokota, J., & Naylor, A. (2002). *Children's books in children's hands: An introduction to their literature* (2nd ed.). Boston: Allyn & Bacon.

LITERATURE CITED

Carle, E. (1984). *The very busy spider*. New York: Philomel.

Cleary, B. (1981). *Ramona Quimby, age 8*. Ill. A. Tiegreen. New York: William Morrow.

Demi. (1990). *The empty pot*. New York: Holt.

Galdone, P. (1979). *The three little pigs*. New York: Clarion.

Grimes, N. (2002). *Talkin' about Bessie: The story of aviator Elizabeth Coleman*. Ill. E.B. Lewis. New York: Orchard.

Henkes, K. (1991). *Chrysanthemum*. New York: Greenwillow.

Hyman, T.S. (1983). *Little Red Riding Hood*. New York: Holiday House.

Kasza, K. (1987). *The wolf's chicken stew*. New York: G.P. Putnam's Sons.

Lester, H. (1990). *Tacky the penguin*. Ill. L. Munsinger. Boston: Houghton Mifflin.

Lobel, A. (1970). *Frog and Toad are friends*. New York: HarperCollins.

McKissack, P. (1986). *Flossie and the fox*. Ill. R. Isadora. New York: Dial/Viking.

Rathmann, P. (1995). *Officer Buckle and Gloria*. New York: G.P. Putnam's Sons.

Say, A. (1993). *Grandfather's journey*. Boston: Houghton Mifflin.

Scieszka, J. (1995). *The true story of the 3 little pigs by A. Wolf*. Ill. L. Smith. New York: Dutton.

Sendak, M. (1963). *Where the wild things are*. New York: Harper & Row.

Shannon, D. (1998). *No, David!* New York: Blue Sky/Scholastic.

Shannon, D. (1999). *David goes to school*. New York: Blue Sky/Scholastic.

Shannon, D. (2002). *David gets in trouble*. New York: Blue Sky/Scholastic.

Steig, W. (1982). *Dr. De Soto*. New York: Farrar Straus Giroux.

Steig, W. (1990). *Shrek!* New York: Farrar Straus Giroux.

Teague, M. (2002). *Dear Mrs. LaRue: Letters from obedience school*. New York: Scholastic.

Wells, R. (2001). *Bunny party*. New York: Dial/Viking.

White, E.B. (1952). *Charlotte's web*. Ill. G. Williams. New York: Harper & Row.

Willems, M. (2003). *Don't let the pigeon drive the bus*. New York: Hyperion.

17

Bringing the Best Characters Into Middle School Classrooms

Janis M. Harmon, Terri Willeford, and Michelle S. Kenney

Janis Harmon, Terri Willeford, and Michelle Kenney show why it is critical to listen to the voices of middle school students when choosing characters for the classroom. Student recommendations provide insight into the kinds of characters that they will find most compelling and appealing.

YOUNG ADULT NOVELS ARE AT THE HEART OF MANY literary experiences for middle school students. Students are captivated by plots ranging from fresh takes on ordinary problems to extraordinary encounters and wild adventures. Plots work best for students, though, when populated with unique and significant characters that they "love, hate, and never forget" (Hipple, 1992, p. 3). Characters are pivotal to students' literary meaning-making experiences (Langer, 1995) because students identify with, respond to, and even *become* the characters in their best-loved books (Martinez & Roser, 2003). Characters play an important

What a Character! Character Study as a Guide to Literary Meaning Making in Grades K–8 edited by Nancy L. Roser and Miriam G. Martinez, with Junko Yokota and Sharon O'Neal. Copyright 2005 by the International Reading Association.

role in extending and expanding the literary development of middle school students.

Given the increasing number of young adult books published today, however, the task of deciding which books to bring into the classroom has become more challenging than ever. Keeping an eye on what students like to read, a finger on district-mandated reading lists, and a foot in the door of the library to find out what titles are available is a balancing act. Ideally, classroom book choices offer students compelling characters in action, but in reality book choices do not always offer characters that are memorable to students. The voices of students need to be heard throughout the process of determining the books—the characters—that claim class time. Your students' recommendations can provide insight into what they particularly seek out and value in characters. With that in mind, review the characters that follow—characters that middle-grade students say they find unforgettable—for what they reveal about the vulnerable, complex, identity-seeking worlds of middle schoolers.

The Memorable Character Survey: Prompting Students to Think About Characters

In order to ascertain which characters middle school students find memorable, we began the project. The survey examines the characters selected most frequently, what students remember about their memorable characters, and student reactions to characters.

In the survey, seventh and eighth graders on two campuses in two different school districts were asked to name and describe "memorable characters" from their reading. Collectively, the 224 students who participated represented a diverse population in terms of both socioeconomic status and ethnicity, including Latino, African American, and Anglo students in both urban and suburban areas. At the outset, we realized that we could not simply ask students about their most memorable characters without first preparing them to recall and think deeply about the books they have read and the characters they have met. For this reason, the teaching framework in Table 17.1 was implemented.

Before we began, we were uncertain about which characters students would select as most memorable. Surely, some would gravitate to our own personal favorites, especially the ones that were required reading, such as Byron and Kenny in *The Watsons Go to Birmingham—1963* (Curtis, 1995)

TABLE 17.1   Teaching Framework for Character Survey

1. Ask students to think about all the books they have read since last year (or during middle school). As a class, brainstorm a list of books students have read. Write the titles on chart paper.
2. Allow students time to talk with one another in a group to recall books and characters. This will help students who do not remember specific titles and characters. Have each student complete a handout of a three-column table with the two headings "Title" and "Characters." The third column has no heading.
3. Conduct a class discussion about what makes a character memorable and write student responses on chart paper.
4. Have students write "Most Memorable Character" as the heading of the last column of the handout. Then ask students to think about which character(s) stands out the most for them and to write the names in the last column.
5. Ask each student to select one character and complete the questions in the Memorable Character survey.
6. Have students form groups to collectively highlight one character for a class exhibition. Ideas for the exhibition include a one act play, poetry, tableaux, poster displays, Readers Theatre, character symbols, visual representations, and character enactments.

and Jonas in *The Giver* (Lowry, 1993). We even speculated that students might find the characters from our carefully chosen read-alouds to be most memorable. How could Jeremiah in *If You Come Softly* (Woodson, 1998) or Julie from *Flipped* (Draanen, 2003) not leave a lasting impression with at least some of the students?

Nevertheless, knowing the wide range of interests and abilities of students at this age range, we put aside our expectations and reminded ourselves that students had met many characters in their self-selected and assigned reading, and undoubtedly had discovered memorable characters we had yet to meet.

The Wide Variety of Books and Characters Chosen by Students

Young adolescence is a time marked by distinct physical, social, emotional, and cognitive changes that keep middle school students constantly moving and shifting as they seek to understand themselves and their role in society

(Irvin, 1998). Moreover, this variability in their overall development is reflected in their reading; their book choices cover a wide range, from picturebooks to the classics. This varied pattern holds true in their selection of memorable characters.

Across both campuses, one of the most surprising findings is the great variability in student choices of most memorable characters.

Choices of Students at the First Campus

On the first campus, 127 students nominated 71 different characters as most memorable. Of these 71, only 13 were selected by more than one student, and only 8 were selected by more than three students, indicating how variantly the students had read, how little they agreed on what made a memorable character, or both. No character was nominated by more than 19 readers—and that "most memorable" character was Harry Potter (Rowling, 1998). Harry Potter's popularity was not surprising given the current international attention and films.

The relatively new characters who garnered multiple mentions on the first campus included not only Harry, but also Stanley and Zero of *Holes* (Sachar, 1998), Jamie of *A Walk to Remember* (Sparks, 1999), and David of *A Child Called It* (Pelzer, 1993). The selected characters that seem to have stood the test of time included Brian of *Hatchet* (Paulsen, 1987), Kevin of *Freak the Mighty* (Philbrick, 1993), and Scout of *To Kill a Mockingbird* (Lee, 1960).

The next five most memorable characters (mentioned by at least three students) on the first campus were Sara (*A Little Princess*, Burnett, 1990) Nancy Drew (*The Secret of the Old Clock*, Keene, 1930), Kenny (*The Watsons Go to Birmingham—1963*, Curtis, 1995), Buck (*A Call of the Wild*, London, 1903), and Ron (Harry Potter series, Rowling, 1998–2000).

Choices of Students at the Second Campus

The 97 students surveyed at the second campus chose 65 different characters. Fifteen of these characters were selected by more than one student, but only five characters were selected by more than three students. Again Harry Potter made the "top five" list, this time joined by Steve (*Monster*, Myers, 1999), Nick (*Night Hoops*, Deuker, 2000), Callie (*Cut*, McCormick, 2000), and Matilda (*Fever 1793*, Anderson, 2000). Several of the top characters were from books written by highly regarded authors, such as Walter Dean Myers and Laurie Halse Anderson. Ellie of *If You Come Softly* (Woodson, 1998), and Winnie of *Tuck Everlasting* (Babbitt, 1975) were also two of the top selections.

Why Students Choose Particular Characters

Students considered the reasons for their character selections and responded to two open-ended probes:

1. What do I especially remember about the character?
2. All students in middle school should know _____ (character) because _____.

Students also responded to three probes to explain their choices:

1. I can identify with this memorable character in the following ways...
2. I enjoyed reading about this memorable character because...
3. This character made me think about...

These three probes helped students elaborate and verify their responses to the first two questions.

For the top eight characters selected at the first campus, enjoyment was the primary reason given for the choices, with the exception of David in *A Child Called It*. They were outraged about what happened to David. In contrast, for the top five characters selected at the second campus, students gave three reasons: (1) "identified with," (2) "enjoyed," and (3) "caused me to think about." Overall, more emphasis was placed on characters who both brought enjoyment and made students think.

However, some students in these classes felt they also could relate to the situations or feelings of characters such as Nick of *Night Hoops*, Steve of *Monster*, and Callie of *Cut* (McCormick, 2000).

Attributes of Memorable Characters

To better understand students' choices, we looked at the facets of characterization students mentioned in their responses—both external attributes (e.g., appearance, gender, age, ability, behavior, and actions) and internal attributes (e.g., traits, interests, feelings, values, motives, and relationships).

External Attributes

Approximately half the student responses referenced external features of characters, including their behaviors, actions, and appearance. Looking carefully at the category of behavior and actions, we noted that students nominated characters that are realistic, amusing, admirable, and engaging; for example, characters were considered realistic when their actions and behaviors paralleled the student's own life, as in the following response about Jonas in *The Giver* (Lowry, 1993):

> He always said what was on his mind. He always thought about things. He was always asking about things and [wondering]. I can relate to that. I have to ask questions about things that are questionable.

Students also identified with the problems and situations that the characters experience. We found a few sobering responses from students whose lives mirrored those of the characters; for example, this one from a student who identified with Steve of *Monster*:

> He and I get accused of crimes and stuff we didn't even do. We had a hard time growing up. Steve and I are alike because the way he got in trouble is the same way I get in trouble when I don't even do anything.

Another student noted similarities with Tommy of *Reviving Ophelia: Saving the Selves of Adolescent Girls* (Pipher, 1994):

> Right now I'm thirteen years old and I too have problems like hers and sometimes the only way to relieve myself is to cut myself, but my mom took me to a Ph.D. and I sort of stopped. But unless it's something real extreme I won't do it.

Some students simply enjoyed reading about characters whose actions and behaviors were believable, as illustrated in the following comment about Brian of *Hatchet*:

> I like stories that involve survival. I like how his mind reacts to things and he's human. He a regular kid doing something extraordinary.

Some students liked characters who experience funny moments, such as the time when Deeni, in the book of the same title (Blume, 1991), "kissed a guy, but when she kissed him, his tooth broke." Other amusing characters were Eliza of *Death From the Woods* (Aubert, 2001) who "was funny and the way she cussed in her mind and what she thought of people were funny too." Still other students admired characters who do unusual things, such as Mullet Fingers of *Hoot* (Hiaasen, 2002), a character who "can catch mullet with his hands, keep poisonous snakes, catch gators, and is just all around interesting" and, once again, Brian of *Hatchet* who "is really cool in the way he makes fire and kills birds for food and builds his house."

Another external attribute students noted about characters was appearance. Some students liked characters with unusual or unique appearances, and some liked characters with appearances that reminded them of themselves. One student was enamored with Aquamarine (*Aquamarine*, Hoffman, 2002) and thought that "she is very beautiful with sparkles and stuff. In my head the shine I had pictured on Aquamarine made her be bright in my head and that is what caught my attention." Another student noted that Kenny of *The Watsons Go to Birmingham—1963* "has a lazy eye like me" and that this similarity "made me more interested to see if he was any more like me."

Internal Attributes

In addition to external features, students' responses to characters' internal attributes accounted for over one third of the total responses. Of that one third, the majority of students referenced bravery, intelligence, adventurous spirit, humor, friendliness, devotion, innocence, independence, confidence, and determination. One student admired Scout of *To Kill a Mockingbird*, and felt that Scout had many fine attributes that others should emulate:

> She wasn't afraid to be different than all the other girls her age. She wasn't influenced by what everyone else thought. She was outspoken, brave and tried hard in everything she did. She was not only your "typical tomboy," but somebody who tried hard in things she didn't want to do (for example, be ladylike). She was down-to-earth and tough. She was a leader and influential. She was what all the boys want to be.

Many students selected memorable characters who were especially brave; for example, Harry Potter captured the attention of one student who felt that "his courage is spectacular. He never gives up and he fights for everyone even if they don't like him." Other notably brave characters students chose were drawn from books that differ in genre, time, and the gender of the protagonist; for example, Brian (*Hatchet*), Deeni (*Deeni*), Ariel (*Before the Dawn*, Collins, 2002), and John (*Nightjohn*, Paulsen, 1993).

Julie of *Flipped* made a strong impression on one student, who mentioned that Julie "made me laugh, cry, and enjoy myself. The thing that made me laugh was her personality. The thing that made me cry was her caring for the tree by their bus stop." Another student admired Jamie's fierce determination, independence, and selflessness in *A Walk to Remember*:

> She does what she wants to do. She thinks what she wants to think. Nobody's opinion is important but her own. Her last priority is herself, and she never has time for herself. The kids at school don't know her and they think she's a loser. But the people who take time to know her, love her.

Students also noted characters' feelings in about one fifth of the responses. The majority of the feelings mentioned were negative feelings, such as frustration, fear, stress, anxiety, and sadness. Students wrote that they shared these same negative feelings with the characters; for example, one student shared Sara's frustration in *A Little Princess*, admitting, "I can identify with her because my dad is in the army and sometimes he has to leave for months at a time, and it's also very frustrating." Another student found parallels in Antonia's life in *Define "Normal"* (Peters, 2003) with that of her own:

> We are both trapped and stressed out. We both have annoying siblings, a family life that is nowhere near perfect, and a personality that doesn't exactly fit who we really are. I can also identify with her because we are both overworked perfectionists.

While many students identified with these negative feelings, other students used them as a basis for selecting a memorable character, as did one student who focused on Tara's feelings of fear and distrust in *Kissing Doorknobs* (Hesser, 1999):

> She goes through a stage where she doesn't trust other people and is unsure about other people's thoughts and intentions. She is also afraid of her own mind, life, and fate. It wasn't until she found someone like her that her paranoia ended.

Characters That Make Middle Schoolers Think

Students' most memorable characters made them think. Several themes emerged in their responses, including life lessons, "if I were the character" musings, self-reflections, personal connections, and thoughts about character situations and issues. Some students said a character reminded them of the important things in life, such as "standing up for what you know is right" as modeled by Perloo in *Perloo the Bold* (Avi, 1999). Other excerpts representative of students' thoughts about characters and life lessons include the following.

> About Jamie of *A Walk to Remember*:
> You have to make the most of life. She barely had time to live and she still put others before her. If you want to do something, do it yourself, don't let other people do it for you.

> About John of *Nightjohn*:
> How cruel people were to the slaves and how we have to be brave and step up to the plate.

Some students took the "if I were the character" stance and thought about their reactions to the characters' situations; for example, one student thought about Harry Potter and "how cool it would be to be a wizard and have magical powers. Also play a game on a broomstick flying 50 feet in the air. He made me think how cool it would be to live in a castle." Another student mused over what it would be like to be Brian of *Hatchet*: "He made me think about what I would do if I were in the situation. Also I began to plan it out just in case it did happen." This stance demonstrates the power characters have to entice students to step into a story world and engage in vicarious experiences.

Other characters made students reflect about their own lives and connect to people in their lives. One student was grateful for kind parents after reading about Dave in *A Child Called It*: "How lucky I am to have nice parents that treat me well. He also made me think about how cruel some people can be." Surprisingly, another student said that Piglet of *Winnie-the-Pooh* (Milne, 1926/1994) reminded her of herself: "He is just like me. I would let people walk all over me and I never did anything about it. I would never stand up for myself." Other responses along similar lines included the following.

> About Scout of *To Kill a Mockingbird*:
> How I need to live life to the fullest and have fun. I just need to be myself and not worry about pleasing others.

> About Shawn of *Stuck in Neutral* (Trueman, 2000):
> He made me think that how lucky I am to be healthy and how important it is to have a good time in your life and spend it wisely.

Some characters made students ponder about global issues and life situations, such as Charlie in the classic *Flowers for Algernon* (Keyes, 1995): "Charlie made me think about how our society treats the mentally challenged...one of the major problems in society. He made me stop and think if an operation would actually cure mental disabilities." Antonio of *Home of the Braves* (Klass, 2002) made one student think about "how hard it would be to move from a foreign country like Brazil, be on the Brazilian National Team, then be on a horrible soccer team and then move to Barcelona." Jonas of *The Giver* spurred another student to become philosophical about life and to ask deep questions:

> What is the meaning of life? How does it work? Are we supposed to know what to do with our lives? How does life work? Jonas made me think about all of that when he discovered about the ways of his town.

Choosing Characters for Your Own Classroom

The characters you allow in your classroom can have an important impact on your students. According to the students surveyed, some characters become a special part of students' lives and serve as mirrors for self-identification. Characters provide vicarious moments of pure enjoyment, but also offer opportunities for serious reflection.

Students want to read about realistic characters whose problems and life situations mirror their own. They also want the comfort of reading about characters in more extreme and dire circumstances that are not part of their own lives. Books with realistic characters include *Cheating Lessons* (Cappo, 2002), in which the main character faces a dilemma when she finds out that a teacher cheated to get students qualified for a quiz bowl, and *A Corner of the Universe* (Martin, 2002), in which Hattie suddenly finds out she has a mentally disabled uncle and must deal with the changes his presence brings.

Students also like to read about admirable characters who exhibit behaviors and traits worth emulating; for example, the courage and determination of Crispin in *Crispin: The Cross of Lead* (Avi, 2002) and the thoughtfulness and caring exhibited by Eric in *Staying Fat for Sarah Byrnes* (Crutcher, 1993).

The antics of humorous characters also draw students in. They easily chuckle when reading about Vince Luca's disgust for his father's "business" in *Son of the Mob* (Korman, 2002) and laugh out loud over Bryce's ignorance about chickens in *Flipped*.

It is important to honor student choice of books and provide a library stocked with books that have many varied and interesting characters—not only recently published young adult books, but also timeless classics that are sometimes overlooked. Middle school students need opportunities to meet a wide range of characters of their own choosing.

Memorable characters punctuate the lives of students with questions and wonderings, thrilling and electrifying moments, and even empty spaces for students to fill. Some characters cause students to ponder their reactions and feelings in situations, as does Jonas in *The Giver*. Other characters pepper students' lives with insights and exclamations, such as Scout in *To Kill a Mockingbird* and Ron, Hermione, and Harry in the Harry Potter series. Still other characters, such as Steve in *Monster*, allow students to muse over issues of guilt or innocence. Such characters need to reside in middle school classes so that students can become acquainted with them, and decide for themselves which are truly worth remembering.

REFERENCES

Hipple, T. (1992). The universality of the young adult novel. In V.R. Monseau & G.M. Salver (Eds.), *Reading their world: The young adult novel in the classroom* (pp. 3–16). Portsmouth, NH: Heinemann.

Irvin, J.L. (1998). *Reading and the middle school student: Strategies to enhance literacy.* (2nd ed.). Boston: Allyn & Bacon.

Langer, J.A. (1995). *Envisioning literature: Literary understanding and literature instruction.* Newark, DE: International Reading Association; New York: Teachers College Press.

Martinez, M., & Roser, N. (2003). Children's responses to literature. In J. Flood, D. Lapp, J.R. Squire, & J.M. Jensen (Eds.), *Handbook of research on teaching the English language arts* (2nd ed., pp. 799–813). Mahwah, NJ: Erlbaum.

LITERATURE CITED

Anderson, L.H. (2000). *Fever 1793.* New York: Simon & Schuster.

Aubert, B. (2001). *Death from the woods.* London: Hodder & Stoughton.

Avi. (1999). *Perloo the bold.* New York: Scholastic.

Avi. (2002). *Crispin: The cross of lead.* New York: Hyperion.

Babbitt, N. (1975). *Tuck Everlasting.* New York: Farrar Straus Giroux.

Blume, J. (1991). *Deeni.* New York: Laurel Leaf.

Burnett, F.H. (1990). *A little princess.* New York: Signet Classic.

Cappo, N.W. (2002). *Cheating lessons.* New York: Simon Pulse.

Collins, M.A. (2002). *Before the dawn* (Dark Angel #1). New York: Del Rey.

Crutcher, C. (1993). *Staying fat for Sarah Byrnes.* New York: Bantam Doubleday Dell.

Curtis, C.P. (1995). *The Watsons go to Birmingham—1963.* New York: Delacorte.

Deuker, C. (2000). *Night hoops.* Boston: Houghton Mifflin.

Draanen, W. (2003). *Flipped.* New York: Knopf.

Hesser, T.S. (1999). *Kissing doorknobs.* New York: Laurel Leaf Books.

Hiaasen, C. (2002). *Hoot.* New York: Knopf.

Hoffman, A. (2002). *Aquamarine.* New York: Scholastic.

Keene, C. (1930). *The secret of the old clock.* New York: Grosset & Dunlap.

Keyes, D. (1995). *Flowers for Algernon.* San Diego, CA: Harcourt Brace.

Klass, D. (2002). *Home of the braves.* New York: Frances Foster.

Korman, G. (2002). *Son of the mob.* New York: Hyperion.

Lee, H. (1960). *To kill a mockingbird.* Philadelphia: Lippincott.

London, J. (1903). *A call of the wild.* New York: Macmillan.

Lowry, L. (1993). *The giver.* New York: Bantam.

Martin, A.M. (2002). *A corner of the universe.* New York: Scholastic.

McCormick, P. (2000). *Cut.* Asheville, NC: Front Street.

Milne, A.A. (1994). *Winnie-the-Pooh.* New York: Dutton. (Original work published 1926)

Myers, W.D. (1999). *Monster.* New York: HarperCollins.

Paulsen, G. (1987). *Hatchet.* New York: Bradbury.

Paulsen, G. (1993). *Nightjohn.* New York: Delacorte.

Pelzer, D.J. (1993). *A child called it.* Omaha, NE: Omaha Press.

Peters, J. (2003). *Define "normal."* Boston: Little, Brown.

Philbrick, R. (1993). *Freak the mighty.* New York: Blue Sky Press.

Pipher, M. (1994). *Reviving Ophelia: Saving the selves of adolescent girls.* New York: Putnam.

Rowling, J.K. (1998). *Harry Potter and the sorcerer's stone.* New York: Arthur A. Levine.

Rowling, J.K. (1999). *Harry Potter and the chamber of secrets.* New York: Arthur A. Levine.

Rowling, J.K. (1999). *Harry Potter and the prisoner of Azkaban.* New York: Arthur A. Levine.

Rowling, J.K. (2000). *Harry Potter and the goblet of fire.* New York: Arthur A. Levine.

Sachar, L. (1998). *Holes.* New York: Farrar Straus Giroux.

Sparks, N. (1999). *A walk to remember.* New York: Warner Books.

Trueman, T. (2000). *Stuck in neutral.* New York: HarperCollins.

Woodson, J. (1998). *If you come softly.* New York: Putnam.

Part V

Character
Redux

18

Toward a Theory of Character in Children's Fiction

Maria Nikolajeva

Maria Nikolajeva challenges educators to move toward
a theoretical understanding of character in traditional
and contemporary children's literature. Her central
tenet is to consider characters less as real people
captured on paper and more as an author's purposeful
design. In classroom book talk aligned with this
position, students may consider how and why
characters play out their roles in the ways they do.

Why should teachers have a "theory" of
characters in children's literature? It is not enough to
answer, "because we haven't had one to date," or
"because there is nothing that supports teaching like
a good theory." Nikolajeva, Professor of Comparative
Literature at Stockholm University in Sweden, has
answered the question like this: A theory of character
is necessary because it undergirds how teachers
approach and interpret literature. She claims that
teachers have had two mantras—two standby
questions—that they use when reading fiction with

What a Character! Character Study as a Guide to Literary Meaning Making in Grades K–8 edited by
Nancy L. Roser and Miriam G. Martinez, with Junko Yokota and Sharon O'Neal. Copyright 2005
by the International Reading Association.

students: "Who is the main character?" and "With which character do you identify?" (The latter question is reshaped for young readers by asking, "Who would you most like to be friends with?") Neither of these questions moves students to the core of literature.

This scholarly and thoughtful work gives weight to the notions, roots to the intuitions, and depth to the probes of this book. Read this chapter not as a roadmap or recipe, but rather as a philosophical and historical treatise. Consider how your own theory of character (understanding and teaching) is affected or made clearer by your growing realization of the creation, roles, purposes, and interpretation of character in children's books over time.

THEORETICAL APPROACHES TO LITERARY CHARACTERS have oscillated between two extremes: characters as mere agents in the plot and characters as complete psychological beings (Chatman, 1978). Subsequently, the central question in discussion of literary characters is whether they should be perceived and analyzed as real, living people or as purely textual constructions. Rimmon-Kenan (1983) has described this polarity as mimetic versus semiotic. Mimetic comes from the word mimesis, which means imitation. Semiotics is a theory of sign, or using signs—including words, pictures, gestures, and sounds—to think and communicate. A mimetic view of character, then, is based on fiction as a direct reflection of reality. A semiotic approach presupposes that, like all other text elements, characters are verbal signs, made of words alone, and have no referents in the real world. A mimetic approach treats characters as individuals, while a semiotic approach treats them as linguistic entities.

A Mimetic Approach

Let's consider the relevance of the two approaches for children's literature. Mimetic characters allow and sometimes require that we go outside the text and construct the character from our own experiences. We can try to explain character behaviors by considering social origin, ethnicity, gender, culture, and upbringing (about which we may or may not glean anything from the text). In children's novels, we also expect child characters to behave consistently with what we know (from child psychology) about their cognitive level, emotional (in)stability, and so on.

The danger of the mimetic approach to characters is that we can easily ascribe features that the author had no intention of providing, and we may even apply stereotypes, such as "girls always like gossip," "boys are naughty," "school teachers are insensitive," and so on. We can further ascribe to characters backgrounds not found in the text, merely on the basis of our own experience. Driven to the absurd, this approach results in the type of questions ridiculed in the famous essay title "How Many Children Had Lady Macbeth?" (Knights, 1965). In children's literature, similar absurdities would be considering how Tom Sawyer (Twain, 1876/1987) has been affected by measles, or whether Heidi (Spyri, 1884/1995) was nursed by a wet nurse. It is sometimes *too* easy to speculate about characters; for example, claiming that a character is evil because his mother was unkind to him, or that parent characters are neglectful of their children (when the "neglect" is essential to the child characters' freedom to explore the world on their own).

Literary characters do not necessarily have to behave the way real people do; they do not necessarily have to follow prescribed behavior patterns or the expected course of development or disturbance. Let me give an example. How shall we judge Edmund's behavior in *The Lion, the Witch and the Wardrobe* (Lewis, 1950/1994)? Perhaps as a way of excusing Edmund's choice of the wrong side in the battle of good and evil, C.S. Lewis gives us some hints about Edmund's having attended the wrong kind of school. If we approach this text with a mimetic perspective, we might speculate about Edmund's being a middle child, perhaps neglected in favor of his older and younger siblings. We may think of dozens of reasons why Edmund needs to take revenge. We could hypothesize that he is suffering from separation trauma, or from extensive fear of air raids since the children have been evacuated from war-threatened London. We could interpret his falling for the White Witch's charms as an indication of his dependence on his mother, and his immediate dislike of Aslan as a prime case of Oedipus complex. We could discuss his personality from different angles, dwelling on a child's natural vanity and desire for attention, or even on the effects of poor nutrition at his boarding school. Yet, in doing all this, we would be stepping outside the text—and applying our knowledge of human nature, of child psychology, of British history, social culture, and more.

A Semiotic Approach

On the other hand, we may simply state that the plot of *The Lion, the Witch and the Wardrobe* demands a traitor, and that Edmund's behavior is not motivated by his psychological properties, but exclusively by the textual conditions. This would be an example of a semiotic, or nonmimetic interpretation. Naturally, we should remember that literary characters are, by definition, more semiotic than real people are, because they are part of a design or a creation. If we assume that characters are textual constructions (semiotic entities), we must then extract the essential traits of the characters exclusively from their words and actions. Further, we can argue that because characters have no existence outside the text, if nothing is said about a character's background, then this background never existed. A semiotic approach mandates that if the text offers nothing about Edmund's parents, we have no reason to speculate about his relationship with them.

Hochman (1985) argues that a single theoretical approach to character is not possible, since authors' attitudes toward characters have changed throughout history, just as views on human beings have changed. I find this observation especially relevant for children's literature, because the changing views on childhood affect the way characters are presented.

Changing Views of Character Across Time

It is commonly believed that young readers, compared with adult readers, are more interested in plot than in characters. Certainly, early children's books imitated traditional folk narratives that are unmistakably plot oriented, and explored the flat, static characters only as a way to clarify the moral(s) of the story. The first adaptations of adult fiction into children's stories (e.g., *Robinson Crusoe*, Defoe, 1719/1983; *Gulliver's Travels*, Swift, 1726/2003) usually cut away most of the character development and focused instead on the plot.

Even today, the vast majority of children's books are plot oriented. This includes both formulaic fiction and novels of quality. Aristotle (1997) argues that characters are subordinate to the plot, and their function in a literary work is merely to perform actions. In other words, Aristotle maintains that agents are indispensable to a literary work, while psychological characters are optional. This distinction, primitive as it may seem to theorists today, is reflected in traditional children's fiction, in which characters' actions are more important than their psychological traits.

Like Aristotle, 20th-century formalist and structural theorists—who focused on the form and structure of literary text rather than its content—view characters merely as agents who perform certain actions and therefore have no psychological features. They contend that characters have certain fixed roles; for example, Vladimir Propp (1928/1968) identifies seven such roles in tales of magic: hero, false hero, quest object, dispatcher, donor, helper, and villain. Since children's literature historically grew out of folklore, most of these roles are found in classic children's fiction. In *The Lion, the Witch and the Wardrobe*, the four children are a collective hero (possibly with Edmund as the false hero), the White Witch is the villain, Aslan is the dispatcher, the Beavers are the helpers, Father Christmas is a donor, while summer and peace in Narnia are the achieved object of the quest. Similarly, in *The Adventures of Tom Sawyer* (Twain, 1876/1987), Tom is the hero, Injun Joe the villain, Huck Finn his helper, Becky the "princess" to be rescued, and so on.

Because formal and structural models describe characters in relation to plot, and only superficially in relation to one another, these models do not allow deep analysis of the characters' traits or inner life. Such models have been successfully applied both to folk tales and formulaic fiction (criminal novels, mystery, adventure, horror, romance), but, as Chatman correctly notes (1978), formal approaches are seldom applied to contemporary psychological novels because the critics and readers of such novels are interested in *why* characters behave the way they do. When Chatman claims (1978, p. 131) that formalist theory of character is "inadequate," he presumably means that it is inadequate for analyzing complex contemporary characters in character-oriented narratives.

Todorov (1977) makes a fundamental distinction between plot-oriented and character-oriented narratives. I find this distinction crucial for any further discussion of character in children's fiction. It is meaningless to analyze Dorothy in *The Wonderful Wizard of Oz* (Baum, 1900/2001) in psychological terms, because she only has one feature: she is good; and only one quest: to return home (the plot objective). The formal model is more than adequate to describe the characters in *The Wonderful Wizard of Oz*. However, there has been a notable shift in Western children's fiction, beginning in the 1960s, to psychological novels that reflect a profound interest in character. It is, therefore, pointless to apply Propp's aforementioned seven character roles to *Bridge to Terabithia* (Paterson, 1977) or to *The Planet of Junior Brown* (Hamilton, 1971). The shift to psychological fiction has resulted in a tendency to evaluate the literary quality of all contemporary children's fiction by characterization rather than by plot.

Character-Oriented Perspectives

Henry James (1884/1972) rejects the division of fiction into plot-oriented novels and novels of character. He points instead to the interconnection of character and action: "What is character but the determination of incident? What is incident but the illustration of character?" (p. 37). Despite this assertion of balance, James pays substantially more attention to character than to any other aspect of text. Character is for James the focus of fiction, and all other elements of the text, such as plot, setting, subject, and style, are subordinate to character. Moreover, in his assessment of plot and action, James gives priority to internal events and actions, which are by definition character-bound; his own novels are the best illustrations of this principle. Further, James distinguishes between characters—fully developed psycho logical beings—and figures, or types, which may illustrate actions or situations, but are not as artistically sophisticated as characters. For him, the psychological dimensions of literary characters are the foremost criteria of merit, and characters lacking psychological depth are artistic failures.

Consistent with James's view, Bradley's (1904/1993) treatment of characters in Shakespeare's plays is as if they are living people. He assembles their personalities from psychological traits that are partly explicit in the texts, partly implicit, and partly determined by readers' understandings of human nature. Bradley ascribes characters a high degree of motivation, which lies beneath their actions and reactions. He also ascribes them moral qualities based on their actions, seeking a psychological explanation for those actions.

Author-Oriented Theories

The tradition originated from Romanticism regards the literary text, including characters, as the expression of the author's mind (e.g., Abrams, 1953). The biographical approach to fiction, dominant in literary criticism during the 19th century, views characters as mouthpieces, the bearers of authors' ideas. This approach is seldom discussed in contemporary criticism, perhaps because it is considered obsolete. It has, however, been revived in two radically different theoretical directions: the psychoanalytical and the sociohistorical.

A psychoanalytically oriented biographer views characters as projections of the author's psyche and treats characters' problems as direct reflections of the author's problems. It is fairly common to search for the origins of famous characters of children's literature, such as Peter in *Peter Pan* (Barrie, 1906/1991) and the prince in *The Little Prince* (de Saint-Exupéry, 1943/2000), in their authors' childhood traumas (e.g., Rose, 1984; von Franz, 1981; Wullschläger, 1995). Even though viewing authors' literary work as confessional testimony may throw some light on them, parallels between text and authors' lives do not add significantly to the understanding of their characters. Even so, this approach should certainly not be neglected in an overview of theories.

Another author-oriented approach, which can be labeled ideological, has resulted in considerably more solid theoretical stances. Its foremost proponent is Mikhail Bakhtin (1990), who, in his essay "Author and Hero in Aesthetic Activity," introduces some major notions about literary characters serving as authors' mouthpieces. For Bakhtin, characters are deliberately constructed by the author to express views, and therefore, may have little to do with human nature or psychology. Although Bakhtin was by no means a Marxist, his position is not far from the Marxist notion of characters as bearers of the ideology of their social class, or the feminist views of characters as bearers of the ideology of their gender. This may seem to have little to do with children's literature, but it is important to note the parallels with critics who view children's books exclusively as educational and ideological vehicles—and their characters, therefore, as bearers of "right" or "wrong" values.

In traditional children's literature, adults provide young readers with clear-cut morals and characters that function as mouthpieces for the author's didactic views. One of the best examples is the cricket in *Pinocchio* (Collodi, 1891/1988), treated in criticism as the voice of conscience (see Zipes, 1997).

Reader Response Perspectives

Contrary to author-oriented theories, reader response criticism presupposes that the reader constructs the character, alongside all other elements of the text. Hochman (1985) claims that the impact on the reader is the most essential function of the character. There is, however, little in reader response criticism that is focused specifically on character, so its approach to character is largely an inferred one. Chatman (1978) speaks repeatedly about characters being assembled and interpreted by the audience; Hochman (1985) describes readers "retrieving" characters from texts, arguing that readers relate the information they get about characters partly to their life experience, and partly to their previous reading. In this respect, each individual reader's previous experience is decisive for the interpretation of character. Iser's (1974) notion of textual gaps suggests that the text may deliberately leave certain character traits unspecified to be filled in by the reader, and further, that each reader fills these gaps differently.

IMPLIED READERS. Eco (1979) and Culler (1975), as compared with Iser, believe authors construct an implied reader and then use inherent features of the text to guide (or manipulate) the reader to adopt certain interpretations. In children's fiction, such guidance or manipulation is generally stronger than in adult literature. A children's book author, for example, may be more explicit about character traits, behaviors, and motivation than authors who are writing for adults; therefore, the construction of the implied reader is more conscious and deliberate for a children's book author. This makes reader response theory (in some respects) more pertinent to children's fiction. I venture that young readers feel stronger empathy with literary characters than do adults, and that children's book authors appeal to their readers' feelings in more immediate ways.

For children's fiction, it may be necessary to identify specific types of implied readers—and examine how they "retrieve" characters differently. The primary audience of children's literature is children, and the secondary audience is the adult mediators. A children's book does not necessarily have adults as its implied coreader; the demands adults put on characters in terms of unity, consistency, or complexity are not relevant for the child reader.

The implied reader also may be sophisticated or unsophisticated (or competent/incompetent in Eco's terms). An unsophisticated reader, following the plot and focusing on events, will perhaps miss most of the clues given in texts concerning the personality of the characters and may not find them important—at least in an initial read. Eco (1979) states that understanding characters is part of literary competence, and a competent reader will know how to retrieve a complex character from features presented in the text.

There also is a difference between readers across time and space, or, in Jauss's (1982) terms, a shift in horizon of expectations. Mark Twain's or Louisa M. Alcott's contemporaries understood their characters differently than we do today. There have been changes in expectations and values, reevaluations of gender and race, and changes in the current interpretive communities (Fish, 1982). Similarly, Swedish readers understand Twain and Alcott differently than American readers. Each interpretive community will have a slightly different understanding of characters in any given novel depending on its historical and cultural context.

THE IMPLAUSIBILITY OF SELF-REFLEXIVE CHILD CHARACTERS. The drive to reduce characters to the level of purely textual constructions is a natural consequence of the development of contemporary mainstream fiction. American New Criticism (as represented by Booth, 1961) has been especially hard on character. Postmodern and poststructuralist views of literature and art have taken the defamation of character further still. These views question the stability and unity of the individual, thus claiming that literary characters as psychological entities are impossible and unnecessary.

The self-reflexivity of contemporary characters in mainstream adult literature can never become a prominent feature of children's fiction, because a self-reflexive child character would, in most cases, be psychologically implausible. This does not indicate that children's literature is lagging behind, but rather that it runs parallel to the mainstream. In offering a theory of characters in children's fiction, we cannot directly apply models available in the mainstream criticism, because the objects themselves present a significant difference. There are, however, valuable tools offered by each of the theories that can be adapted to analyze characters in children's fiction.

Using Mimetic and Semiotic Approaches

Although I definitely lean toward the semiotic end of the spectrum, I agree with Chatman (1978) when he states that a reasonable approach is something between the two polarities (i.e., mimetic and semiotic). However, I do not share Chatman's desire to reconcile the two views; they are fundamentally incompatible. A mimetic approach inevitably results in treating characters as psychological entities, while a semiotic approach suggests characters are textual constructions. In certain types of narrative, characters are more prominent, and thus more psychologically motivated, while in others they are subordinated to actions and therefore reduced to elements of plot design.

The view of character depends on the actual reader's sophistication. An unsophisticated reader may follow the plot of *The Golden Compass* (Pullman, 1996) or *Bridge to Terabithia* (Paterson, 1977) without paying attention to the psychological subtleties of the characters; a sophisticated reader will, in the same texts, concentrate on the characters and put high demands on their mimetic qualities. Neither view is "better" or more correct, and the concepts of mimetic and semiotic interpretations of characters should not be perceived as evaluative.

In children's literature scholarship, a long-enduring bias toward mimetic interpretations of characters calls for special scrutiny of its concepts. Literary characters are indeed constructions—fictitious figures rather than actual human beings. They have no will of their own, and do not have to behave consistently. It is therefore advisable to avoid analyzing them as if they are human beings, claiming for instance, "He does this because he wants...." Instead, the question could be posed as to why the writer has chosen to have the character act in a certain way—even though the writer may have successfully created a psychologically plausible character.

Unsophisticated readers tend to concentrate on plot rather than character. A great number of children's literature critics question contemporary children's novels on the basis of their "lack of plot" and their focus on characters and relationships. At the same time, formulaic fiction has been accused of deficiency in characterization, and subsequently in artistic merit, without acknowledging the textuality of characters as part of the genre specifics. These common attitudes call for a deeper understanding of the function of character in a narrative.

The Ontological Status of Fictive Characters

E.M. Forster (1927/1985) argues that, in real life, people have remarkably limited possibilities for knowing anything about others and their backgrounds, thoughts, and feelings unless they are told. Conversely, in literature, people are frequently allowed to learn everything about a character (Homo fictus versus Homo sapiens), right down to the tiniest detail.

Hochman (1985, p. 59) develops Forster's statements, noting that in order to "retrieve" characters from texts, readers connect them to their experiences of real people; yet real people and literary figures are not identical in their ontology (theory of existence). Hochman does not reject Forster's views, but corrects them slightly. Because literary characters do not exist, readers cannot interact with them physically or mentally, or interfere with their actions. We cannot stop Othello from strangling Desdemona. We cannot warn Jess in *Bridge to Terabithia* against going to the Smithsonian with his teacher when we sense that something will happen to Leslie in his absence.

Literary characters are written once and for all. They have no background other than that provided by the text. However, unlike real life, literature provides all the relevant information about characters, and authors arrange this information into coherence. We may not know everything about a given character, but we know all we need to know. We make constructs on the basis of limited information, just as we do with real people. Yet, real people are opaque, whereas literary characters are transparent. Characters are also more structured than real people. They have motives and values. They are connected to the overall structure of the text within which they appear. In fiction, only central characters are complex and coherent, while peripheral characters seldom show any complexity. In real life, all people are presumably equally coherent. Yet we certainly know more about the people in real life who are closest to us (central), while peripheral characters in our lives may seem quite one-dimensional. Literature, in this respect, is like life.

The ontological status of characters, that is, the reader's understanding of their relationship to reality, presents some specific challenges in children's fiction because characters act within nonmimetic modes considerably more often than in the mainstream. As often as not, characters in children's fiction are animals (or even inanimate objects) rather than human beings. Even when they are human beings, they may appear in fantastic settings and situations that eliminate the need for background information. When reading about human characters, readers fill the gaps in the characters' backgrounds with their own previous experiences. They assume that they once had parents, that they were born and then grew to their present state, and so on.

In a fantasy such as *Winnie-the-Pooh* (Milne, 1926/1994), the need for background is eliminated by the premises of the narrative. The characters have no background, even though Piglet claims to have a grandfather called Trespassers W., and Owl claims to have an Uncle Robert, whose portrait he has on the wall. However, the toys have no past. We do not know and cannot know anything about the characters apart from what we read in the text. When first Kanga and Baby Roo, and later Tigger "arrive" in the forest, we do not ask where they come from and what they were doing before. On a metafictive level, we may assume that the boy, Christopher Robin, gets new toys for his birthday or for Christmas. In the fictive world of the forest, they simply "arrive" and the boy–ruler dismisses the question posed by his subjects, just as an insensitive parent may dismiss a question from a child about the "arrival" of a new sibling.

Character Background

There seem to be differences among genres in providing character background. In adventure stories, the background is often of no importance. Thus, we know that Tom Sawyer is an orphan, brought up by his mother's sister, and also that Sid is his younger half-brother. However, we do not know anything about Tom's parents. Tom does not seem to have any memory of them or feel grief. How long have they been dead? Did Tom and Sid have the same mother and different fathers, or did Tom's mother die in childbirth? If Tom's father remarried, what happened to his second wife? Has the father left the family to seek his fortune elsewhere, like Huck Finn's? These questions (cf. "How Many Children Had Lady Macbeth?") are ultimately insignificant because the parents have no function in the plot other than being absent, and since the novel is plot-oriented, the main character is not burdened by identity crises arising from his orphaned status. On the contrary, in a predominantly character-oriented domestic novel, for instance, *Heidi* (Spyri, 1884/1995) or *Anne of Green Gables* (Montgomery, 1908/1982), the background of the protagonist is carefully accounted for, because it is essential for character's quest for self.

Based on real-life experiences, readers build on assumptions while constructing the complex portraits of literary characters: They were born, had a childhood, attended school, can be injured, cannot fly, need food and sleep, and are mortal. These assumptions represent the "default value"; in order to assume anything else, the readers must be informed. To these assumptions, the readers must also add their knowledge of the social and historical backgrounds that may have shaped the characters' personalities. Any unusual experience necessary to understand characters' present position or state of mind has to be presented in the narrative, explicitly or implicitly; everything else is fruitless speculation. We cannot claim Tom Sawyer is naughty because his father was an alcoholic or his mother had unchaste habits.

From Opaque to Transparent

Several critics, following Forster's ideas, argue that literature allows us to gain an intrinsic knowledge of other people, while in real life we only have intrinsic knowledge of ourselves and extrinsic knowledge of other people. While real people are always opaque, literary characters may be presented in a vast continuum from opacity to full transparency. For Forster and many other scholars, this is the main attraction of fiction. The ways readers come to know and understand characters represent epistemological questions (questions regarding experience and knowledge).

Historical and Social Context

Hochman (1985) emphasizes the importance of historical and social context in the understanding of character. This is extremely important in children's literature because young readers may not be aware of the change in values over time; for instance, child abandonment and abuse were once acceptable acts in children's literature, but not today. Readers cannot judge a parent beating his children in a Victorian novel by the same measure used to judge a contemporary parent. The societal norms encoded in such adjectives as *nice, virtuous, well-mannered,* and even *pretty* differ considerably over time and from culture to culture. However, readers do not always have the knowledge of exactly what these qualities denoted in their time. Young readers, lacking such knowledge, can fall victim to racist, sexist, and other types of prejudice through characters.

Character Traits

What is the minimal amount of information needed about a literary character? As compared with real people, literary characters are always incomplete. What number of words is sufficient for a reader to construct a personality? A name alone might be enough. Indeed, many peripheral characters in literature are little more than a name. (In a central character, readers certainly expect more than a name.) On the other hand, a name is not in itself necessary to understand and relate to a character. A first-person narrator may omit his or her name, remaining anonymous throughout the novel, and yet be revealed as a complex character. This is less typical in children's fiction because names have a strong connection with identity, and it is therefore believed that young readers need a name to associate with the character.

Age, gender, and race may be minimal requirements to know a character. Readers assume that characters have an age, even though age is not necessarily revealed explicitly. Readers determine the age of characters from their social position, their childhood memories, their reading or music tastes, and so on. Further, if a character has parents and grandparents alive, we assume that he is young; if she has children and grandchildren, we assume that she is old. In children's literature, the scope of a character's age is limited by the concept of childhood as such: By "child" we normally mean an individual up to age 11 or 12 years.

Characters also have gender, if only revealed by the pronouns *he* or *she.* Theoretically, however, it is possible to manipulate a text so that the character's gender is not disclosed. In combination with gender-neutral names, this device allows the character's gender to remain ambivalent, especially in a first-person narrative.

Race may not be mentioned in a text but can be inferred from the plot, setting, and other textual elements. In such novels as *Roll of Thunder, Hear*

My Cry (Taylor, 1976) and *The Planet of Junior Brown* (Hamilton, 1971), the characters' race is essential to understand both the events and the situation; however, the characters are not specifically presented to the reader as people of color. Often, if a character's race is not mentioned, readers may judge it by some "default value."

Aristotle (1997) claimed that characters should only possess one of two traits: noble and base. In many cases this is also true about characters in children's fiction: They can be easily divided into "good guys" and "bad guys." The traits of noble or base—good or bad—are revealed primarily through character actions. Adopting the protagonists' views, readers perceive all actions geared toward their ascent as noble, while all actions bringing about their descent or destruction as base. Readers do not speculate about the villain's motivation for being mean, since being mean is the only trait a villain can have. Readers also have a repertoire of actions that they inherently evaluate as noble or base. Helping other people is noble; stealing, cheating, lying, and killing are base. (However, these values are not absolute; in fact, in Greek tragedies, even heroes engage in stealing, cheating, and killing.)

In psychological novels, readers expect characters to have traits other than merely good and bad. Even so, readers expect the traits to add to a consistent whole. These traits may not necessarily be revealed all at once, nor are they all necessarily revealed by the same means, such as through actions. Readers get to know literary characters successively—from a number of incidents—in a way similar to getting to know real people; there is, however, a profound difference. Because literary characters are created by writers, contradictory information may be given through various characterization devices; for instance, a character's self-evaluation may contradict another character's opinion, or even the narrator's overt comments. Writers may choose to omit essential information or withhold it until later. In fact, readers are rarely interested in all properties of a character. Instead, they ask what "knowing" is sufficient to understand a character in a particular text. In children's literature, this question is especially relevant; young readers may misjudge characters or fail to assemble a number of traits into a whole.

Characterization Devices

How is information about characters revealed? Chatman (1978) suggests that readers register every trait they encounter in a character and add them up into what he calls a "trait paradigm" (pp. 126–188). Every new trait may slightly or substantially change the perception of a character. Compare the combination, *brave + clever* to *brave + stupid*. The second example probably equals *reckless*. Likewise, the value of *generous* changes in the combinations *rich + generous* and *poor + generous*. The combination *brave + clever + generous* almost adds up to *perfect*. These are, of course, primitive examples, because even in very simple stories, characterization is usually significantly more complex, but the examples illustrate Chatman's trait paradigm.

By contrast, Rimmon-Kenan (1983) suggests the idea of a network of traits, indicating that a character is not made out of a sum of traits but of a complex system of interactions. If Chatman's paradigm is a list, then Rimmon-Kenan's network is a three-dimensional geometric. Rimmon-Kenan distinguishes between direct definition (by which she means narrative statements, such as "She was stupid.") and indirect presentation (including actions, speech, external appearance, environment, and analogy).

Authors use a broad spectrum of characterization devices in fiction. Description and narration are two devices in which characters are the most opaque. Readers become acquainted with characters more or less in the same manner that they become acquainted with real people, seeing their external appearances and hearing somebody's direct judgment of them.

In characterization by actions and reactions, characters are still relatively opaque; however, readers are sometimes allowed to follow them through events and situations that would be impossible with real people (e.g., accompanying a character on a lonely and dangerous journey or witnessing private acts).

Characterization by speech brings us closer to characters' inner worlds, especially if we assume that they are sincere in what they say. Internal representation, that is, portrayal of inner life, makes characters completely transparent in a way no real person can ever be, not even someone we know intimately.

Character Interaction With Plot

Because conventional children's literature is plot-oriented, characters are essentially revealed through their involvement in the plot. Most plots in children's fiction are indeed constructed in the traditional manner: with a beginning, a middle, and an end. A standard plot begins with an exposition in which characters and setting are introduced. A vast number of children's novels open with the characters' physical dislocation, so that the characters are presented not in their usual surroundings, but in alien ones—sometimes idyllic, sometimes threatening, sometimes undetermined—allowing the reader to guess whether the new situation is benevolent or not. Other children's novels introduce protagonists in their normal environments, into which an unusual element is brought—whether exciting or dangerous. The characters' reactions to their changed situation is an excellent way to expose their most prominent traits.

In any case, some change in the character's situation is essential to set the plot in motion. However, unlike adult protagonists, child characters seldom, if ever, can decide their fate themselves. They do not choose to leave home, but are forced to do so by the adults; for instance, Heidi is first taken to live with her grandfather in the mountains, then ruthlessly and without warning snatched away and placed in a family of complete strangers. Similarly, Tom in *Tom's Midnight Garden* (Pearce, 1958/1987) is sent away to stay with his relatives, despite his violent protests. Some young characters do run away from home; however, this is nearly always provoked by some action on an adult's part, as in *The Adventures of Huckleberry Finn* (Twain, 1884/2003).

In most stories, children's and adults' alike, characters are introduced at the moment of crisis, that is, in extreme situations, dislocated, exposed to dangers or emotional disturbances, in which they are forced to act heroically. The crisis brings about loss of innocence, resulting in knowledge, insight, and maturity. Character traits are revealed prominently under such conditions; therefore, it is natural for authors to portray characters in out-of-the-ordinary settings (see Nikolajeva, 2002, pp. 198–222). When some children's books are accused of having "unbelievable plots," it is a consequence of overall mimetic attitude to literature.

Resolution

After the character has been taken through complications in a rising action that reaches the climax point, a resolution (or falling action) follows. Resolution does not imply the solution of the conflict; it is merely the part of the plot following the climax (the culmination or turning point of the plot). The character's participation in the resolution allows a good deal of characterization. The final pages of *The Lion, the Witch and the Wardrobe*, which describes the children's happy rule as the kings and queens of Narnia after the victory over the Witch, is a good example.

Resolution should not be confused with denouement, when the fate of the character is known, the initial order restored, and the narrative brought to closure. For a child character, closure can be either a further empowerment or a disempowerment. When Tom Sawyer finds the treasure and, albeit indirectly, wins over Injun Joe, he not only enhances his position as a hero, but gains higher status in adult society. The Pevensie children, on the other hand, return from their adventures in Narnia and are stripped of their regalia, wisdom, and glory.

Closure

It is further necessary to distinguish between structural closure (a satisfactory round-up of the plot) and psychological closure (bringing the protagonist's personal conflicts into balance). In a children's story these typically coincide. When Pinocchio is transformed into a human boy, the plot is concluded, and his conflicts with external enemies as well as with his own self are solved. Peter Pan's victory over Hook is synchronized with Wendy's accomplished quest for self and her readiness to go home.

However, the structural and psychological closure may stand in discrepancy to each other, as in *Homecoming* (Voigt, 1981): The arrival at their grandmother's house is a natural way to finish the Tillerman children's journey; however, it does not solve the main conflict of the story, does not bring back the children's mother, and does not necessarily promise an easy and happy future for the characters. The structural plot is concluded; the "human" plot is left open ended. The ironic title adds to the ambiguity of the ending. In terms of characterization, psychological closure is more interesting than structural closure.

The happy ending—which in most cases presupposes a combination of structural and psychological closure—is something that many adults immediately associate with children's literature, and that many scholars and teachers put forward as an essential requirement in a good children's book. Folk tales always have a happy ending, expressed by the coda "lived happily ever after." Because children's fiction borrows many of its structures from folk tales, traditional children's books have happy endings, at least superficially: Dorothy returns home, the White Witch is eliminated, the treasure is found, and so on. In contemporary novels for children, there is some deviation from the obligatory happy ending. Instead of a closure rounding off the plot, a new opening or aperture for the character is presented.

Aperture

Unlike a structural open ending, aperture does not imply the possibility of further character development (providing an opportunity for a sequel), but an indeterminacy concerning both what has actually happened and what might still happen to a character. Aperture is thus an ending that has a variety of interpretations. Aperture in fact precludes a sequel because the course of further events would be radically different. Thus, aperture leaves it for the reader to decide what has happened to the character, what may happen next, and sometimes even what conclusions the character must draw. Aperture occurs in *The Catcher in the Rye* (Salinger, 1951): Has Holden been cured now? Will he manage to attend a new school? Will he live up to the expectations his parents and the society have for him? Aperture also occurs in *The Brothers Lionheart* (Lindgren, 1973/1996): Is Rusky dying at the end or has he actually been dead all along?

Would a sequel depicting Holden adjusted to societal norms satisfy the reader's appreciation of this complex character? Would a sequel depicting Rusky's further adventures in the next world add anything to the moral dilemma of the protagonist? Aperture stimulates the reader's imagination in a way traditional closure can never do. On the other hand, it may leave a less sophisticated reader frustrated. Even so, aperture seems a more natural ending for a children's novel because child characters are always left halfway in their maturation; they are by definition not fully developed as individuals.

The dominant ending of the mainstream novel, marriage (with all its variations, implying the protagonists' reunion with the objects of their desires) is seldom employed in children's fiction. Its variant, the child's reunion with the missing parent, is sometimes employed (e.g., in *The House of Arden*, Nesbit, 1908/2000; *The Secret Garden*, Burnett, 1911/1998; and *The Neverending Story*, Ende, 1979/1997); however, the power position in this event is not the same as in marriage. Reunion with a parent brings the child back into parental protection, limiting the freedom that the protagonist has enjoyed during the parent's absence. Further, in contemporary children's fiction, a pseudoreunion is more likely, in which the recovery of the absent parent brings disappointment rather than joy. In *The Great Gilly Hopkins* (Paterson, 1978), Gilly's recovery of her mother implies the loss of her foster family, which she has learned to value—an important insight that marks the character's substantial growth. The example shows very well the relativity of a happy ending and the way aperture reveals characters' emotional maturity.

Character Types and Their Interaction With Plot

In order to understand the character's role in the plot, consider two main types of characters according to their power position: the underdog and the trickster, both originating from folklore. The most common hero in a folk tale is an underprivileged child, the youngest son or daughter, or a child of unknown origin. At the end, the hero finds fortune, love, and a kingdom, triumphing over those who seemed more clever and stronger in the beginning.

The abandoned orphan is the most typical character in children's fiction. The degree of abandonment may vary from physical to emotional. Tom Sawyer's and Anne Shirley's parents are dead. The March sisters' father is away at war (*Little Women*, Alcott, 1868/1968). The parents of the four children in *The Lion, the Witch and the Wardrobe* remain in London, and the children are free to have their adventures. Such children, whose parents are not central, are *functional orphans*.

While the underprivileged child is the most widespread in contemporary psychological children's novels, the trickster is more common in entertainment literature. Tom Sawyer is a trickster. Jacob Two-Two is a trickster. Many "naughty boy" books, such as *Just William* (Crompton, 1922/1994), have the same origin. A tomboy girl, such as Jo March or Anne Shirley, alludes to a trickster figure as well, while in *Pippi Longstocking* (Lindgren, 1945/1950), a girl plays a typically male trickster role.

Both the underdog and the trickster are characters who, as the plot progresses, change their power position from low to high—or at least higher. This is what accounts for intrinsic hope and optimism in children's literature. This upward plot movement is typical in fairy tales and in classic novels. In ancient literature, Renaissance drama, and in contemporary mainstream novels, protagonists start by having power and lose it as the plot progresses: the tragic plot. In Greek tragedy, characters are subjected to Fate; in Shakespearean dramas, they often bring about their own defeat. Contemporary adult characters lose their life partners or friends, fail in their careers, face a major illness or death, and so on—a consistent and definitive downward movement. While a conventional plot inevitably finds solutions for these problems and restores the power balance, most contemporary existential novels, including young adult novels, leave the plot unresolved or show the protagonist's defeat, including (in extreme cases) death or suicide.

In a children's novel, however, a downward movement is unlikely. The temporary defeats that a child protagonist may experience are usually followed by success. If they are not, the protagonists' young age leaves open many possibilities. They can repair their social relationships and reestablish broken bonds with their parents; they can improve their academic records and athletic achievements; they can recuperate after traumatic losses. Thus, a protagonist of a children's novel is seldom, if ever, depicted as an ultimate failure, a being without hope.

On the other hand, it certainly takes some sophistication to see the positive aspects of endings that superficially seem tragic. When the Little Mermaid (Andersen, 1974) sacrifices herself rather than kill the prince and be saved (the original story is radically different from the Disney version), readers often fail to realize that she has in fact attained the promise of what has been the object of her quest, an immortal soul. In *Bridge to Terabithia*, readers may be thoroughly upset by Leslie's death, but for Jess it provides a substantial thrust toward spiritual maturity. In fact, the ending shows him at least partially recuperated and definitely strong enough to go further.

The ends of stories, especially in contemporary children's fiction, reveal characters, posing more questions than providing answers.

Causality and Motivation

In real life, we do not necessarily see events around us in a cause-and-effect relation. In literature, we expect that if an event or an action is depicted it must be important to the plot. Causality also is a powerful means of revealing character; for instance, Pippi moves to Villa Villekulla *because* her father has disappeared in a storm. Although Pippi could have reacted to her father's absence differently—by taking over the ship and becoming the sea captain herself—her character is revealed to us through her decision to start a new life. Similarly, the White Witch enchants Edmund with Turkish Delight *in order* to prevent Aslan from taking power in Narnia. The witch's behavior reveals her as evil because the reader knows that Aslan represents goodness. Without this knowledge, readers would judge the witch as generous and benevolent. When reading novels, readers do not consciously make all the causal connections, but the ones they do make certainly help them assemble the image of the character from the details provided.

Readers also expect characters to have motivations for their actions. In his discussion of the structure of romance, Frye (1976) points out the difference in design between realism and romance. In realism, readers expect a good deal of logic in the events and motivation behind the character's behavior; in romance, the demand for logic, consistency, and continuity is considerably weaker. The characters behave in a certain way simply because the plot requires it of them. Many critics have pointed out that the literature of romance is, to a high degree, based on coincidences; and children's literature, with its strong inherent links to romance, has the same tendency.

Readers expect characters in realistic children's novels to behave reasonably within the scope of their cognitive potentials, but more readily accept fantasy characters' behavior according to the plot design; for instance, a fantasy hero fights the dragons because this is his role in the story and not because he has high moral standards and a strong sense of right and wrong. Frye (1976) points out that the less displaced—or the closer to traditional narratives—the characters are, the more rigidly they follow the prescribed patterns of behavior. However, readers ascribe all characters certain motives, whether ethical or material, altruistic or selfish. Such a motive may be fighting evil (the Pevensie children fight the White Witch because it is the right thing to do), revealing external secrets (Tom Sawyer exposes the murderer because it is morally correct), eliminating dislocation (Dorothy goes through the trials in the land of Oz because she wants to go home), finding one's identity (Gilly is reluctant to accept Maime as a substitute parent because she feels strong bonds with her biological mother), or fulfilling desire (the Arden children keep going into the past because they hope to find a treasure and become rich).

What clearly follows from this argument is the fact that readers cannot always draw conclusions about characters on the basis of their behavior and motivations because these may be wholly dictated by the plot. Further, the demand for motivation leans on the general approach to literary characters. As Scholes and Kellogg (1966) point out,

> Characters are concepts in anthropoid form or fragments of the human psyche masquerading as whole human beings. Thus, we are not called upon to understand their motivation as if they were whole human beings but to understand the principles they illustrate through their actions in a narrative framework. (p. 88)

That is, if we liberate ourselves from the view of literary characters as living human beings, we will not seek any motivation behind their actions, but instead try to examine the writers' design behind them—working to understand character just as we do to make sense of story.

REFERENCES

Abrams, M.H. (1953). *The mirror and the lamp: Romantic theory and critical tradition.* Oxford, UK: Oxford University Press.

Aristotle. (1997). *Poetics.* Montreal, QC, Canada: McGill-Queen's University Press.

Bakhtin, M. (1990). Author and hero in aesthetic activity. In M. Holquist & V. Liapunov (Eds.), *Art and answerability: Early philosophical essays* (pp. 4–256). Austin: University of Texas Press.

Booth, W.C. (1961). *The rhetoric of fiction.* Chicago: University of Chicago Press.

Bradley, A.C. (1993). *Shakespearean tragedy* (3rd ed.). London: Macmillan. (Original work published 1904)

Chatman, S. (1978). *Story and discourse. Narrative structure in fiction and film.* Ithaca, NY: Cornell University Press.

Culler, J. (1975). *Structuralist poetics: Structuralism, linguistics, and the study of literature.* London: Routledge.

Eco, U. (1979). *The role of the reader: Explorations in the semiotics of texts.* Bloomington: Indiana University Press.

Fish, S. (1982). *Is there a text in this class? The authority of interpretative communities.* Cambridge, MA: Harvard University Press.

Forster, E.M. (1985). *Aspects of the novel.* San Diego, CA: Harcourt Brace. (Original work published 1927)

Frye, N. (1976). *The secular scripture: A study of the structure of romance.* Cambridge, MA: Harvard University Press.

Hochman, B. (1985). *Character in literature.* Ithaca, NY: Cornell University Press.

Iser, W. (1974). *The implied reader: Patterns of communication in prose fiction from Bunyan to Beckett.* Baltimore: Johns Hopkins University Press.

James, H. (1972). *Theory of fiction.* Lincoln: University of Nebraska Press. (Original work published 1884)

Jauss, H.R. (1982). *Toward an aesthetic of reception.* Minneapolis, MN: University of Minnesota Press.

Knights, L.C. (1965). How many children had Lady Macbeth? *Explorations,* 1–39.

Nikolajeva, M. (2002). *The rhetoric of character in children's literature.* Lanham, MD: Scarecrow.

Propp, V. (1968). *Morphology of the folktale.* Austin: University of Texas Press. (Original work published 1928)

Rimmon-Kenan, S. (1983). *Narrative fiction: Contemporary poetics.* London: Methuen.

Rose, J. (1984). *The case of Peter Pan, or the impossibility of children's fiction.* London: Macmillan.

Scholes, R., & Kellogg, R. (1966). *The nature of narrative.* New York: Oxford University Press.

Todorov, T. (1977). *The poetics of prose* (Trans. R. Howard). Ithaca, NY: Cornell University Press.

von Franz, M.L. (1981). *Puer Aeternus: A psychological study of the adult struggle with the paradise of childhood* (2nd ed.). Santa Monica, CA: Sigo.

Wullschläger, J. (1995). *Inventing Wonderland: The lives and fantasies of Lewis Carroll, Edward Lear, J.M. Barrie, Kenneth Grahame, and A.A. Milne.* London: Methuen.

Zipes, J. (1997). *Happily ever after: Fairy tales, children, and the culture industry.* New York: Routledge.

LITERATURE CITED

Alcott, L.M. (1968). *Little women.* New York: Little, Brown. (Original work published 1868)

Andersen, H.C. (1974). The little mermaid. In *Hans Christian Andersen: The complete fairy tales and stories* (Trans. E.C. Haugaard). New York: Doubleday.

Barrie, J.M. (1991). *Peter Pan.* New York: Viking. (Original work published 1906)

Baum, L.F. (2001). *The wonderful wizard of Oz.* New York: HarperTrophy. (Original work published 1900)

Burnett, F.H. (1998). *The secret garden.* New York: HarperTrophy. (Original work published 1911)

Collodi, C. (1988). *Pinocchio.* New York: Knopf. (Original work published 1891)

Crompton, R. (1994). *Just William.* New York: Macmillan. (Original work published 1922)

Defoe, D. (1983). *Robinson Crusoe.* New York: Atheneum. (Original work published 1719)

de Saint-Exupéry, A. (2000). *The little prince.* San Diego, CA: Harcourt. (Original work published 1943)

Ende, M. (1997). *The neverending story.* New York: Dutton. (Original work published 1979)

Hamilton, V. (1971). *The planet of Junior Brown.* New York: Macmillan.

Lewis, C.S. (1994). *The lion, the witch and the wardrobe.* New York: HarperCollins. (Original work published 1950)

Lindgren, A. (1950). *Pippi Longstocking.* New York: Viking. (Original work published 1945)

Lindgren, A. (1996). *The Brothers Lionheart.* London: Hodder & Stoughton. (Original work published 1973)

Milne, A.A. (1994). *Winnie-the-Pooh.* New York: Dutton. (Original work published 1926)

Montgomery, L.M. (1982). *Anne of Green Gables.* New York: Bantam. (Original work published 1908)

Nesbit, E. (2000). *The house of Arden.* New York: Dutton. (Original work published 1908)

Paterson, K. (1977). *Bridge to Terabithia.* New York: Crowell.

Paterson, K. (1978). *The great Gilly Hopkins.* New York: Crowell.

Pearce, A.P. (1987). *Tom's midnight garden.* New York: Yearling. (Original work published 1958)

Pullman, P. (1996). *The golden compass.* New York: Knopf.

Salinger, J.D. (1951). *Catcher in the rye.* New York: Little, Brown.

Spyri, H. (1995). *Heidi.* New York: Puffin. (Original work published 1884)

Swift, J. (2003). *Gulliver's travels.* New York: Penguin. (Original work published 1726)

Taylor, M. (1976). *Roll of thunder, hear my cry.* New York: Dial.

Twain, M. (1987). *The adventures of Tom Sawyer.* New York: Puffin. (Original work published 1876)

Twain, M. (2003). *The adventures of Huckleberry Finn.* New York: Penguin. (Original work published 1884)

Voigt, C. (1981). *Homecoming.* New York: Atheneum.

Conclusion

Where Do We Go From Here?

Miriam G. Martinez and Nancy L. Roser

HE CONTRIBUTORS TO THIS VOLUME HAVE LOOKED
at character in children's books from multiple perspectives. They
have shown that characters need not be just like us to offer us better
understanding of ourselves. We have learned that writers and readers create
characters together, that characters don't all come from one place, and that
their origin may lie in mystery. In his introduction to *Bless Me, Ultima*,
Rudolf Anaya (1972/1999) explains that "Ultima appeared to me and
instructed me to make her a character in the novel" (p. vii). Henry James
(1881/1983) never forgot a remark from Russian novelist Ivan Turgenieff
on the centrality of character: The story always began for Turgenieff "with
the vision of some person or persons, who hovered before him...interesting
him and appealing to him just as they were..." (p. vii). It was then that the
author knew he must find the story for his characters—the right
relationships, the situations that would draw them out, and derive "the
complications they would be most likely to produce and to feel" (p. vii).
For Anaya, James, and Turgenieff (and for other authors and theorists as
well), character is the horse that comes before the cart that is plot.

Each contributor to this book has argued persuasively that understanding character is central to understanding narratives. Even so, character
is just one element within the inextricable mesh that shapes a literary work.
We understand that any literary element becomes more or less central
depending upon the work as a whole, and that it is the intersection of
character and context that yields the potential for story (Harvey, 1966).

What a Character! Character Study as a Guide to Literary Meaning Making in Grades K–8 edited by
Nancy L. Roser and Miriam G. Martinez, with Junko Yokota and Sharon O'Neal. Copyright 2005
by the International Reading Association.

Awareness of those intersections also makes for stories being read more thoughtfully and sensitively.

As teachers and students gather in groups to talk over books, they may want to consider how character intersects with other literary elements. In *The Midwife's Apprentice* (Cushman, 1995), for example, the shifts in setting mirror the changing emotional states of Alyce, the young protagonist. The book opens in bleak winter, and Alyce (called only Brat early on) sleeps in a dung pile to avoid freezing. Without home, food, or anyone to care for her, she seems as devoid of hope as the landscape. But as winter becomes spring, Alyce's circumstances slowly shift, and for the first time she begins to imagine a future. By considering the interplay of character and setting, readers can live deeper within the novel's mood and metaphor.

The authors of this text have emphasized that teachers who help children "latch on to character" have one way of leading them through the twists and turns of the story mesh. The authors have suggested practical ways to rely on the understanding and interpretation of character as a first step in becoming better readers of literary texts. For, at some place within literature study—some medial place between appreciation and dissection—must lie the goal of growing "better readers," the purview of schooling. At some point between prescriptions for teaching literature and the total abandonment of the literature curriculum lies the opportunity for teachers to serve as literary guides through the narratives that are right for their children.

We know that careful reading demands attention, speculation, inference, imagination, and a willingness both to judge and suspend judgment—all aspects of effective comprehension instruction (Duffy & Roehler, 1989; Fielding & Pearson, 1994; Pressley, 2000). In this volume, teachers have been reminded to closely link effective cognitive strategies with the possible literary understandings of each unique text. We believe this is where comprehension strategy instruction and the study of literature naturally intersect. When readers of *The Midwife's Apprentice* hope that Alyce will help young Will successfully deliver the calf, they are *predicting plot* (i.e., character in action). When they sigh with satisfaction as the clever Alyce tricks the narrow-minded townspeople, they are *inferring character traits*. Readers who can sense the sparkling spring morning on which Alyce makes her first visit to the manor are *visualizing setting*. It will be within our teaching at the intersection of cognitive strategies and literary elements that we help students become closer readers of narratives.

Understanding the complexities of a character (such as Alyce) may lie at the very heart of literary meaning making. There are three other necessities: (1) good stories in which these divergent, complex and changing characters act their roles; (2) receptive students open to stepping into story worlds (Langer, 1995); and (3) insightful teachers equipped with sufficient instructional strategies to guide literature explorations—the very kind of instructional strategies that the authors in this volume have described.

REFERENCES

Duffy, G.G., & Roehler, L.R. (1989). Why strategy instruction is so difficult and what we need to do about it. In C.B. McCormick, G. Miller, & M. Pressley (Eds.), *Cognitive strategy research: From basic research to educational applications* (pp. 133–154). New York: Springer-Verlag.

Fielding, L.G., & Pearson, P.D. (1994). Reading comprehension: What works. *Educational Leadership, 51*(5), 62–68.

Harvey, W.J. (1966). *Character and the novel.* London: Chatto & Windus.

Langer, J. (1995). *Envisioning literature: Literary understanding and literature instruction.* New York: Teachers College Press.

Pressley, M. (2000). What should comprehension instruction be the instruction of? In M.L. Kamil, P.B. Mosenthal, P.D. Pearson, & R. Barr (Eds.), *Handbook of reading research* (Vol. 3, pp. 545–562). Mahwah, NJ: Erlbaum.

LITERATURE CITED

Anaya, R. (1999). *Bless me, Ultima.* New York: Warner. (Original work published 1972)

Cushman, K. (1995). *The midwife's apprentice.* New York: Clarion.

James, H. (1983). *Portrait of a lady.* New York: Bantam. (Original work published 1881)

Author Index

Note: Page numbers followed by *t* indicate tables.

Subject Index

Note. Page numbers followed by *f* and *t* indicate figures and tables, respectively.

DONOR ROLE, 186

DOROTHY, 186, 202

DOWNSTAIRS CHARACTERS, 50–51

DRAMA, 83–95; books for, 88*t*; planning for, 87–90; pleasure and, 92–94; procedure for, 89–90, 90*t*; social nature of, 86–87

DREW, NANCY, 171

DROP EVERYTHING AND READ (DEAR) TIME, 107

E

EASY-TO-READ PICTUREBOOKS: for Readers Theatre, selection of, 100–101, 101*t*

EDMUND, 184–185, 201

EEYORE, 117*f*, 121*f*

ELIZA, 173–174

ELLIE, 171

E-MAIL. *See* keypal journal

EMPATHY, 85

ENGAGEMENT: character and, 85–86; in primary grades, 166–167

ERIC, 177

ESPERANZA, 79, 115–116, 115*f*, 126, 130

ESSAYS: and fiction, 20–21

EULA, MISS, 18–19, 22–23

F

FACIAL EXPRESSIONS: and character, 136–138

FALSE HERO ROLE, 186

FEELING: in characters, 22, 98; in memorable characters, 175

FICTION: children's, theory of character in, 182–204; personal essays and, 20–21

FICTIVE CHARACTERS: ontological status of, 191–195

FIGURES: versus character, 187

FISHER, PAUL, 50

FLAT CHARACTERS, 155

FOLKLORE: drama on, 87

FORMAL APPROACH TO CHARACTER, 186

FOX, 97, 103–105, 161

FRAMING: and character, 142–143

FROG, 163–164

FUNNEL, MRS., 34

G

GAUGING, 116–117, 117*f*

GESTURES: and character, 138–140

GLORIA, 164–165

GOLDILOCKS, 138

GRACE, 139

GRANDFATHER, 165

GRANGER, HERMIONE, 178

GRAPHIC ORGANIZERS: for drama, 92–94

GROUP SIZE: for Readers Theatre, and book selection, 98–99

H

HAPPY ENDINGS, 198

HARRY, 98

HEIDI, 197

HELPER ROLE, 186

HERO ROLE, 186, 200

HEWITT, ROBBIE, 16

HIGGINS, M. C., 128

HISTORICAL CONTEXT: and character, 193–194

HOPKINS, GILLY, 126, 199, 202

HOPPER, EDWARD, 145–146

I

IDENTIFICATION, 85

IDEOLOGICAL APPROACH TO CHARACTER, 188

IKE, 164

ILLUSTRATING, 113–114

ILLUSTRATIONS: and character, 134–153, 156–157; text and, 151–152

IMPLIED READERS, 189

IMPROVISATION, 91–92; books for, 93*t*

INTERPRETATION: dramatic, 91–92

ISABEL, 41–42

NATIONAL BLACK THEATRE, 64
NELSON, PUTNAM, 15–16
NICK, 172
NOBLE TRAITS, 195
NORMA, 32
NYASHA, 148

O

O'HARA, SCARLETT, 26, 28–30, 34
OLIVIA, 137, 145
ONTOLOGICAL STATUS: of fictive
    characters, 191–195
OPAQUE CHARACTERS, 193
OPPRESSED CHARACTERS: and discussion,
    130–132
ORPHAN CHARACTER, 200
OWEN, vii
OWL, 117f, 121f, 192

P

PALETTE: and character, 144–146
PARENT CHARACTERS, 184
PEDRO, 126
PERFORMANCE GROUPS: size of, and book
    selection, 98–99
PERITEXT: interpretation of, 147–149
PERLOO, 176
PERSONAL ESSAYS: and fiction, 20–21
PETER PAN, 198
PETER RABBIT, 146–147
PHYSICAL TRAITS: text and, 158–159
PICKETT, BILL, 118
PICTUREBOOKS: character in, 6–7,
    156–157; illustrations and character
    in, 134–153; images of character in,
    136–141; for Readers Theatre,
    selection of, 99–101, 100t–101t
PIGLET, 176, 192
PING, 165–166
PINOCCHIO, 198
PLEASURE: and drama, 92–94
PLINKETT, KATHY, 33–34
PLOT: and character, 43–48, 196–202;
    character types and, 200–201; in

children's books, 185; narratives
    oriented to, 186; predicting, 206;
    student development and, 4; in
    young adult novels, 168
POET: as creator of character, 54–69
POLLOCK, JACKSON, 145
POSTMODERNISM/POSTSTRUCTURALISM:
    and character, 190
POTTER, HARRY, vi, 171, 174, 176, 178
PRIMARY CLASSROOM: character in,
    154–167
PROMPTED RESPONSE JOURNAL, 75;
    literature for, 77t
PROPORTION: and character, 142
PRYNNE, HESTER, vi
PSYCHOANALYTICAL APPROACH TO
    CHARACTER, 187–188
PSYCHOLOGICAL CLOSURE, 198

Q

QUEST OBJECT, 186
QUIMBY, RAMONA, 163

R

RABBIT, 121f
READER RESPONSE APPROACHES TO
    CHARACTER, 188–190
READERS: implied, 189
READERS THEATRE, 64, 96–110; in
    bilingual classrooms, 105–107; book
    selection for, 97–101; characteristics
    of, 96–97; and literacy program,
    107–108
REALISM, 201–202
RED RIDING HOOD, 142, 148
RELATIONSHIP WEB, 118
RESEARCH: and character, 15
RESOLUTION, 197–198
RESPONSE JOURNAL, 74–78; literature for,
    77t
RITTER, ROBERTA, 50
ROB, 32
RODZINA, 73
ROMANCE, 201–202